ONE HOT SUMMER IN
ST PETERSBURG

by the same author

DRUG TALES
APRIL ASHLEY'S ODYSSEY
SATYRDAY
THE UNDERBELLY
TO NOTO
20TH CENTURY CHARACTERS

ONE HOT SUMMER IN ST PETERSBURG

Duncan Fallowell

JONATHAN CAPE
LONDON

First published 1994

1 3 5 9 10 8 6 4 2

First published in the United Kingdom in 1994 by Jonathan Cape
Random House, 20 Vauxhall Bridge Road, London, SW1V 2SA

Random House Australia Pty Ltd
20 Alfred Street, Milsons Point, Sydney, NSW 2061
Australia

Random House New Zealand Ltd
18 Poland Road, Glenfield, Auckland 10,
New Zealand

Random House South Africa (Pty) Ltd
PO Box 337, Bergvlei, South Africa

Random House UK Limited Reg. No. 954009

A CIP catalogue record for this book
is available from the British Library

ISBN 0–224–03623–8

Typeset by Deltatype Ltd, Ellesmere Port, Cheshire
Printed in Great Britain by
Clays Ltd, St Ives plc

To ——,
wherever you are

CONTENTS

DREAM

CHAPTER ONE

The Beyond   3
The First Night   7
Lucky Bananas   10
Next Thing   17
The House Of Friendship   18
Are You Ready To Die?   23
It Begins   26

CHAPTER TWO

Sonya Telephones   29
Lack Of Information   34
3 Stately Borzois   37
La Luna Verde   40
Sonya Rings   42
Sunday Morning   43
A Lemon Is Mentioned   45
A Nuclear Submarine In The Foyer   46
Dmitri   48
Back At The Flat   56
Beginning To Rave   57
Serafima Is Bashing Away   66
Heaven   78
Nina Rings   80

CHAPTER THREE

There Is In St Petersburg An Englishman   86
How Does He Find It So Far?   91
The Day Of The Dacha   94
The Day Of Petrodvorets   100

NIGHTMARE

CHAPTER FOUR

This Evening The Air Is Iron-Coloured   103
Another Thing Happened   109
Next Day I Land   112
Vertigo   118
The Scented Villain   124
The Return Of Camilla de Martino   130
More Shocks   134
Food   145
Time To Go   149

CHAPTER FIVE

The Humidity Is High   152
To-Day Is The Day   157
Staring Into Space   166
Don't Bother To Wrap Me Up   173

CHAPTER SIX

Meet Maxim   176
In The Kitchen   179
From Death's Door To Jetset   180
The Dynamo Club   188
Get It From The Inside Out   193
I Do Ring   198

REALITY

CHAPTER SEVEN

At First   205
Rodion Says   210
The Palace Is Ablaze With Light   212
The Magic Theatre   215
I Am Ablaze With Light   218
Giselle And Pop-Mechanika   224
Grace, The Serbian Girl   226
Will Dima Never Stop Springing Surprises?   227

CHAPTER EIGHT

Picnic At Pushkin   238
Saturday   248
He Smells And Tastes Of Heat And Soap And Smoke   251
Walking Back Towards The Road   252
Sunday   255

CHAPTER NINE

The Ship To Anywhere   258
Feminist Film Party   265
The Consignment Of Caviar   273
The Party At The End Of The World   276
Navy Day   287
Jill   290
I Do Not Know How   292
Didn't Move An Inch   294
Osip In The Ice-Cream Parlour   295
Is It Possible To Know A Russian?   300
Walking Back Along Nevsky Prospekt   306
Dima   308

POSTSCRIPT

DREAM

CHAPTER ONE

The beyond . . . . Let your mind slide there . . . . . Do not be afraid . . . Breathe deeply. Bestir yourself. And clamber out of the circle of your confidence . . . Rising from the sucking mud of encumbrant habits, slipping the net of accumulated duties, feel the cranium strain across its crown and split! and through the yawning aperture you ascend all moist and fresh into a shuddering space. Up, up, through levels of diminishing inertia. Up, up, stretching the rubbery membrane of your backward glance beyond its powers of inhibition and – pop! – you . . . are . . . free . . . . .

Above the crags and ravines and fallow pools of all that is familiar, across tracts of preconception, and through the banal vistas of truncated hope, and out the other side, let the moving light of your attention dare to go. Faster – cleaner – keep on. In the exhilaration of a reduced and streamlined identity, in this progressive nakedness of being, keep on, keep on, keep on, so that eventually, inevitably, your point of focus, like a slowing comet, encroaches upon the brink of an unknown region, of something completely new. Do not be afraid. Burst the threshold into curiosity and beyond. Keep on, looking down upon a landscape of strangely coloured exhalations and magical shapes until . . . until the velocity of escape is etherealised upon an atmosphere far away, and the expended thrust falters and descends in a ball of extreme wariness towards some prickly cluster which, expanding by degrees, you can in due course clarify as the scintillant and ornamented topknots, detailed in a macabre glow, of an improbable dream city. You are   falling

down

down

down down into the coruscations of a different magnetic field, down through a layer of hectic points and swooning curves, of aerial statues in surprise and rooftop beasts hunched in grimace, of glittering schemes of cool or feverish fantasy between earth and sky . . . and so down to the mid-floor of a great stucco building . . . and down into a room . . . (phew, tush, fold wings) . . . where 4 creatures are about to begin dinner, where it is 10 o'clock at night, with full sunshine outside and very hot . . . and in clingy black tights and a man's striped shirt, a woman wheels a hostess-trolley into the most formal chamber of her gloomily cavernous home. You . . . . . grin like an idiot – at her, at the trolley, at the 2 other guests, at the walls, at the brown upright piano, at the 2 sewing-machines, at the tablecloth. The trolley, constructed from tubes, is rickety and one of the wheels squeaks. But it is laden with delicious food which the woman places on the dining-table: red caviar, red tomatoes, pink radishes, black bread, white bread, yellow butter, yellow potatoes, pale green cucumber, dark green herbs, grilled veal, and a jug of cold water and a refrigerated bottle of white alcohol dripping with condensation.

'Please,' she says through the miasma of humid uncertainty, serving up meat and potatoes, 'eat.'

In an awful hush I lift the knife and fork; 6 eyes are upon me; I insert something in my mouth, bite, and say 'Good.' As a seismic wave of relief passes through them, 3 pairs of shoulders settle downwards like geological plates, and they also begin to eat.

'Vodka?' she asks with a coy tilt of the head.

'Da,' I reply grinningly, in almost my only word of their beautiful language (and I have yet to master the thistlelike alphabet). Still reeling from shock, having landed only moments ago, I suppose this grin – which I'm trying to dislodge but it seems fixed there in plaster – is a propitiatory reflex covering the fear and chill innocence I feel. Alone among aliens, denied all customary retreat into the protective sophistications of one's tribe, my nudity borders on the desolate: a castaway tensely scanning the natives. So I eat.

The woman is in her middle 30s and, though unnerved by this thing which has suddenly come to lodge with her, she is a natural and good-natured flirt. Parting bee-stung lips and flapping her eyelashes, she imbibes a fuscous liquid which she calls 'Pierpsy'. The 2 other guests, both men, drink icy spirit from small glasses emptied in one gulp. Observing my sips, they ask 'Do you not like vodka?'

Net curtains stir as an antique tram rumbles by in the dusty street below. But there is no breeze. The air is gluelike and mosquitoes move sluggishly about the room. I stare at a photograph opposite and the shorter, darker of the 2 men says 'Yes, Serafima was the ballroom dancing champion of our country –'

'Oh,' she interrupts, waving a petite hand bashfully, 'long time ago,' and adds with a concerned look 'Please – eat – more . . . but I still love to dance.'

Nervousness makes eating difficult and I am harried by a recurrent thought: what the hell am I doing here? She dabs her mouth with a small triangular paper napkin; a glass of them stands in the centre of the table. At one point our eyes meet and are held, only for the briefest moment, yet long enough for a glance to become a gaze of conspiratorial candour, acknowledging our mutual and inquisitive ignorance. Then she disappears into the kitchen with the trolley, waggling her bottom in a paso-doblé.

The 2 men, who speak excellent English, ask if I am interested in mountain-climbing, to which the reply is 'Niet.' The shorter darker livelier one, Jo, bursts into laughter and claps his hands, congratulating me on my accent, while the long thin pale reticent one, Leonid, hovers at the gate of a smile. I cringe and knock off the remaining vodka as Serafima drags the trolley – squeak squeak squeak – back into the room, bearing a large apple tart and pot of cream. Something warm and furry is rubbing against my leg.

The flat is of the Dada school of art, having a quality of makeshift in many of its accoutrements. Water pipes are visible, and rusty or badly painted. Rigmaroles of electric wiring and socketry are pinned to the walls like ivy. The bathroom is basic, home to a degenerate gas heater which after various jabs and strokings can be persuaded to spout a curmudgeonly amount of warm water. The loo likewise is basic, home to a cat tray. Furniture, some pieces quite noble, is either damaged or brand new, mostly the former. An array of glum ornaments stands about. Few of the movables have any connectedness: random totems triumphantly connived for in the social struggle. The wall plaster is in bad condition, papered over but the paper peeling here and there, patched with diverse rectangles, the whole disintegrating faster than it can be disguised. These motley walls enclose a general high-ceilinged dimness, and dimness was at first my most vivid impression, of the city as we drove into it, of the flat as we entered it, as though everything were dissolving into everything else in a haze of dust and faded colours. It is a dimness which immediately absorbs the attention, for once the eyes have adjusted, they discern an extreme and lively mellowness, a visual world animated by having no hard edges.

'Do people in London have flats as big as this?' wonders Leonid. I am startled, since he has hardly spoken. But emboldened by the echo of his own voice and seeing me say yes to more vodka, yes to more pudding, he leans forward and declares, with an eccentric shine in his eye, 'This is how rich people eat.'

'What about the telephone?' I ask.

'She has – of course.'

'I mean, how do I use it?'

Jo and Leonid look at each other and shrug: 'You pick up the piece on top and – but your hostess will show you.'

'No, how do I pay for the calls?'

'Your hostess pay.'

Serafima is looking worriedly from one face to another.

'I'll be using it a lot,' I say, blushing.

'Lot easy! Telephone easy!' she laughs, sending up a cloud of smoke – Serafima is a coffee and cigarettes person.

Through a process akin to badminton, I discover a superb fact: telephone calls within the metropolitan area are free. Heating and gas operate on a similar principle. No wonder the place is bankrupt. But thereby the telephone becomes the bloodstream of the city, conferring on it a cellular cohesion, making of it a grand village. The phone rings constantly, even in the flats of not very nice people. But there is no directory for private subscribers – these numbers are divulged to one personally.

The gentlemen prepare to leave – Leonid agrees to take me on a motor tour to-morrow for $20 – and as they walk into the hall, I realise that the squeaking is not the trolley's but comes from the dry, old, springy parquet floor – so it will be impossible to come in late or go for a 4 am pee without being detected.

Serafima asks 'What time do you get up?'

'No particular time. Not early.'

'Good.'

Why does she look so sad when she smiles?

The first night is memorable for what doesn't happen. It doesn't get dark. The mosquito repellent *Shooh!* doesn't work. I do not sleep. The bedroom, which Serafima has vacated, is large, with pretty flowered wallpaper and a colourprint of a cataclysmic scene – either the Last Day of Pompeii or the Destruction of Sodom and Gomorrah. On the other wall is a child's painting of a ship at sea. The room is equipped with stark brown cupboards, shelves with books, 5 satin roses in a vase on the desk, but instead of proper curtains to blot out the giant window, there is merely a pair of thin pink and cream drapes suspended from a bobbled pelmet and tapering to 2 knotted balls halfway to the floor. This guarantees a flood of photons through the small hours. I catch Serafima before she subsides onto the sofa in the Best Room, and she unearths a piece of navy blue velvet, hooking it across the lower panes, but it would still be possible to read a newspaper in here. Therefore over my face I fix a black mask, courtesy of British Airways.

At 2 am it is absolutely silent, except for mosquitoes singing in the ears, and one is absolutely awake. I dab on more *Shooh!*, put in earplugs, and resettle back into blindness. By the London clock it is only 11 pm. Oh, this mask is maddening and makes the eyes puffy! I drag it off, perceive some lessening of the light outside, and go to the window. One of the earplugs hits the floor. The courtyard is not much to behold, a well of mustard wash, featureless windows, tarmac, corroded kingsize dustbins, several heavily bruised vehicles parked awry. But overhead – what a rich and luminous peachy blue! As though the peach and the blue yearned to be lavender . . . The phrase 'white nights', which the locals use to describe these summer nights when darkness never comes, is neither appealing nor just. These is nothing white about this one – it is deep with gorgeous colour. But I am hot and sticky and slug whisky from the duty free bottle and throw myself onto the bed and feel the heat breathing out of my naked body, the heat which is so unexpected.

Yes . . . what the hell am I doing here . . . nothing too special, I'm afraid. I've come to work quietly on a novel. It is set in the English countryside and I can't write English settings very well if I'm in England. Before, one could *visit* Russia (although I only ever had 1 day in Moscow). Now, for the first time in nearly 100 years, it is possible to *be* here. Am I the first foreign writer to come for such a purpose? To hang out? Cheap room, cheap living, maybe some sexual opportunity. Not many distractions. I mean, I know that Russia is in utter turmoil. But I hope to avoid it.

But why St Petersburg particularly? I know nothing of St Petersburg and know no one who lives here. I have no connection with the place whatsoever. But . . . . . . in 1961 my father returned home with a gramophone. We'd had a gramophone before but the new machine played LPs. My parents are not great classical music buffs but they do enjoy it and among the records which made their appearance that Christmas (alongside Connie Francis and Handel's *Messiah*) was Rimsky-Korsakov's *Scheherazada* – Ernest Ansermet conducting l'Orchestre de la Suisse Romande, in mono – and it turned out to be the most thrilling music I'd ever heard in my life. At the age of 13 I was *gone*, slaughtered by sound (and even now, when I know it so well as one of the clichés of the repertoire, it retains its intoxicating power; there is a rendition on Melodiya, from the USSR State Symphony Orchestra conducted by Yevgeny Svetlanov, which is devastating). The programme of the work begins and ends with tales of the sea, and from the sleeve notes it transpired that Rimsky-Korsakov had been a naval cadet in St Petersburg and was later Professor of Composition at the Conservatoire there. So the effect of this music was not at all to act as an introduction to the *Arabian Nights* or the Islamic world, but to imprint on my imagination the idea of St Petersburg as a place ineffably fabulous.

Russian music became a food; I consumed everything from Glinka to Shostakovitch. This was made easier when my father undertook a contract to supply the Supraphon Record Company of Czechoslovakia with wire merchandising racks. Suddenly our house was a-slither with piles of free records from behind the Iron Curtain. Why Russian music particularly should strike me in this way I do not know. The chromatic poignancy of its melodic lines, that haunting eastern or bluesy catch, the brilliance, the vigour, the melancholy, the spaciousness, all this stole my heart and made me upset and excited, and reached a climax in the works of Rachmaninov. But that doesn't fully account for a response which had the intimate force of an atavism. How wonderful to have been the unsuspecting recipient of a splash of Russian blood! (although, to my limited knowledge, all forebears have been English). I also devoured books on the subject. Did you know that Rimsky-Korsakov composed the Andante of his First Symphony, the first symphony ever by a Russian composer, in 1862 while on naval duty at Gravesend?

So maybe this was the beginning of it, of why whenever in later days 'St Petersburg' appeared on the printed page it gave off sparkles, of why when 'St Petersburg' flashed on the departure board at Heathrow this afternoon, it seemed the most glamorous possible destination. And yet – there is also a curious sense of having been delivered up, of having had only a very limited say in the matter, as though an intrigue of arcane forces compelled me hither out of enigmatic necessity. You see, it all happened so quickly – I am hardly aware of any interval between the decision to come and finding myself here.

The omens however were not altogether encouraging. My original place of accommodation in Ulitsa Khalturina, adjacent to the Winter Palace, fell through at the last moment. Whether literally or figuratively I never knew – either would be possible. Leonid found an alternative and less epicentral abode in the late 19th-century part of town but I was not reassured when we pulled up outside to discover that the English agents, Tim 'n' Terry, had the name of the street, the number of the building, the name of the landlady all wrong. OK, so it's a funny language, you're forgiven, but it means that no post from England will arrive – not that it would've arrived anyway. Let it be said at once that Tim 'n' Terry, Jo 'n' Leonid, perform travel miracles in freakish circumstances. They are enterprising and big-hearted, trustworthy and flexible. I commend them to the Queen of England when she comes. But I was a new boy on this run and somebody could've warned me of the calamitous state of all Russian domestic buildings – it's as if an earthquake rippled through town just a couple of days ago – it was a shock. And teenage boys were scuffing shiftily about the entrance to the courtyard. 'Don't let people know you are foreign,' said Leonid unnervingly as we climbed out of his dented Lada. He looked as though he were gearing up for a funeral – I now know it to be his normal face.

'But it's obvious I'm foreign.'

'Yes, it is!' blurted Jo. They'd both collected me from the airport – and what a riot that was, 2 hours in an impacted scrum trying to locate one's bags before someone else took a fancy to them. A planeload of Russians returning from Istanbul at the same time, importing plump mysteries in dozens of black bin liners done up with fawn tape, had it worked out little better than we did . . .

At the bottom of the staircase to my new home I looked upwards. Concrete walls, painted dark green to the level of a theoretical dado rail, ascended through repeating right-angles into blackness despite the light of day. Windows were thick with dirt and mostly cracked. Cigarette ends littered the steps. But we did not climb. A lift like a vertical coffin slid down to greet us.

As she opened the worn and padded maroon front door, her prettiness was astonishing. This wasn't your usual idea of a landlady: blonde hair pinned up, lithe figure, large blue eyes of a merciful sweetness and fright. Behind her an abyss of shadows. How do you do.

'First – slippers!' she said with pert movements and a quick laugh. The comforting oriental custom of leaving one's shoes in the hall obtains here too. I presented her with a giant tin of Quality Street chocolates. She gave polite thanks but did not look at it, dumping the tin nonchalantly on the nearest table as though this luxury were something she saw twice a day at least.

And so here I am.

What will to-morrow bring? There's the motorama with Leonid. And I have promised to deliver at some point a book from one Robin Milner-Gulland in Sussex to one Emelyon Lenko on the Field of Mars, and a CD player from a mum called Jean to a daughter called Katya. I want to walk everywhere! Since this town has by all reports become rather dodgy of late, perhaps I should enquire about a bodyguard – and an interpreter – and a masseur – apparently, with the rocketing exchange rate, one might sustain an entourage . . . . No sooner has the light begun to wane than it begins to wax . . . . Feel wired up – slug more whisky – turn onto my left side and the other earplug drops out. I gaze across the room to the ship at sea. It has a tall funnel and radiates dark blueness, but no soothing marine undulations reach me.

Lucky Bananas. Stagger out of bed, brush teeth, and into the kitchen where Serafima looks as though she has staggered out only moments before. In a powderpink dressing-gown she is blinking groggily through cigarette smoke, trying to light the gas. It's nearly 10 am and the television's on, an American soap opera called *Santa Barbara*. The colour of the picture is good – but it flickers constantly.

'Put your head out of the window,' she says, 'and feel how nice it is.' The exterior thermometer has already climbed to 27 degrees C. When I turn round, there sits on the table an impressive-looking bowl of porridge, containing chopped walnuts and topped with homemade jam and smetana (soured cream). I chew and stare at a dripping tap plumbed through from the bathroom over a tiny sink. Scrubbing brushes are worn down to their gums and the scourer is threadbare. Serafima sips her coffee, halfwatching the TV . . . It feels good.

D: What do you think of Americans?

S: I don't know any. But my friends who do, say they are . . [She consults a dictionary lying beside the ashtray] . . simpleton, fool.

D: That's a slightly sweeping judgement. They are very successful.

S: Oh yes.

D: Maybe one has to be a bit foolish to be successful.

S: But you mustn't have only money in your heart, it's bad.

D: What do you think of the English?

S: Snob . . . And the Swedish we say are computers.

Sergei, Serafima's 7-year-old son, arrives from out of town with his cousin Igor who humps in flagons of water. Sergei is a redhead and is covered with mosquito bites which he scratches into bloody scabs. Igor switches the television over to weight-lifters: tall blond one, square oriental one, medium brown one, short hairy Turkish type, all Russian.

'This water doesn't need to be boiled', explains Serafima, 'because it is from the countryside.'

'Can I have some please?' There's a throb behind my eyes – vodka and whisky don't mix. Ozzie gives my calf a furry rub, the white tabby with ginger trimming who when stroked rolls onto his back and vibrates his legs like a doxy. Serafima's son named him after an English pop singer.

'My other son did.'

'You have another son?'

'He is 18.'

'You look too young.' It's true. She must've pushed the boat out early. (As I shall discover, quite a lot of Russians do.)

'Thank-you,' she says, drawing in her lips. 'He lives with his father in Pushkin. But next year he will live with me. He is very good boy. He tells me everything.'

On the box, weight-lifters give way to gymnasts preparing for the forthcoming Olympic Games, and I try the number for Emelyon Lenko. No reply. Try another number, Ennio Nicotra's, a Palermo contact; success; we've never met but he extends an invitation to dinner early next week.

Leonid turns up looking as though he's received a death threat, in time to say good-bye to Serafima who is dashing to her English lesson – something comes away from the wall in her hand and she sighs 'I must decorate.' Leonid changes money, thousands of roubles for my dollars; I turn off the gas ring which is still burning, and out we go.

In a glare of sunshine St Petersburg begins to zoom towards us, its manifold façades sliding back on right and left in 2 endless strips of architectural plates. This is a city not of houses but of palatial blocks built on wide streets and canals; and because height was always restricted, and the terrain is flat, they are under a huge sky. Despite ubiquitous dust, the confectionary colours of the stucco come through. Golden domes and spires break the pitching, chimneyed roofline with an opulent energy. Occasionally there are green trees and everywhere fanciful bridges over curving streaks of water. For a Londoner each view has an unearthly emptiness and integrated beauty that is spell-binding.

Leonid swerves to avoid a heap of rubble which rises up on our side of the road (there's plenty of rubble around but no rubbish – they must recycle everything), bounces into and out of a pothole, and we hit Nevsky Prospekt. Crowds! Traffic! But almost at once we veer out of it and round to the right, round to the left – a jostle of cadets in white caps skip between cars and bubble off across Palace Square, the Winter Palace shimmers past in an electrifying dazzle and is gone . . . Leonid sweats at the wheel.

'Such a beautiful day.'

'I hate the heat,' he replies. 'I like winter. In winter you can cross-country ski.'

'My God, that's a beach in the centre of town!'

And it is – the genuine article, a long golden strand running beneath the bastions of the Peter and Paul Fortress on the bank of the Neva, chock-a-block with sun-worshippers, a few of whom venture into the oily brown slurrups of water. The Neva is very wide and so the heart of the city is an enormous expanse of water, majestic and irregular; closer examination reveals its majesty to be riven with dangerous currents and eddies.

Up at the Kirov Park, where riders and keep-fit enthusiasts strike heroic attitudes, Leonid points out Sosnovy Bor, the local nuclear power station trembling 60 kilometres away across the Gulf of Finland. It spat out some quite nasty stuff just before I arrived. Back down Kirovsky Prospekt with its mountainous apartment blocks, designed by and for laudanum-swilling neurotics circa 1900 – over Kirovsky Bridge – another

park, and a technicolor prodigy! What in heaven's name is it? (My solemn
cicerone offers information only upon request.)

'Church of Blood.'

'Why?'

'On site of Alexander II's assassination.'

'Ouch. Can we get some mosquito repellent?'

Back in Nevsky Prospekt he pulls over beside a tumble of tarmac and
loose kerbstones and we enter a nondescript door into a spartan room.
Chemist, yes. Repellent, no. Nevsky Prospekt incidentally is the only
thoroughfare in St Petersburg which is busy – and it's *always* busy. The
pavements are lined with market stalls, and alongside them chorus lines
of individuals stand motionlessly, each holding up a single object for sale
– a book, a bottle, a jumper, anything. The heterogeneous crowd surges
past them – office workers, shoppers, families, students, tourists, old
men with a row of military medals pinned to frayed jacket, gypsy beggars
barefoot and filthy. The young people are strikingly sexy, with a dash of
bravura or fierceness in them and something spaced-out too. Slavs often
have remarkable eyes and mouths. The weakest feature is the putty nose
but this often confers charm to a face which would otherwise be too
superb. The racial mix is very apparent and their bodies are well-made,
thanks to work, exercise, national service: straight backs, firm limbs, a
natural physical confidence in the walk. Girls show their legs in very short
skirts, and boys their muscles in tight coloured singlets. It is quite
believable that these people have been Europe's most resolute 20th-
century empire builders. But the hard life tells. Evidence of physical
damage is widespread among all categories, often carried off with flair:
scars, bandages, arms in slings or plaster, bashed noses, black eyes,
purple bruises. Yes, damage can be colourful – uncovered lesions are
marked with medicated paint in red, orange or green.

And uniforms can be colourful. These are no longer the uniforms of
cavalry officers of the Imperial Guard who wore white elkskin breeches,
nor those of the Circassian Guard who wore white kaftans with gold belts
and high white lambskin caps; but they are nonetheless very colourful by
non-royal standards. Black, grey, white, blue, green, khaki, decorated
with gold and red; caps forward over eyes or level or on backs of heads,
belts round trousers or round the waist of jackets Cossack-style, trousers
over boots or tucked into boots; uniforms singly or collectively wherever
you look. This prevalence is not threatening because the men inside them

do not strut. They are part of the normal human round, picturesque, often at ease, chatting, smoking, sometimes relaxed to the point of loucheness.

Near the chemist a kneeling peasant woman is striking the pavement with her head in an even, trancelike rhythm. A young man, in black Cossack-style uniform with gold pips and buckles, stops and extends his hand. She takes it and the 2 of them in the pell-mell of pedestrians remain frozen thus: he bent over at an unnatural angle as though he'd quite like his hand back eventually, she in padded rags holding it, staring at nothing, drinking the touch.

Eye contact and talking to strangers are permissible. Russians, however, can totally ignore a foreigner in their determination not to reveal how very interested in you they are. An Afro-American passes by, wearing a scowl and a T-shirt with *Enjoy Shopping* across the chest. A simoom wind shoots briefly down the streets. Dust clicks between my teeth.

We try several more chemists but without luck so, impatient to lose my rouble virginity, I turn to bananas. The banana-seller is in his early 20s, stockily built, with a scar running horizontally from the left-hand corner of his mouth, and chrome hair in a crewcut. His outfit is well-chosen (blue denim suit and mirrored sunglasses reflecting purplish silver) and when he holds up a large bunch of yellow bananas the whole effect is iconic. They are per kilo almost twice the price of a bottle of vodka – and vodka recently shot through the roof. Leonid looks away bemusedly.

'Lucky bananas,' says the seller. 'This first summer we have.'

'You speak English!'

'Sure. Banana the status snack! Usually I don't sell bananas. I am helping my friend.'

'What do you usually do?'

'Usually I sell anything.'

'Do you have anything anti-mosquito?'

'No. But after they get you,' he says, finally coming out from behind the disconcerting shades, 'put soda on the bites.'

We take off past the Moscow Station, rattle down to the Alexander Nevsky Monastery (where the quintessence of damage is lined up in the Avenue of Cripples: bundles with missing parts, whole missing sections, each with its grimy upturned hat on the pathway), sweep up abreast the river to the blue and white, gold-tipped ensemble of the Smolny Convent.

Observing a few silent minutes in front of it, while Leonid mops his deliquescence, the question which forms itself is: is this the prettiest arrangement that was ever put up anywhere in the world?

'There are no traffic jams. Oh yes, *there's* one.'

'No. It is petrol queue. What's a kilometre long and plays chess? The St Petersburg petrol queue.' That snuffling flu-like noise must be Leonid's laughter.

Back at the flat, Serafima puts on the kettle and asks 'What do you think of our city?' and I reply 'Have a banana.' It is attractive the way Russians say our city, our country. From the Best Room comes the thundering alacrity of Michael Jackson L-O-U-D.

My head is a jangle of snapshots but it is now clear that I am living in a unique habitat, a great 18th- and 19th-century city that is *absolutely complete*. This is the only thing which is clear, and the joy of it makes one afraid, that its completeness will not survive, because from a maintenance point of view we are in a disaster zone. What makes the historic centre complete is not simply that all the buildings are present – though for a major city of 5 million inhabitants that is unique enough – but that there is none of the commercial clutter which overlays every other city of comparable size. Also, Soviet architects were here enlightened on the subject of context. At the few infill sights created by the war they produced (during the height of the Modern Movement) buildings in a vigorous classical style. Even Stalin respected the skyline.

And the atmosphere is extraordinary. Atmospheres plural. One detects several, interlaced or opposed, generating an eerie momentousness: everything acquires a significance beyond the immediate. Hence there is an expectant air: you feel the town longing to dance or maybe sock you in the jaw, preparing to spring into shrieking life beneath its shame, neglect and confusion. Definitely confusion: in one of the 2 capital cities of a philosophy, social system and empire which collapsed suddenly, recently, utterly. A zany holiday mood: this is the hottest summer for years; the population is tanned and half-dressed; never seen so many painters setting up their easels out of doors. A mood stoical and blasé. A sense of freedom bordering on wildness: the absence of control and organisation, so different from my own society, can trap one in vortices of vertigo. A sense of menace: the least claustrophobic city on earth, all disposed in a dreamy looseness, and yet tensions crackle directly onto the skin. This will have to do for now. It is inadequate. I am aware of an enormity I cannot get to grips with.

I leave a message on Katya's answerphone. Serafima cooks dinner in white shorts and a white top with lace covering the upper side of her breasts between which a small silver cross continually disappears and reappears. 2 boys play improvised tennis down in the yard while a third teases a mongrel dog, making it yap. Members of an odd species of bird, like a particoloured cross between black crow and grey pigeon, are clubbing out there on the tilted rooftop in the evening sun. Serafima fries chicken pieces using nut oil from a jar beside the stove. She often fries, while on the shelves a team of black and red enamel cooking pots, painted with flowers, remain unused – perhaps they were a wedding present. To-morrow she will swim in a lake near her sister's and invites me, but I am calling on the House of Friendship to find out if they can fix me up with some gymnasts – there could be an article in it.

'Do you like Márquez?' she asks.

'Yes.'

'I am loving er Hundred –'

'Years of.'

'Alone.'

She drops her eyelids, heaves, laughs, lights a cigarette . . . . . Should I? Or am I fooling myself that she is interested? I cross to the gas ring and turn it off but she says 'No, no, I make coffee in a minute', so I relight it with a match, singeing a knuckle. But although it isn't what I want, I cannot rid myself of the feeling that it would be the proper and gentlemanly thing to do. It is amazing this womanly way she has, without the slightest direct reference, without the slightest breach of etiquette, of making me feel guilty for not making love to her. Why does she not have a scramble of suitors on the phone and at the door? There is something valiant about Serafima but she isn't really the solitary type – inside there is hunger and restlessness.

Ozzie has taken to usurping my bed. I put him out and prepare to sleep but the light (though its presence outdoors all night long is a great anti-mugging device) is no inducement and probably one shouldn't try too hard – go with the flow and all that. But what flow? I can't detect any flow . . . Liberated from the tyranny of night and day, the locals keep the oddest hours. Serafima says some people walk around all night – lovers, loners, insomniacs, bandits, misfits. So far everyone I've met seems to be a misfit (which is always a great help). Another cat is snoozing in the gutter outside the window. I tap the glass to say hullo, what's the secret, but it moves jerkily away, lacking its front left paw. At about 2 am sleep descends for the first time since my arrival.

Next thing – a banging on the door – spasm of shock – I open up – Serafima's bleary eyes flicker back at me out of the gloom: 'Telephone, Duncan. I say he sleep. But she say wake up him.'

Oh God – my father's had a heart attack, mother been strangled, brother electrocuted, sister car crash, flat gone up in flames – the playing cards of disaster snap in the brain as I wrap a towel round my waist – squeak squeak goes the parquet . . .

'Howdy-doody,' says a slightly manic voice. Jill, one of my oldest friends – and I could kill her.

'You're drunk!'

'No I'm not!' She's mightily offended and pissed as a newt.

'Do you know what the time is here? 2.30 in the morning. I just get to sleep and –'

'I didn't know.'

'I just got to sleep for the first time . . .'

'I didn't know the time was different.'

'Where on earth do you think you're phoning then?'

'Oh God, I screwed up, I screwed up!' and she puts the phone down on me.

'Anything bad?' says Serafima.

'No, just a friend. I'm sorry.'

'No problem. I understand.'

And she does. Russians realise that because of the lack of lines into the country, foreign calls sometimes come through at anti-social hours. But that's not Jill's excuse. She's just sloshed and wants to be goofy. In fact it's not that difficult phoning in to Russia. It's phoning out that's the problem. To phone out you must book the call 4 days in advance.

Hot and bothered. Can't get back to sleep. Ugh, what's that? Oh – Ozzie wants sex or something – I throw him out!

The House of Friendship – it's in a dopey state that I meander towards it. En route my attention is first caught by hundreds of cabbage white butterflies obliterating a sheltered corner. They certainly don't swarm like that in Berkshire . . . No, no – I see now what it is – people have stuck to the wall a mass of handwritten advertisements which are fluttering in the breeze; this impromptu bulletin board is a very Russian piece of ingenuity. If you tried to start one up in Notting Hill you'd be arrested for defacement – or charged a fee.

The second thing to be noticed is a pair of men on the opposite side of the road, near the pavilions leading up to the Engineers' Castle. These pavilions, of utmost originality, are 2 of the happiest things in the city, sort of neo-classical baroque or Vanbrugh in fairyland, oval birthday cakes with flattened ends, attic panels, rusticated stucco, and columns. If I fail to mention them again it is not because I don't often stop to study and adore these, well, should I instead be calling them 'lodges' or 'villas'? But they have such a look of vernal pleasure about them that 'pavilion' seems right – but anyway, they are not the rub. To begin with it is a straightforward scene, the pair of men walking along, talking, clerkish with briefcases. Then suddenly they halt – and start to fight. Talk about out of the blue. And real fisticuffs. Heavy punches are thrown before they lock into a wrestle, both faces gasping, bloodshot. A terrible fury has arisen in them. The larger has the smaller by the tie and is twisting him round against a wall, while the smaller kicks back aggressively with his brogues. And, as suddenly, they abdicate the contest. Like schoolboys who've declared pax, the muscles ease, the clothes are adjusted, and they continue along the street as though nothing has happened, the very model of bureaucratic convention.

Oh dear I've been going the wrong way – refer to map – upside down – yes, along here . . . The House of Friendship is a government international-liaison organisation, the legacy of Soviet days, and is housed in the 19th-century Shuvalov Palace. Mmm, very nice – the building has cherubs along the frieze and is on that part of the Fontanka where the canal (which they call a river) gently bends and passes under the equine statuary of the Anichkov Bridge, making blond perspectives to bewitch the soul: lines of pillared palaces crinkle in a heat-haze above bronze-coloured water . . . . .

Within the Shuvalov, Mrs Podnak in a big red blouse takes charge of me. 'The first thing I want to tell you,' she says, jabbing a ball-point into a notepad, 'is that Nevsky Prospekt was not like this before. All these traders are not typical.'

'Shouldn't they sell things?'

'They feel they can stand there and sell anything! They should all be put in *a special place*. It's ugly.'

'I do love it.'

She goes blank for an instant behind her spectacles, then lunges forward. 'But our city is not this – it is a museum city!'

'It's falling down.'

'Jolly well right there. And the problem also is the mafia.'

'Yes, freedom can be messy.'

'We have gone from total protection to total exposure. They throw us off a cliff and say fly! How can we help you?'

'I'd like to meet some gymnasts. And some ballerinas.'

Her nostrils flare slightly in suppressing a yawn and she says 'Let me introduce you to Sonya, my assistant.'

A slim and sultry woman with long black hair sidles into the room. She is about 45, elegant in blue pleated skirt, white blouse and pearls, and speaks in a hypnotic drawl touched by an almost Scottish burr. 'I know the kind of people writers like to meet,' she says, flicking back a stray lock of hair.

This is Sonya, very languid, very cultured, lover of Bath and York, erudite upon Shelley and the Brontë country. She can transfix you with a flow of stories about St Petersburg and its buildings, explaining who was murdered where, so that it is with reluctance that one interrupts this brilliant and inexhaustible fleuve in order to alter its course. In her casually replete manner, she escorts me through the state apartments of the palace, so reminiscent of the First Class waiting-rooms of a Victorian railway terminus – most are assigned to 'conference' purposes and all have ruched net blinds to protect the interiors from light – whereafter we descend to the House of Friendship café for refreshment.

'Can I have that please?'

'Borzhomi,' she breathes, 'Stalin's favourite mineral water. Where are you staying?'

'Baskov Pereulok.'

'Ah, near the KGB Headquarters.'

'There are some mad 19th-century buildings there too.'

'This we call "cock".'

'You do what?'

'Cock, cock. This florid merchant design of things, from the 19th century in St Petersburg, we call it the Cock Style.'

'Why?'

'It's obvious. You know what a cock is?'

'I believe I do.'

'The hen's husband. Therefore it's called the Cock Style because it is full of display and puffed-up like a cock. Do you know what is one of my favourite pastimes? To visit the countryside and look at the cocks. They are so varied, so beautiful, so puffed-up, so splendid! Russians love cocks. In Yugoslavia they love peacocks – but we love just cocks. Some are quite small, some very big – white ones, red ones, brown ones – no 2 cocks are the same. But all of them are wonderful! It is traditional in Russia, when you enter a village, to be presented with a white cloth sprinkled with salt and pepper, and embroidered on the cloth is always – cocks. Oh, I love cocks!'

As Mrs Podnak joins us, Sonya says to her, in a less fulminant tone, 'He chose Stalin's favourite mineral water.'

'From the good old days,' I say jocularly.

'Jolly well right good old days!' proclaims Mrs Podnak with some emotion, glaring at me through her spectacles.

'All the raw material is here,' I speculate, 'for St Petersburg to be one of the smartest cities in Europe in 50 years' time.'

Sonya moons out of the window: 'I shall not see it.'

'I'm trying to persuade a friend of mine to open a bookshop.'

'Let me tell you,' says Sonya, 'that near to the Russian Museum is a forgotten club which before the Revolution was called the Wandering Dog, the resort of talented bohemians. It has wonderful wall paintings done by artists of that time and has for many years been locked up, waiting. I'd love to see it used again.'

'But would he get enough passing trade there?' I ask. One suddenly feels expert in such matters – most Westerners get attacks of entrepreneurialitis in this new Russia.

'It is a very beautiful space.'

'But the passing trade, Sonya,' echoes Mrs Podnak. 'Would he get enough of it?'

'You see, with the ozone layer disappearing so fast,' I continue, 'no one will want to go to the beaches of the Mediterranean. They will all be crowding north to the pleasure domes of St Petersburg. It's obvious.'

'Do you think it possible?' whispers Mrs Podnak, her eyes growing large and lustrous behind the spectacles.

'After 75 years of repression there'll be a supernova of creativity!'

'Yes!' chorus the 2 women.

'Unless . .'

'Unless?' They peer closer.

'Unless the mafia chokes it.'

'By the way,' says Sonya, 'our ozone layer is extremely thin because we are close to the Arctic.'

'Oh . . . Then whatever happens, *don't* let them knock down the buildings. The architecture is your guarantee of a future. Unless you are very determined, opportunist builders will happily destroy this town like piranha fish on a drowning man.'

'Our city receives 25% of Russia's total budget for restoration,' says Mrs Podnak, her eyebrows arched with pride.

'It's not enough,' says Sonya. 'I am very worried about a corner site near the Astoria. It was the old Paris Hotel, very fashionable before the Revolution, and waiting 10 years to be restored. Soon it will collapse all by itself and –'

'If you want to meet any officials,' says Mrs Podnak cutting in, 'that can be arranged.'

'I don't think so.'

'But if you change your mind . . .'

'You won't forget – gymnasts. And ballerinas.'

'I'll get onto it,' says Sonya with a dreamy cackle.

From the plastic bag which I carry round like a Russian in preference to anything more mugworthy, I draw out a small bottle of Floris's Edwardian Bouquet Concentrated Bath Essence, hesitate, then present it to Mrs Podnak as the superior party. She exudes a rich, deep, genuine smile, and suddenly as radiant as a teenager, blinking bashfully, she says 'Please think of the House of Friendship as your second home.' Tripping down the grand staircase, I hum 'Shuvalov to Buffalo'.

A fresh wind has got up and blown the sky into a clear bell of blue. Flakes are flying off the lime trees and whorling about like carnival confetti. Between the electrically erect Church of Blood and the voluptuously coiling art nouveau gateway to the Mikhailovsky Gardens, where tennis players pop on the courts, a thin knock-kneed man, trolling along in flared jeans and Joe Orton cap, bounces up and asks 'My poems?', opening a shoulder-bag of hand-printed works. I decline and without pause he bounces over to someone else who also declines. His indefatigable pursuit of customers is admirable but almost too abrupt to succeed – he is too much to swallow in 3 seconds and one is making the instinctive reflex of refusal without really wanting to.

Ahead is the Field of Mars at whose heart burns the Eternal Flame. It is planted with mauve and white lilac, and inside one of these coppices 2 girls are embracing softly. A little further on, sheltered from the wind, is a spot to sunbathe with fruity views. Opposite, through trees, stands a straw-coloured edifice with portico, pediment, giant order rounding the corner, and a floral frieze to add luxury. These palatial blocks which line the streets go by the name of 'Dom', ie. house. To the left rises the Church of Blood, *Scheherazada* made matter, towers in torsion, outcrop of mirth and mosaic, diaphanous and palpitating like a Big Top above the surrounding strata of classical taste: a conjunction of genius. And to the right –

Oh . . . no more for a minute . . . . . My head falls back among dandelion clocks in the uncut grass, and whiffs of lilac scent drift into the nostrils. Here I am the only sunbather. Perhaps it smacks too much of hedonism near a memorial: although Russians have gone right off labour, they sometimes seem rather nervous of falling into pleasure. No doubt Mrs Podnak would disapprove of the way I'm throwing out my arms and legs – but one has to say, the inner Podnak resilience is quite amazing, given that all her external certainties have been decimated. Sonya on the other hand is a natural swimmer. Part of her is an artist and thrilled by the berserk dance of a Russia unchained.

Only as the body subsides into relaxation, each widening parameter of the descent signalled by asymmetrical twitches, do I realise that it has been gripped by a terrific tension. When this realisation has been fully achieved, it begets a tiny worry which duly initiates the reverse process, and I start to wind up again, my aplomb in stripping off on this particular grass, near this particular flame, decreasing proportionately. There is distant music. In the Summer Garden, to which I take myself, a small scratch band is playing Latin-American-dictator rumbas and tangos with pizzazz, with swing, and the diabolical rat-a-tat snare drum giving a Kurt Weill touch. Tears fill the eyes but only one spills over.

By the time I get home, the wind has blown dust into everything:

throat, lungs, hair, clothes, shoes, socks, between toes, and especially under fingernails which should be kept very short in St Petersburg. Try the Lenko number again (the kitchen phone has acquired a new sticker: Don't worry, Be Happy) and a young woman answers, speaking broken English in an accent which isn't Russian. He's not there. He's away until the end of August. 'But I have some books to give him from England.' OK, she says, bring them round to-night. After a fast dinner of soup with a little rice in it, meat-filled ravioli pouches, carrots and potatoes sprinkled with coriander and dill, followed by cake and strong tea, I wash, change, and rush out again as Serafima says 'Duncan, you can invite your friends here. It is not a problem.' (I have since discovered – in Poznansky's biography of Tchaikovsky – that the Russian word for cock qua cockerel also [like the English word] connotes 'penis'.)

Are You Ready To Die? The Lenko flat is on the Field of Mars – in the block with the giant order rounding the corner. Which is known as the Writer's Block. The path to almost any Russian flat, even in the grandest architecture, is via a staircase inky and forbidding. How did the Communists so alter gracious buildings as to create such a phenomenon as the death-staircase? Despite the pervasion of white nights, I remember most of these hanging graveyards as stripped of lightbulbs, windowless, black as hell. Glimmers of wan illumination may fall on broken floortiles, chipped marble steps, ravaged banisters of wrought iron, forgotten landing fireplaces, damaged stucco swags overpainted beyond recognition. And in buildings of the later 19th century, thanks to the glorious gurgitations of the Cock Style, staircases can attain to a degree of Frankensteinish horror that is well nigh sublime. Those of the earlier, neo-classical period however are more simple, and this particular one in the Writer's Block (built circa 1825?) is not too bad, grim without being actively malign.

Like Serafima's, the front door is padded, for noise and to absorb the shocks of attempted break-ins, but it carries a panoply of bolts and locks far in excess of hers. Beyond it lies another world. Though not large, the rooms are finely proportioned, cube-shaped, and they sparkle with cut and cobalt blue glass, gilt lamps, empire furniture, chandeliers, pictures, cabinets of books.

'Yes, I know,' chuckles its occupant. 'When Russians come they say ah, it is like before the Revolution!'

She is about 30, with lively Latin looks, and a quality of eupeptic optimism which turns out to be an incorrect assessment: it is only the style in which she approaches thoughts of doom. Her head is wrapped in a buoyant turban and she proffers a fruit, an unusual lemon-shaped orange with the smooth, waxy, slightly translucent skin of a medlar.

'Do you know what it is? Neither do I. Drink?'

'Water please. Boiled is OK. I drink so much water in this town, don't you?'

'You drink boiled water?' Beside the fruit bowl lies an invitation to the War and Peace Ball in London.

'Um – yes.'

'Careful! Boil several times – at least 3. I drink only bottled.'

'We also have countryside water which we don't boil.'

'Ugh! What countryside? It may be radioactive. Would you like a cognac as well?'

'I'd prefer vodka.' (I've taken to tippling vodka, though I never much cared for it before. In moderation it has emollient properties without blurring the perception.)

'I'll take a cognac. They never discuss the radioactivity. They never discuss the real problems. Don't swim.'

'I packed my trunks.'

'Don't swim in the sea or in the lake or in the swimming-pool!'

'A swimming-pool can't have radioactivity.'

'Why not? And there will be other activity. Like germs.'

'They put in chemicals.'

'Yes, my God, and what chemicals! Would you like some caviar?'

'Is it radioactive?'

'I don't know, but the Caspian Sea certainly is.'

She returns from the kitchen with white bread, butter and a tin which she opens. 'This is red caviar. I prefer it. Would you try it for me?'

'Of course. Why?'

'Maybe it is bad. Sometimes they do something awful at the factory. Only buy in a tin, never in a glass – they can open the couvercle and mix with rubbish.'

'This is good.'

She tries it too, savouring without haste, and says in a ruminative voice 'Yes . . . mmm . . . this is a good one.'

'I've already had dinner.'

'What did you have?'

'Like ravioli with minced-meat inside.'

'Typical Russian dish. Do you know how they do the minced-meat?'

'No . . .'

'They mix the meat with newspapers.'

'That's an interesting recipe but I'm sure Serafima –'

'And there are no proper controls, so the animals have diseases.'

'Why did you bother to come to Russia?'

'I love it! Salut to Peter the Great! It's his birthday to-day. Salut to Pushkin! It was his birthday on Saturday.'

Her name is Mira Apraxin, of Russian father, Spanish mother, living in Belgium. She is here to learn the language and unearth some roots. Despite her background, her whole manner is Parisian and it is odd coming across this frantic French routine in St Petersburg.

'The shock is not only when you arrive in this place,' she says. 'There is another shock perhaps greater – when you return to your country and you can hardly communicate with your friends. I was so angry to-day! A boy tried to charge me $6 for a T-shirt! I said I have only roubles and he said no problem, give me 600 roubles, and I said are you mad? Some men in Russia work a whole month for 1,000 roubles. I made a fight and eventually he admitted that he gets only 10%. The rest will go to the mafia. So nothing changes – the strong people get everything, the poor people nothing. It was always like this here. I said don't you mind being exploited? He looked blank.'

'Maybe he was lying. Maybe he gets 30%, 40%.'

'You are right. Reality in Russia is a fog! I went to the old Apraxin Palace yesterday. Strange feeling . . .' She falls silent for a moment. '. . . . Cognac doesn't go with caviar. I'll change to vodka. Should I mix?'

'Have a glass of water first. Is that candelabrum made of Siberian jasper?'

'Probably. If you eat caviar when you drink, you don't get drunk. That's what they say. The caviar absorbs the alcohol. Take more vodka, eat more caviar!' She makes the beau geste with a beringed hand. 'Let me tell you – I wanted to have feast, mixing different groups like we do in the West, to make new chemistry. So I tried it. No good! The temperature was ice. Russians are *so suspicious* of each other. Never again shall I try it.'

And they don't understand about going out. When I say "Let's go out," they say "Why?" '

'Maybe you're with a funny lot. My landlady loves going out. So do I.'

'Bravo! Then we can go out!'

'She swims in the lake too.'

'But not in the sea I hope. Finland is very worried. They offer money to clean it up but Russia says clean up what? there is no problem.'

'Stop! For the next 10 weeks I'm going to believe the Russians.'

'They lie a lot. After several hundred years of living in a police state, it comes naturally. The real problem is nobody knows what's happening. The world's biggest country is – I don't know how to say in English.'

'Dissolving?'

'More.'

'In chaos? . . . . In *rotting* chaos?'

'Um . . '

'In meltdown?'

'That's it! In meltdown.'

'Listen, for the past year I've had eczema on 3 fingers. Radioactivity must be good for it.'

'Ah, eczema!' she exclaims, throwing up her eyes and showing her palms in gleeful response to a new ghastly theme. 'It is the latest disease in Europe! Everybody has it!'

'No, what I want to say is that in the short time I've been here, my eczema has cleared up, gone away, kaput, niet, zilch! Miraculous.'

'Don't be impatient,' she says, eyes laughing, both hands adjusting her turban, 'it will return.'

'Maybe not. Maybe I'm past the point of return now.'

'Yes, I know that feeling,' she says and looks out of the window with a rueful expression. 'What's the worst thing you ever heard?'

'Um . . .' I think for several seconds – so many awful things but the question has cancelled every single one. Then a recollection, and gazing at the vodka bottle, down which droplets of condensation run like tears, I say 'Sumo wrestlers have a special servant to wipe their bottom.'

It Begins. Walk along any street. Every 50 feet or so you will encounter an opening, large enough to take a lorry, into an inner courtyard. These are rarely ceremonial entrances. Most seem to have been crudely punched through the ground floor, a television-screen-shaped access into the heart of the tough life behind the delectable façade, a succession of private video clips at your shoulder as you walk along – man playing with cat, girl calling upwards, woman in rags hobbling with a stick to a bench. And sometimes children playing – but not as often as you'd expect. These are not spaces of boisterous expression. The clip is always specific, the courtyard possessed by a preponderating reserve, an underlying quiet and stillness into which the specific event is re-absorbed. City of 100,000 courtyards, none of them pretty – their accursed or ominous or defaced beauty is almost never compromised by a tree or a window box – usually it's debris and dustbins. Many are masterpieces of a nostalgia infinitely subtle in its gradations of decay. And all are brim-full of stories.

As often as you pass one of these openings, you will pass a telephone kiosk or hooded wall apparatus, probably inoperative, certainly with glass smashed. Cracked and broken glass is everywhere. Green glass, brown glass, white glass. The streets, yards and staircases are glass-splashed, urine-splashed, vomit-splashed. Unidentifiable vapours hang among rusty pipes. Electric wires snake up outside walls, up lamp-posts, across streets, swing aimlessly, exposing the population to rude awakenings. You are in a place of physical danger – loose steps, holes, things sticking out. You will be grazed, slapped, stabbed by inanimate objects. Plants push through pavements from the soggy earth below, making volcanoes of asphalt over which you stumble, or they dangle green arms from mouldering cornices and attics, pieces of which fall on you. Cobbles tumble askew among tramlines, railings are buckled, fences twisted, walls cracked or stained or pitted or dripping, sometimes no more than vertical rubble. Brickwork flushes red beneath a rout of stucco.

Mrs Podnak sighs 'It was not like this before.' But to wreck the physical tissues of a metropolis to their very pith takes a long period of time. Most of the last 100 years. And here we are at the end of the 20th century in an arena of anachronisms, both of past and future, which render the place timeless. Take a look through windows – minor clerks organise the distribution of army underwear in a count's faded smoking-room – half a rococo boudoir to store dried beans – an old lady typing in

the corner of a scruffy ballroom wipes the heat from her brow. Between
dilapidated columns, an industrial tower or radio mast, remote in the
peripheral distance, blinks and beckons from an electronic utopia to
come, which when you reach it, by taxi or underground or a leap of the
imagination, is far more pregnant with catastrophe than is the old city –
though both are the more exciting for that. And yes, it is hot indeed.
Unsteady and sepia-tinted, St Petersburg floats on mud in a hot humid
summer, networked by canals whose steep banks of pink granite channel
a liquid which changes from black to purple to bronze to dark blue for
reasons best known to itself. Mira is right about reality here being a fog. I
have to write down every task otherwise I forget it, otherwise its reality
does not impinge. I do not only mean appointments, things to see, things
to buy, but well, for example, on my list for to-morrow I have put 'Shave'.

O seething and sleazy necrosis shot with paranoia! So magnificently,
heart-rendingly beautiful and full of dread! Derelict from end to end,
from top to bottom – I emphasise: you cannot imagine the splendour of
this. It has to be witnessed. Everything broken. Not only cars, clocks,
taps, windows. Also hearts, minds, memories, insides. Everyone has to
make it up as they go along, day by day. We are living in a giant do-it-
yourself kit. Therefore the mystery, the spirit, the drama are not broken.
On the contrary, they are invigorated and flow as fluid pigments in coils,
spasms and fitful lines through the days and nights of the city. And on the
day following the conversation with Mira – out of all this swirling dinge
and lurid angst and breathless impressionism – there appears a bright
golden face. It is in clear definition, smiling hesitantly, and of a freshness
which disorientates, in that one is for a second magnetised by this quality,
rather than curious as to who possesses it. A young cadet from the nearby
Dzerzhinsky Naval Academy is, perhaps, asking me for a cigarette. This
is a frequent request in Russia, I should have got the hang of it, but I am at
a loss and he notices that. Removing his cap out of courtesy, he runs a
hand through curly blond hair in a shy gesture. I smile uncomfortably,
say 'Niet' in the hope that this is a plausible reply, and walk on through
the Gorky Gardens. But annoyed by my feebleness, by the automatic
shrinking away from contact like a tense tourist frightened of being taken
advantage of, I stop and turn round. But he has vanished. Really I must
start carrying cigarettes – I have 200 Camels at the flat, always my basic
puff, but I gave up years ago. Not long afterwards I shall discover that his
name is Dmitri.

CHAPTER TWO

Sonya telephones and says 'The gymnasts and ballerinas are a little complicated. I am trying. For the moment, would you like to visit a sculptress and a poet?'

We meet at the House of Friendship in the evening and she introduces her son Rodion. He is small, bespectacled, with a mischievous face, and pulls a paper from his rucksack.

'This is *Hotel*,' he says, 'my new magazine.'

Among the texts are plenty of cartoons and photographs of naked women: obviously an avant-garde production.

Sonya, chic in black suit and discreet jewelry, tosses her hair: 'Hm, the new sexuality . . .'

'What are the stories about?'

'Everything. Sex mostly,' replies Rodion, screwing up his face in a mudlark grin. 'I take the photographs myself.'

We walk to Ulitsa Tchaikovsky where heavy brown iron gaspipes are laid above the pavement. Children jump up and down on them. Another scowling staircase – as I stumble, Rodion says 'We have problem for lightbulbs. Most are made in Armenia. Now we cannot get them. It's the same with fridges – biggest factory is in Baltic States.'

The door is opened by a girl with Jimi Hendrix hair and we remove our shoes. The release of the foot from its bondage, this greater contact with the floor, always eases the soul. We cram into a tiny kitchen as best we can, Sonya almost out in the passageway. Masha the Sculptress makes a fuss of her, nods at me, and keeps stirring the pot. An Airedale bounces in.

'Radek!' rebukes the girl as the animal slobbers. The name is short for Rudyard as in Kipling. Their previous dog was called Keats.

'What do you think of the English?' I enquire, finding my soul not so very eased after all.

'They like jokes,' laughs the girl (who is the daughter of the house). 'And they love their traditions. And they don't like immigrants.'

'How can that be?' I protest. 'We have the most cosmopolitan society in Europe.'

She replies, with an effective tremble of the hair, 'Maybe the immigrants like you!'

'It is also very well known', adds Sonya, stretching with her head, long neck and upper body as far into the kitchen as she can, 'that the English are the most romantic people in Europe. Oh, it was always my dream to cross the English Channel in a northerly direction – and I did it! The place I would most like to live in the whole world is Oxford.'

It comes over the radio – putsch in Moldavia.

'Every day, something more,' mutters Masha the Sculptress, slapping a cup of very strong tea in front of me. There is no milk. Masha is stout in a colourful knitted jumper and black track-suit trousers. Muscular hands betray her calling – or she could be a pianist – or a labourer (you see quite a number of female labourers around, carrying buckets of rubble).

Her husband, Misha the Poet, lanky, sitting in the corner, leaning sideways, hands trapped between his knees, complains 'An ice-cream is more expensive than a ticket to the Kirov! Ridiculous!'

'Mafia block food supplies,' announces the Sculptress, echoing the radio news as she moves among the rudimentary tracklements of her galley.

Sotto voce, Sonya says 'Masha and Misha are not very happy.'

The Poet conjures up a thick typescript and dumps it in my lap: a study of Russian poetry, complete with annotations and final corrections. His life-work, it was ready to go – and cancelled on the eve of publication. The state publishing house had run out of money.

'I work up there.' Misha points to an eyrie contrived near the ceiling, reached by a step-ladder, and secured by a florid wrought iron balcony salvaged from some falling façade. 'I can be Juliet,' he says, 'and Masha can be Romeo by the stove.'

Her knitted bulk turns, slaps a plate of bread and a dish of sprats on the table, and commands me to eat.

'They are from the Neva,' says Rodion with a provocative twinkle, tucking in at once.

Masha had many sculptures completed, ready to adorn the Institute of Agronomy, but now they sit in her workshop because the Institute has no money to pay for them. Sonya explains this to Masha's accompaniment of despairing grunts. The state system of arts patronage and control has passed away. For new artists, whose ingenuity is a response to vicissitude, the possibilities are now limitless, but for the older ones . . . I fancy there is no place for this Sculptress and this Poet between the pages of *Hotel*. Beached by history, Masha slaps another cup of very strong tea in front of me and a chunk of boiled fish and says something.

'Masha wants to know what you think of Russia,' interprets Sonya in her best charm school manner.

'Too soon to say.'

'Say something.'

'I'm dislocated. Rhythms are fractured. Sleep up the spout –'

'Up the what?'

'Insomnia. Things, people, emotions don't connect in the way I'm used to. I sometimes feel about to cry for no explicable reason. One minute I feel a target, next minute I feel invisible.'

'It will get worse,' nods Rodion.

'And at the same time, better,' nods Sonya, patting my knee. 'You will accept it more. But our world, you cannot envisage it! For example, we have no judicial system. It was crushed by the Communists.'

'No one knows who the land belongs to.'

'University professors are walking the streets trying to sell their shoes.'

'At least you have oxygen now?' I venture.

'We can breathe but we cannot eat.'

Neither can I very well. Chewing is easy, deglutition is not. I know it's churlish in the face of their generosity but after a number of well-intentioned assaults upon it, I summon up the courage to push away the plate.

The Sculptress inhales the kitchen and exhales a short phrase. Rodion translates: 'Masha says you will not get more tea until you have finished your fish.'

'I don't want more tea.'

'You have forgotten how to eat simple things,' says Sonya in a muted wail. 'You are accustomed to strawberries and cream and bananas. But now you must learn to eat like a peasant.'

Her raillery returns me to the struggle but I cannot manage the heavy egg roe which gives off a discouraging fume.

'That's the best part,' says the Sculptress unrelentingly. Thin rays of aggression out of her eyes bring hotness to my skin. From neck upwards I am transformed into a bunch of thorny roses and chilli peppers. But I'll be cudgelled only up to a point. My ego stirs, and I quietly and decisively place knife and fork together. Russians traditionally leave their knife and fork angled and apart on the plate, but I feel she grasps what my own gesture purports.

Rodion suggests opportunely 'Would you like to see the roof?' And he leads me there, via secret entrances, steps and attics, trailed by Radek and the daughter. One last narrow wooden walkway over plaster and insulation between beams, through a glazed trapdoor and . . . air! light! space! wind! breathe in deeply and breathe out nerves . . . 'It is like a Braque,' he says.

An immaculate roofscape, of interlocking triangles and trapezoids in dull red and green and silver, recedes on all sides, interrupted only by the looping bite of the Neva. The roofs are made from a metal alloy which booms when you walk on it and we are perched triumphantly on a booming apex. Radek, who has been dragged hither much against his will, looks ready to shit himself with terror, his paws slithering frantically on the steep inclines, while the girl pulls him up by a throttling lead and laughs, her Hendrix hair spangled with horizontal light from a huge scarlet sun hanging above the river.

'In Islam,' she says, 'the roof is women's territory during daylight. If a man goes onto the roof during the day, he creates a scandal.'

'Look,' says Rodion, pointing to a grey and turquoise beetle across the water, a clanking robot from *The War of the Worlds* lifting its antennae to the left of the *Aurora* cruiser. This is St Petersburg's mosque, built between 1910 and 1912, in a manner influenced by art nouveau ('the modern style' as Russians call it) and presaging art deco. It is currently being renovated by Muslims.

'Rodion is an expert on our city,' says the girl, 'especially on the secret courtyards, the black life we call it, the life behind the façades.'

Back in the kitchen he says 'I can take you for a walk on Sunday. To some terrifying places.'

'I however shall be unable to accompany you', his mother regrets, 'because on Saturday I go to Zelenogorsk for my annual holiday. Government dacha. The name means green hill and, oh yes, it is very beautiful place where little gothic villas, with carved balconies and old furniture, fringe the lake.'

As usual I am captivated by her lulling use of English and sensual burr; then Masha slaps more tea down in front of me and a polythene bag of small bagel rings. The tea – no – it is extremely strong, I have downed 5 cups already, it's gone 11 pm now, I'll never sleep. Enough. Thank-you.

'But we thought you would like it after being up on the cold roof,' whines Sonya with a frown.

'It wasn't cold. Honestly, Sonya, I'll never sleep if I keep drinking this.'

Masha slaps down a cup of hot water, a welcome substitute, with a surly twist of her body. Russians, through years of hardship, consume anything that's put in front of them. Not to do so seems an unpardonable affectation. So what! I shall defy this conspiracy to pour more tea down my throat. Why must they make me feel I've given offence merely by refusing an extra cup of tea? Is one not allowed to hold a little to one's own nature? Hoping to make amends I resort to the bagel. But it is so hard I am unable to break it either with teeth or fingers. Rodion, delighted by my quandary, giggles and demonstrates the technique, holding it at an angle in his palm and pressing hard. The knack however eludes me . . . . moments tick away and I'm becoming the centre of attention again as all minds focus on my desperate involvement with the bagel. Will it? Or won't it? Unable to withstand a combination of subtle movement and force of will, its adamantine integrity eventually succumbs. I look up, expecting a round of applause, but they merely start snapping away with their own bagels. Masha is the supreme master at it – the bagel only has to see her coming in order to pulverise itself in self-abasement. I put a small piece in my mouth hoping it will soften which, after being lobbed about by the tongue, it slowly begins to do; then all at once – it's pulp. Radek dribbles hopefully in the wings, longing for the bagel which won't, which resists every approach, which is then tossed out of the circle of humanity and into the jaws of a dog. All bagels play hard to get but rare is the bagel which truly prefers pets.

The Poet, shifting lankily, turns to the wall and says 'I feel like an insect, trodden on, crushed, just managing to crawl forwards a centimetre or so.'

'But Russia is still the best place!' trumpets the Sculptress. 'We have a crisis. But it is the biggest, the best, the most *magnificent* crisis in the whole world!'

In the background, on the radio, the Kremlin Clock strikes midnight. The daughter laughs, showing white separated teeth.

Lack Of Information. On the rising floor of the darkly illumined lift at Baskov Lane are 4 or 5 cardboard cigarette ends. In the 1960s Imperial Russian Cigarettes, constructed with such cardboard extensions, could be purchased in large, square, tissue-lined, flip-top boxes from a shop in the Burlington Arcade. They were handmade above the premises by 2 old ladies. An alternative, more compact variety was Chaliapin Cigarettes. And yet another: Cairo Cigarettes, untipped, oval, done in an oblong, powder-blue, tissue-lined, flip-top box of 50, with a mosque printed on the lid and on the cigarette paper too – Benson & Hedges introduced them at the time of Edward VII's visit to Egypt and, incredulous though you will be, they were banned only recently by a European Union diktat – as assuredly Imperial Russian Cigarettes would have been, had they endured, possessing as they did a rich aromatic oriental tobacco, an immense length due to the incorporation of the hollow cardboard filter (which would be squeezed flat at its end prior to ignition, to create as it were a built-in cigarette-holder), and for being, perhaps most culpably of all, absolutely the grandest cigarettes available anywhere – oh, those giant creamy boxes gallooned with a fine maroon line and emblazoned with the Romanov coat of arms! But alas the 2 old ladies passed away without finding anyone to inherit their rolling technique. All this sort of thing survives longest in London which, since the eclipse of Italy in the 18th century, has been the world capital of dress and articles for gentlemen as has Paris over the equivalent period for gentlewomen. However, this local – and presumably original – variety of the card-tipped cigarette, on the rising lift floor, is considered the lowest smoke by Russians.

Squeaking through the hall, I spy Serafima rapping on the phone in the kitchen. She puts it down, pours me a shot of vodka, and says 'Katya telephoned.'

'Where are the KGB Headquarters?'

She flaps a hand over her shoulder.

'What are they up to these days?'

'Nobody knows,' she says, adding with a tinge of exasperation 'This is the problem with Russia to-day – lack of information! Are you hungry?'

'Little bit . . .'

She foxtrots across the room, hacks at something, returns with a plate of damson shortbread sprinkled with sugar. Homemade and tasting of bliss. A number of photographs are scattered on the oilcloth, as though earlier she was musing down memory lane. Here's one of her bikini-clad in the crooked branches of a pine tree on the Black Sea. A leg dangles provocatively. There, under lights, dancing in a beaded and sequined gown, bending backwards, right over, hair almost sweeping the floor. The face of the male partner cannot be seen, only the back of his black-haired head. And here is Serafima with friends, the single woman among couples. While they joke with each other heedless of the camera, she moves out of the collective mood and smiles directly at the lens, addressing the future. This is the pre-perestroika world, naïve, enclosed, lost for ever.

Looking up from the pictures, she says with wistful passion 'There is a very beautiful concourse in Blackpool . . .'

'How does a Russian know that?'

'I am only part Russian. I am also part Tartar. Genghis Khan! Are you frightened?' She doesn't look remotely Tartar.

It's after 1 am. Is it bedtime? That has become a very vague concept of late . . . My room smells fresh from the toiletries in my luggage. Russian rooms don't smell fresh. Cleaning materials are difficult to find and expensive. Not only that. In summer they must keep out mosquitoes and in winter the cold. Not only that. They love a warm fug. A security thing. That their persons are as clean and spruce as they are in this soapless city of dust is a victory of perseverence. Of course they have the 'banya'. There are many enormous bath-houses here. Almost everyone goes to them and so before long shall I.

Putting Ozzie out in the hall, impervious to his leg-trembling pleas, I return to a secret stash of Jordan's Original Crunchy Bars. Most of the goods have been brought over as gifts, but a few are reserved for my solitary pleasure. As though embarking on an adventure of auto-eroticism, I unzip the rigid bar.

When in England my intention of spending the summer in St Petersburg became known, a number of the men said 'Really?' and seemed slightly put out. Most of the women said 'My God! Can we visit you?'

Jennifer Paterson asked 'Is St Petersburg what used to be called Moscow?'

Frances Stonor Saunders warned 'They stab you in the back for your denim jacket' and her brother Alexander said with a leer 'Their health service has collapsed.'

My mother said 'Do be careful' but was very excited, and my father said 'Well done. Where did I put *The Sporting Life?*'

Michael Wylde: 'I want to come and clean all the silver in the Hermitage. They never clean it.'

Von gave me a pot of her marmalade and a universal plug and James gave me my first Russian lesson.

Justin: 'I'm jealous.'

Ed Berman: 'As a foreigner with £100 per week to spend you immediately become a millionaire which is a weird state if you aren't used to it.'

Micky Karoli: 'Watch out for radioactivity. But there's very little AIDS – so far.'

Brian Clark: 'St Petersburg is the extreme of whatever is happening in Russia – and you have extreme mood swings in that city.'

Jane Rayne: 'Do take a kettle. And loo paper. No, do.'

Kate Braithwaite: 'I bet the rats and cockroaches in St Petersburg are *awful*.'

Mr Nagy from the corner shop: 'I wouldn't go there if you paid me double!'

Alexandra said 'Take an umbrella!' and Layla said 'Take cuppa soups and Earl Grey.'

In the end it was so bewildering – this storm of disparate warnings and advice – that the jitters struck, eczema flared on 3 fingers, and I took all: notepads, pins, pens, Polos, visiting cards, soaps, giant tubes of toothpaste, muesli, Sicilian Tarot, syringes, garlic, Marmite, English mustard, earplugs, Sellotape, weighing machine. T-shirts from Boy in the King's Road, 3 homemade dance tapes, Debussy and Ravel piano music, cheapo personal cassette player, camera, films, Rachmaninov's piano concertos, Elmore James, early Rolling Stones, The Hits of Rhythm King, Orlando Gibbons, Swingout Sister, Hendrix, Webern, Dinah Washington, olives à la grecque, Floris Bath Essences, Fortnun & Mason Black Cherry Jam, Earl Grey, Darjeeling, Tetley ordinaire, batteries, small padlocks, Body Shop shaving creams and shower gels, sardines, coffee, Wilkinson twinblade disposable razors (non-swivel), Sicilian sardine pasta sauce, honey, Dettol, Johnson's Baby Oil, eczema creams, potassium permanganate soluble tablets, Pope, *Martin Chuzzle-wit*, T.S. Eliot's *Collected Poems*, Yeats's *Collected Poems*, Baudelaire, dictionaries, Hazlitt's *Essays*, Bacon's *Essays*, Septivon, Bach's Rescue Cream, condoms, KY, Evening Primrose Oil capsules, Brewer's Yeast, Vitamin B12, Selenium, Cod Liver Oil capsules, Multivitamins with extra iron, Edward Green's boot polish, Milk of Magnesia, Vichy Crème Solaire Anti-Wrinkle with Vitamin F Sun Protection Factor 4, Cool Water by Davidoff, Chanel No.5, Trumper's Spanish Leather, Trumper's English Fern cologne, Taylor's Travelling Shaving Brush, anti-crab shampoo, organic flapjacks, Concentrated Travel Wash, peanuts, more peanuts, Kit-Kats, emergency tranquillisers, plastic gloves, blank cassettes, lecithin, Nurofen, cuppa soups, tissues, torch, travelling toothbrushes, corned beef . . . etc . . . etc . . . etc . . . .

3 stately Borzois on 3 strings are waiting at a bus-stop with their master (it was Catherine the Great who made the Borzoi fashionable). The dogs are relaxed to the point of cretinism but the master is on edge. No doubt he is dreading the embarrassments of the forthcoming journey, of having to transport his waist-high charges aboard one of the trams or buses tightly filled with resentful citizens, and he has in consequence adopted a bellicose, confrontational stance undermined by strain around the eyes. People give the whole group a wide berth.

This I notice walking to the flat of Katya who has invited me for tea. She lives at the Fontanka end of Dzerzhinsky Street, a fair distance away. A number of naval cadets are slouching by the Anichkov Bridge during their afternoon break. They separate and one of them starts to walk alone down a side street. The back of his head conveys something and I say hullo! quite loudly. He turns round.

'Minoot. Don't move. Stay there.' Crossing to a nearby booth, I ask for Camels but the nearest they have is Marlboro. When I return and present them to him, he looks exceedingly abashed and blushes vividly but laughs too, revealing a front tooth chipped at 45 degrees.

'We met before. Gorky Gardens.'

'I know,' he says. He looks down at the cap which he is holding between both hands. 'This must be here,' he says, putting it on. 'If officer see . . '

Sailors are the best-dressed people in town. His uniform is well-made from sturdy cloth, the brilliant white top properly seamed. The buckle of golden metal on his leather belt bears the insignia of an anchor intertwined with hammer & sickle – brass maybe? The alloys in this country are different from those in mine.

'Where are you from?' I ask.

'St Petersburg.'

'I mean when you are not at college.'

'Yes – my home is that way.' He waves to the north. 'Where are you from?'

'London.'

'Oh, beautiful.'

'You know it?'

'No.'

'Your English is good.'

'No, no, no. Little, little.'

He has become nervous as though we should not be talking.

'Are you always at college?'

'Next week holiday begin.' A quick smile jumps across his face.

'Perhaps we could go somewhere. I don't speak Russian. You could help.' Then I go blank, can't think of a thing . . .

'Yes. Where do you want to go?' he asks after a moment.

'Oh – anywhere.' We exchange names and I give him my telephone number and say 'Well, um . . .'

'Excuse me, I am sorry,' he says. 'I am late. Thank-you very much for cigarettes. I like it.' And he's gone. How old is he? 18, 19?

Continuing to Katya's, I pause at Lomonosov Square, look up Theatre Street, laugh aloud, and take the rest of the Fontanka Embankment with a happy-go-lucky stride.

A London girl in her late 20s, Katya lives under the roof at the top of a dark bluish-green staircase (which must have been very pretty 100 years ago) in a lair patterned with blue wallpaper. As well as the CD player, her mother has couriered over a roll of cotton wool and a toy hammock for dunking the white Siberian kitten in warm water to clean it.

'And I've brought you olives à la grecque.'

'How did you know olives are my favourite thing?' The telephone rings; she talks and giggles for a couple of minutes. 'That was Vladik. He's a performance artist who became famous for doing Marilyn Monroe. Then he did Hitler. Now he eats too much and is getting fat so he shaved his head and does Khrushchev. He used to be in the army. He wants to go to the Tam Tam Club.'

'Is that one of the places?'

'Another place you can rave is the Planetarium except that the mafia have moved in on it, so now no one really . . . Do you know about the bridge problem? Oh God, you must have some tea. Have you noticed how racist the Russians are?'

She is a jumpy person. Table and chairs beside attic window over-looking yard – television – ghetto blaster – large heater in corner – disarray of newspapers and magazines on floor – postcard of Einstein and photo of her Russian father (who died recently) pinned, among other snips, to the wall – Peter Pannish student pad atmosphere – night nursery in daylight – and the homely impoverishment of most Russian flats. She shouts through from the kitchen 'Then we can go for a walk!'

'What bridge problem?'

'Do you want sugar? Why are you here?'

'To try and establish precisely how Catherine the Great died.'

'The bridges go up at 2 am for 20 minutes. Then again at 3 until 6. So it's a good excuse if you want to stay with someone for the night. You phone up and say "Can't get back. I'm stuck at the Tam Tam." Catherine the Great? Wasn't it a horse or something?'

'Why are *you* here?'

'. . . Sometimes I wonder . . I find it very tricky attempting to do more than one thing a day.'

'The Russians are beautiful, aren't they?'

'Yes, they score high on that. But be quick. They go off early. Not enough vitamins.'

'Eye contact is permissible.'

'Do you think so?' she exclaims. 'I don't!'

'Another thing that's noticeable – recognising you as a foreigner, they immediately look at what you're carrying and immediately look away. It's face – bag – away. Or bag – face – away. And sometimes just bag – away. Do you know Ennio Nicotra?'

'Is he Russian?'

'Sicilian. I have to be there in about an hour. Near the Maryinsky Theatre.'

'Everyone's on flexi-time here.'

'We could walk in that direction.'

Perambulating slum yards, she recounts how, bringing her mother this way on the woman's first visit to her daughter's new lifestyle, they encountered a man emerging from a manhole in a spacesuit, helmet and shoulders dripping with black slime, surrounded by police and on-lookers. He clambered out of the pestilential sewer, dragging behind him a pair of bloated legs. Gradually they settled a discoloured female corpse on the tarmac.

At Ploschad Mira, a locus of vitality and desperation where the poor sell oddments, shooting and fighting are endemic. Its centre is graced by a tangle of rusty girders as though something under construction in a previous era were stopped and left to the elements, like a vast and jilted Anthony Caro sculpture. By now the open-air market has drawn to a close but a few hopefuls stand about, held in a paralysis of 'perhaps'. One man, respectably dressed, is holding up for sale a single rice biscuit in cellophane. Gangs of tramps joke and squabble beside illegal bonfires, swilling spirit from clear glass flagons. And working women walk home across the square with inauspicious dark crusts on the skin of their shins. We pass westwards into a leafier, more placid district with canals.

'In what way racist?'

'Every way. And anti-Semitic. Russians don't work hard and dislike the Jews who do.'

'I met a sculptress who –'

'And they are unhappy that the Jews have another, more prosperous homeland to look to.'

'– seemed typically Russian in her extreme love-hatred towards her country.'

'So many of them want to leave. They've made such a mess of it. When I first came, with the 24-hour light, everything went haywire. Now I have a sort of routine and get up about midday. Occasionally I get attacks of Protestant guilt about not getting up at 8 am.'

Slowly shuffling by on the left is the Yusupov Palace where they murdered Rasputin – or tried to. He survived poison and bullets and they were obliged to push him through a hole in the ice of the canal outside.

'I love it here, but to fall in love with St Petersburg', she sighs, 'is like falling in love with the wrong person – somehow it always lets you down.'

La Luna Verde. Ennio lives in a large unexciting flat near the Conservatoire for which he pays $100 per month. He is studying to be a conductor and will soon marry a dark-eyed Russian girl who looks more Sicilian than he does.

'I live in this town 2½ years and I love it more and more.'

'Does it remind you of Palermo?'

'Palermo? No! I hate Palermo! In all my time here I have no personal experience of violence. But my friend has. He was in Nevsky Prospekt carrying a sports bag and an Armenian pull out a knife and say what is in your bag? My friend run away. My only problem is with the light.'

Sicilian windows have total-exclusion blinds built into their frames and so Sicilians cannot sleep even with a chink of light.

'Correct. But I have the mask!' he exclaims.

'Doesn't it make your eyes puffy?'

'I train myself. Would you like to see how a conductor at the Maryinsky lives? He is my teacher and has no bathroom and no hot water. You see, I am not naïve about this place either. Go into any shop. They are not interested if you buy or not. On such motivation the Communists tried to build a country.'

Haunting my inner ear in this city is Rachmaninov's First Piano Concerto. Snatches, extended waves, echoes of it, keep slipping through my brain like threads of pearls as the streets move underfoot . . . but to Ennio's knowledge it is not on any programme this season.

Spaghetti with tomato sauce and real Parmesan cheese.

'Do you know Camilla de Martino?'

'Yes. I was there to-day with the Consul. But she is out of the country. She is often out of the country. How do you know her?'

'I don't. We have a friend in common.'

Both Sicilians and Russians live in secretive, violent societies governed by fear – and so truth is not a priority – and therefore close relations are especially significant, in Sicily family, in Russia friends. But this is the North, so one is here never subjected to those bovine obsessions of the South – why aren't you married? don't you want children? don't you want grand-children?

In the taxi home I converse in Italian with a St Petersburg girl of transparent, oval-faced, blue-eyed beauty, set off by a concentration of mood which is very Russian in its combination of taciturnity and liveliness. She has already married her Italian, and with her my use of the Italian language is far more fluent than it was with Ennio, partly because I am less ashamed of its crudeness and partly because her straightforward replies are easier to understand. The taxi reeks of petrol and peering through the window at 2 am we see a green moon over the Fontanka, flying above like a kite in the royal blue sky. Surprisingly the firmament is jewelled with stars and appears richer, deeper, darker than usual. Car headlights are on.

Sonya rings. 'I have now established the correct telephone number of the correct person for gymnasts. He is a member of the Sports Committee which is situated in the House of Physical Culture, a very charming salmon-pink palace in Ulitsa Khalturina.'

'Oh good. What does he say?'

'I don't know. I cannot get an answer. I have tried many times but nobody picks up the phone. But I shall keep at it and someone will try while I am away. Do you know what Masha the Sculptress said after you left? That man will never understand Russia or the Russians.'

'Bloody cheek! Tell Masha that I am not interested in understanding Russia. I am not here to understand Russia. And anyway it seems that Russians understand Russia not much better than anyone else. I simply want to spend a few months working quietly. By the way, enjoy your holiday.'

Sonya does not react but as usual continues her train of thought unphased. 'To understand Russia and the Russians you must realise that our life is entirely absurd – and always was. Russia is people playing many parts and pieces of parts in a huge theatre. You are working on this English novel now?'

'Well, no. But I shall when I've adjusted.'

A girl throws a red ball against the side of an abandoned food lorry down in the yard. The lorry never moves. It is always there, rusting in its clumsy position, badly parked in a way that can't even be called perverse because it was done one day entirely without thought – one day – zip – in through the arch – stick it any old place – forget it – bang/thud/thump goes the ball. Serafima is away for the week-end. Cut a slice of damson shortbread and look in fridge – homemade potted meat, homemade sauerkraut, salami. The jug of prepared milk is almost empty. I mix some up from powder. How does she do it so that it isn't lumpy? Mine is always lumpy. Chicken rissoles for dinner. Not sure which oil is the safe one, so fry them in butter. Too much fried food – like Scotland. Not enough fruit and vegetables. These can easily be bought at the Vladimirskaya Market but I'm too distracted, it has to be organised with an interpreter. My stools are not firm and though of varying colour, they have the consistency of cake mixture before it is cooked. Ah! . . . almost dropped the butter dish. The horror of breaking an item in a Russian household – very likely they would treat such an event with the same tightening politesse as they receive presents but oh the dart in the heart! because even with money, many objects can no longer be replaced . . . . . Ozzie scratches on the bedroom door and howls in the hall through the bathyscopic night . . . . .

Sunday Morning. Rodion rings to confirm our appointment and suggests we meet outside the Sredny Prospekt tube station on Vasilievsky Island, near his place of residence. The weather is perfect – warm, sunny, fresh – and in the small public garden in Ulitsa Nekrasova a group of podgy women and men in caps, all faces deeply lined, hold parley. One of the men ambles to the roadside and, pinching the bridge of his nose between thumb and forefinger, voids his snot into the gutter. Otherwise the streets are empty of people and traffic . . . . . The expansive gentleness of Petersburg at times like these no other city can match . . . It survives until Palace Square (my fault; I should have gone over the Kirovsky Bridge) where a hard hectoring voice through a loudspeaker, promoting trips to Pushkin and Pavlosk, drowns out the brass-band-with-pumping-cheeks by the Winter Palace gates. Gypsy beggars, like figures from a mediaeval print, and a vital part of the town scene, are particularly active to-day. A black-eyed tot, struggling with a papoose swathed in dun rag, intercepts me, eliciting a 5-rouble note. This incites the rest of her party, squatting under a tree, to lift their haunches and advance upon her benefactor. Handing over a further paltry note, I call a halt, making a wall gesture with the hands which they prefer not to acknowledge, so I don sunglasses and walk in brisk haute école towards Palace Bridge, torso hot in black T-shirt, legs cool in faded Bristol blue shorts, hailed by souvenir-sellers.

Having misjudged the distance, I am late for Rodion but he is not put out and leads off with a bouncy step, going up on his toes, towards, it is

hoped, some extravaganza of utmost nightmarishness. But not a bit of it –
we enter a cemetery set in wild birch wood with tombs half-hidden in the
undergrowth, a bucolic idyll among the tidal waves of urban dilapidation.
A number of graves have been overturned in the past by robbers
searching out rings and gold teeth. Currently the place is one of the
mafia's dumping grounds for their victims.

'Do you know soup from this one?' he asks, indicating ferns.

'No, only this one,' I reply, indicating nettles.

An uncannily well-paved path – laid for Nancy Reagan's visit – winds
towards a blue and white baroque chapel hidden by trees. The interior
throbs with yellow candlelight. Women in headscarves press mur-
muringly upon conical long-haired priests covered in rhinestones whose
rose-tinted voices ascend from stomach to vault.

Rodion lives in a communal flat. In the courtyard a man is beating a
carpet over a clothesline with a looped carpet-beater. As we climb the
stairs Rodion says with his hobgoblinistic charm 'Do not be afraid. It's
only what happens when for 75 years people don't own the place where
they live.'

'In London we have a different problem – areas of the historic city
pulled down to make money. Capitalism can be very destructive too.'

In the doorway a silent, heavily pregnant figure is silhouetted. 'That's
my wife,' he says as we slide past. Tea is brewed but she keeps to another
room. A copy of *The Spectator* lies on his desk.

'I have a subscription,' he says.

'You are interested in politics?'

'No! We are sick of politics! We want to make our own lives now. I
enjoyed my stay in England. I liked very much the slums of Stepney. And
I made a discovery. In school we were taught that Britain entered the war
because Stalin asked Churchill to help him in his fight against Hitler. It
was only a few months ago in England that I learned about the Hitler-
Stalin Pact which is not generally known in our country.'

A train of thought is triggered which will become increasingly
important in the weeks ahead: lying . . . propaganda . . . self-protection
. . . delusion . . . squirting ink at the sun . . . darkness . . . uncertainty
. . . absurdity . . . fear . . . a lie is also . . . a dream . . . a desire . . . a
hope . . . a wish . . . a creation . . . a disturbance . . .

A Lemon Is Mentioned. At breakfast a brand new gas mask is hanging over the back of a kitchen chair. What does Serafima know that I don't? She isn't up yet. Make tea and toast – switch on box – film about happy peasants with folk music, haystacks, freshly baked bread emerging from the oven like roast babies: it's mentally subnormal – flick – American low-budget film about a woman working at a supermarket check-out who has an affair with a man in a Rolls-Royce: mentally subnormal. Sergei and Igor are staying for a few days. They are fighting in the bedroom. Now Sergei is crying and saunters into the kitchen drying his eyes and prepares himself a bowl of curds from the fridge. Igor follows him in and puts an egg on to boil. Katya rings to say that someone called Nikita will ring. 5 minutes later Nikita rings and I say come round. Serafima lolls against the doorpost, yawning, and enters the kitchen to prepare her coffee, mumbling incomprehensible phrases. She withdraws with the steaming cup to her dressing-table in the hall; it has a high tilting mirror and is strewn with creams, colours and sticks, plus a very heaped ashtray like a pocket Vesuvius. She is late for her English lesson. Nikita, who lives close by, turns up in shades with circular lenses. His hair is cropped very short. I hand him a cup of tea. Leonid arrives to change money, looking harassed and drained (more so, that is, than usual). Between gulping the last of her coffee and flying out the door, Serafima causes a yellow object to materialise on the chopping-board. 'If you want lemon with your tea, Duncan . .' Decidedly casual was her act of prestidigitation but the fruit is a great luxury. Lemons haven't been around for over 2 years.

'Your landlady seems fun,' says Nikita. 'I am having trouble with my landlord.'

'Why?' His sunglasses are like 2 black gun barrels levelled at me.

'I put a certain postcard on my wall.' Nikita is an avant-garde journalist. (Fuses are short in this town. Or endlessly, infinitely long . . .)

On the way out I have a twinge – really, Serafima's locks are nothing compared to Emelyon Lenko's and there's 10 weeks' worth of dollars cash under Ozzie's bum in my bedroom. Money, like lying, is another insidious theme.

'Do you want to come to the Gayfest?' asks Nikita.

'Sure. When is it?'

'A group from Hamburg are helping to organise.'

Leonid is to-day changing roubles at 125 per US dollar – it keeps leaping – and at one of the secondhand bookshops on Liteiny Prospekt I buy a Russian guide to St Petersburg, published in 1913, for 1,350 roubles. The lady in the booth marked Cash, with plastic combs holding back wads of grey hair, counts out the notes twice, checks the sum against the abacus, rings it up on the till. But tills have not kept pace with inflation, so she is obliged to ring it up in repetitions of 90 roubles, the top figure on her machine.

A Nuclear Submarine In The Foyer. So if Russia is this absurd theatre, let's go . . . Michael Stronin is the Literary Director of the Maly Drama Theatre, lately famous for its exuberant and frank treatment of previously controlled subjects such as village life, army life, and every other form of life ('Lots of swear-words and on-stage nudity,' says Nikita). Mr Stronin is standing beside his office desk in gaudy Turnbull & Asser braces, and in a narrow crevice between phonecalls he asks 'How do you find St Petersburg?'

'Strange.'

'So do we.'

He is about to vanish to Wales for his summer holiday – near Ruthin – but arranges for a translator to accompany me to several performances.

The first play is *Home* and the translator, small and doll-like with a mop of brown hair, is waiting at 7 pm outside the theatre in Rubinstein Street. He is in sports dress, having come directly from a Kung Fu training session, and his name is Vladimir Vvedensky (I want to call him VVV but inevitably this gets shortened to VV). After a cordial greeting he explains 'There are 3 variants. 1: we can both sit in the stalls and I whisper a commentary in your ear. 2: you can sit in the stalls and I can relay a commentary from a closed box via headphones. 3: we can both sit in this special glass-fronted box at the back of the circle and I can tell you what's going on in a natural voice.'

'Let's start with No.1 and see what happens.' I propose a fee with that touch of querulousness which attends all such transactions here. 'Is it OK?'

'Fine by me, guv'ner!'

VV is a student of English at St Petersburg University and has a repertoire of Cockney slang derived from the works of Dickens etc. He's writing a thesis on it.

The interior of the theatre is painted black, with Ionic pillars either side of the stage and a chandelier on the ceiling. The audience is well-dressed. *Home* is set in a village in the 1950s and is the third part of a trilogy. An actress sits at the front of the stage weeping over her sad, hard life. Behind her is a bleak set of 5 suspended logs, astride one of which sit 2 actors, their faces in sympathy with hers. They start to sing a dirge. This turns to joy as neighbours arrive and the vodka comes out. They all start to sing a dirge. The Communist Party Inspector is very heartless.

During the interval we eat cakes in the foyer and confront a piece of sculpture with our heads tilting one way then another. It is a chunk of nuclear submarine: a goldfish bowl, containing 2 live goldfish, is embedded in the porthole: beside it hangs a map of its nuclear range.

In the second half of the play there is a wedding, dancing, music. Some girls arrive from Moscow, fashionable in trews. The bad Communist Party Inspector is replaced. Oh joy. By and by they start to sing a dirge.

At the end the audience claps in unison: splash-splash-splash-splash-splash. Very tribal. All the characters had tales of woe but the audience laughed a great deal, not merely snorts appreciative of wit but trails of outright cachinnation too . . .

'Russian joke,' says VV as we debouch onto the street. 'It wasn't in the play. There was a very lazy dog. He was howling for hours and hours. They asked him "Why have you been howling for hours?" and he said "I accidentally trod on my own balls – but I'm too lazy to take my foot off." '
I don't get it.

So I have seen Part 3 of the trilogy first. A few days later I see Part 1. Maybe, because of the vagaries of the repertory system, I shall never be able to fill in the middle. This would be apt. It seems many stories in Russian life have an end followed by a beginning, or a beginning followed by an end, but no middle. Already I have had a number of experiences of that kind, which end before they've begun, or which have no power of duration or development. There are others which have only a middle: suddenly you find yourself in the middle of something but cannot understand how it began and there is no end to it. Or again, something might come to an end – and you didn't even realise it was a story, didn't realise you were involved, but you were and now it's over. Oh really, has it ended? I didn't realise . . . Therefore it is entirely appropriate – even advantageous – to see these plays out of sequence.

Several weeks later I do manage to see Part 2 of the trilogy. Parts 1 and 2 are called *Brothers and Sisters* and when the trilogy opens it is 1941 and the 2 heroes are both 17. The whole work embodies an unprecedented mauling of the Communist way of life in a rural community and, since I don't understand a word, VV gives an unflagging exposition of that life's ghastliness and obduracy. On the first night his translative whispers so antagonised the audience that we took to the glass-fronted box like the 2 goldfish in the sculpture. But I am utterly absorbed. Much of it goes in directly through stomach and heart – the breast heave that is Russia! Socialist Realism has been replaced by social realism and the staging is brilliant. The acting is brilliant. They laugh, cry and play music with complete conviction. VV explains that at drama school one is taught to sing and to play a variety of musical instruments – about this sort of thing, the Russians are far more thorough and highly pitched than we are in the West. The trilogy features a Russian popular march from, I think, the 20s – I've heard it before – it gets under my skin.

'Are they also taught to drink? There's a vast amount of booze in the story.'

'They don't have to be taught. When Maly actors go drinking they give their names and addresses to the barman, so that if they pass out he can put them in taxis. Did you understand this one?' VV slaps the side of his neck. 'It means – let's have a drink.'

'OK. And I'd like to see more plays.'

'That is easily arranged. What else do you need?'

'A good masseur.'

'Right-o, guv'ner. I'll ask.'

Dmitri the cadet rings.

Du: Oh great! I didn't think you would.

Dm: Why not?

Du: I dunno. We can meet?

Dm: Yes. I am free now.

Du: To-day?

Dm: Yes. To-day.

I am beginning to catch on to this Russian immediacy and adaptability. Trying to synchronise is a big problem here. Or rather, paradoxically, in order to synchronise one must suspend the obsession with time. It is impossible to plan a schedule even for a few days ahead. Every appointment should have 'maybe' after it. My diary is full of strikings-out. In this ever-bubbling crucible of St Petersburg, the telephone network is essential to the process of perpetual revision. Officially this may have been a 'closed' society but no more efficient form of jungle drumming than Communism's beloved 'free phonecalls' has ever been devised. But it also maintains liquefaction in an eternal present, deters crystalisation. If Russians had to pay for phonecalls, they'd probably keep more rigidly to appointments. Some hope. As it is:–

X phones, suggests we meet Y.

But I'm waiting for Z to get back to me.

Z doesn't.

Phone X and say OK, we go ahead.

X says OK, he'll tell Y.

Y has now disappeared.

Z rings.

X locates Y, phones me, but I'm out with Z.

Y phones directly – I'm still out.

I return, phone X.

X is at Y's.

Phone Y, X answers, Y not there, his mother's sick.

And so on . . .

I'm alone in the flat before Dmitri comes, walking up and down the squeaky parquet . . . . The bell goes.

A boy in yellow sports top and blue jeans is standing in the doorway. A shock rushes towards and through me. Scrubbed, gleaming, elegant, he looks younger and shorter than I recall. Um . . . I've been *hit* by something. Thrown right off balance. Where to begin? I hear myself say –

'How do you do? . . . . Tea?'

'May I?'

Where did he learn that charming phrase? I don't look. Everything is moving. I look. He smiles rapidly, with nervousness, lips crooked, eyes flicking. The tea is made – one second it's nowhere, the next it's made and miraculously pouring itself out. Punctuality not being a Russian vice, he is 40 minutes late. I wouldn't dream of mentioning it but he points to his wristwatch, puts his head on one side, half closes an eye, frowns, and says 'Sorry.' It's very effective.

'No, no, no problem. Milk?'

'Yes please.'

Where's the fucking milk? Do I have to mix some? Lumps. Ants swarm hotly under the scalp.

'Sugar?'

'Yes please.'

'Biscuit?'

'Yes please.'

'Cigarette? Here – take the packet.'

And suddenly – as suddenly as the tea made itself – we are talking easily and fast, despite a titanic language barrier. Well, there's not much of a barrier seemingly. And the embarrassment ebbs. His uniform made him unreal, an image. But now he is not at all remote. He is here with me.

'I looked at the KGB Building. It is very ugly. The only modern one in this district. And the only one to break the' – pocket dictionary – 'skyline. That was obviously intentional. About 1960?'

'People say there are same number of floors below ground as above ground,' he explains matter-of-factly. 'Some years ago a man on the river saw a pipe from that building pouring blood into the Neva. A . . . excuse me.' Pocket dictionary. 'A tugboat was there churning up the water to disguise it.'

(The operations of state terror, in whatever country, even when lawful within their own systems, are always conducted in secret, never in the public eye, because they know that what they do is disgusting.)

We resort to the dictionary constantly – I shan't keep saying so.

'Have another biscuit.'

'Thank-you. May I?' This time the expression is apropos a paperback lying on the table. He picks it up and opens it gingerly.

'What is the story?'

'It's about a boy of 17 who has no father and whose mother is killed and what happens when he goes to live with another family.'

'Very beautiful story I think,' he says, and bites his lower lip.

'Hope so. I wrote it.' And I hope he's impressed by that. Mutual embarrassment returns, ebbs again.

He says 'You are the first person to speak English I understand.'

We decide to visit the Yelagin Palace and, while looking for a taxi, dodge a drunk with a briefcase winding all over the pavement. 'That's one of my teachers,' chuckles Dmitri. Finally he flags down a car, arranges the fee, and asks me 'Can I sit in the front?'

'If you like.'

The Yelagin Palace is on Yelagin Island, a leafy park in the north of the city. It was built by Rossi between 1818 and 1822, round an earlier core, for the mother of Alexander I. During the Second World War the Germans destroyed it, as they did every other palace outside the Siege line except Lomonosov, but it was subsequently rebuilt and its interiors fastidiously recreated. I wish to go there on a hunch – and because no one else seems to.

The palace overlooks water and park, and because of profuse verdure, has the atmosphere of a country house. A notice announces that the restoration of the garden is imminent but the notice is old and the wilderness riots lazily and unafraid in the sun. The great lawn opposite the entrance front is a lake of tall buttercups, thickly yellow under an azure sky. The entire site is balmy, tranquil, with few folk of any sort.

Dima (the short form of Dmitri) pays for our admissions before I can prevent it. The entrance hall is brown and green, animated by the babyface of a policeman with a pistol in a kiosk. As we pull on cloth overshoes he turns to look at us with a single swivelling movement of the head and back again, like a penny automaton on Brighton Pier in the olden days. The next room, the staircase hall, is pallid with a sugary grey marble floor and Orphic lyres along the frieze. The staircase itself disappears aloft in a series of painfully acute deckchair angles. Rossi must have been a very short man to have supposed it possible to go up without a sense of duress upon the skull (unless this is one of the few survivals from the earlier building).

We do not yet try it ourselves, but continue through several rooms of small and perfect proportions to the first decorative masterpiece, the Porcelain Room, a white and gold cube. The Graces dance in swirls of pastel drapery and garlands, cherubs cavort or pull buxom goddesses in chariots attended by moths and their dainty revel continues past the cornice and into the cove above, but a plain white background always predominates as though the decoration is applied to ice. An ancient attendant sits by the door. Dima puts a question to her and she stands up and begins to talk, or rather, commences to expatiate. Any minor official in Russia has a tape-recorder which plays if you talk to them on duty. The tape plays and plays. He stands respectfully for some time before cutting in with a thank-you and relaying the gist: 'The walls are painted china.'

Next, the Blue Drawing-Room – coooool . . . blue, gold, white, with a suite of bentwood furniture in an unusual and not quite pleasing design – some sort of intergalactic wedding-present from in-laws in the neptunium trade. Each honey door is embossed with the muse Terpischore in gold playing a lyre: their skirts are held up at mid-thigh by what appear to be suspender-belt fasteners.

Passing through double doors, the attention is effortlessly drawn up the full height of the building into a creamy ballooning space coffered in trompe l'oeil. The eyes rotate slowly on the pinion of the neck and descend again via caryatids and Ionic half-columns against curving walls. This is the Oval Ballroom where Pushkin danced, and on the far side sits a woman in socks and sandals, sunk in a book. In the centre hangs a gilt chandelier of Apollonian angels blowing trumpets, clashing cymbals, plucking lyre, harp and guitar. The palace is full of active, corybantic figures and it is apparent that the genus of the entire decorative scheme is music and dance: a very Russian classicism, simultaneously light and rich.

'Do you like dancing, Dima?'

'Yes. Do you?'

'Mmm.'

Really I know hardly more about him than that. That he likes dancing – and that one day he'll be an officer in the Red Navy or whatever they're calling it now. The dancing one might've guessed. He walks with a sailor's gait. I let him move on a little so that I can observe this movement, loose at the hips and knees, no tensions, aware but not self-conscious, the feet advancing somewhere between a scuff and a skip. The springiness of the legs gives the whole body a lilt as it walks which is just this side of a swagger, ie. it expresses blitheness, not the desire to impress. The back is upright without stiffness. The neck is strong and tanned, the hair cropped very short at the sides, left curly on top. In earlier years it would have looked 'military' but this 2-tier haircut is currently fashionable for young men in the West. In terms of presentation therefore, including the casual stylishness of his dress, he could be the son of a businessman in Chelsea, Parioli or Bel Air. But coming closer you quickly discern the 'elsewhere' in features and behaviour. Getting too far ahead, he pauses, standing with feet apart and legs straight, turning from the hips to give me a candid stare. 'Very beautiful,' he says and directs me towards the view of the lake through the crescent of arcaded windows.

After the albino loftiness of the Ballroom, the Red Drawing-Room is hot! with pink and plum silk, the effect deepened by the use of a darker, reddish mahogany for floor and doors, the profound red of polished chestnuts. There is a hint of the Far East, something pagodalike, in the pediments above the doors. Dima blows out his cheeks, exhales, grins, and makes a beckoning gesture into:–

The Long Dining-Room. Above the phantom banquet, along the perimeter of the ceiling pushed softly upwards like the roof of a tent, grisaille pagans process in stately measure, attended by cherubs and satyrs. It's always a bit of a relief when the satyr makes his appearance and ideally it should have been earlier in the scheme because music and dance, like most other activities, should not be chaste. Round the walls a series of flat pilasters, tapering towards the floor, are the last word in tongue-in-cheek elegance, a parody of elegance if that be possible. They are made from scagliola of the most wonderful texture, as though mustard and cream were folded together then flecked with cigarette ash. But the parodic idea is suggested by the capitals: ghouls, with braided hair and the eyes of drug addicts, carry large Ionic volutes upon their heads, and these ghoulish lads are trying hard not to look upwards and giggle. This isn't the grandest room in St Petersburg but it may be the smartest. The air of secret laughter could clinch it.

Down one side, tall mirrors parallel the windows opposite. Dima is checking himself out in the mirrors, passing a corrective hand through his hair, Narcissus moving from pool to pool. I say 'Yes, you look very good.' Caught off guard, he spins round on one overshoe, hunched, colouring, smiling with red lips pressed together. And laughs almost silently, head back and showing dark dental fillings, the only darkness in all that sunny summery head: he is a happy person. Another thing to be mentioned – we have overshoes to protect the beautiful parquet floors but the floors are underwaxed and dull, terribly, unhappily dry.

Coming out from one of the most delightful early 19th-century suites of rooms in Europe (the exterior is more ponderous and spoilt by railings on the roof and an old rusted chimney, but it makes nonetheless a pleasant bow-fronted heap across the water), coming out into sunshine, Dima puts a cigarette in his mouth and intercepts a stranger for a match. Faintly, through the trees, drifts a song from a portable radio. Female voice, powerful, but streaked with melancholy and erotic longing. Sounding far away. There is no breeze. Only stillness and sunshine. And the woman's powerful song far away. Something in it of Samarkand, Tashkent, Astrakhan, and my emotion turns inside, away from the glare of the West, towards the half-hidden romance and cruelty and soft glows of Asia. Yes, I am far away. Dima is leaning against a stone lion, smoking, looking at me.

'Can we find a drink?' I ask.

In the café we are the only customers. There is nothing to eat, and to drink only a tray of white plastic cups containing water and the slightest trace of lemon. Perfectly refreshing. Dima stubs out his cigarette. Then he winks at me.

Buy more lemon water.

Rest and shade in here.

It isn't necessary to speak. I want to speak.

'How old are you?'

'17.'

Like the boy in that paperback of mine. Old enough to have been shaped by Soviet Russia; young enough to have been shaped by Democratic Russia.

'When you are not at college, do you live with your parents?'

We are walking through the park. He is looking at the ground and suddenly lifts his head and looks directly into me with his beautiful greenish blue eyes.

'No, no, no. My mother died when I was baby – but I remember her.'

'And your father?'

'He was officer in Army. Killed in Afghanistan. But he did not like me. My aunt and uncle – they love me. They live by the Black Sea – I go there soon for my holiday. You can come with me.'

'Let me think about it. But you said you live in St Petersburg –'

'Yes. South-west of centre.'

'You said north.'

'No, no. Near Obvodny Canal. You can visit my home. But it is in a bad part. Sometimes I read at night and hear shooting. Turn out the light, wait 15 minutes, turn it back on, continue to read.'

'Is there much shooting?'

We have crossed into that portion of Yelagin Island known as the Park of Culture and Rest, with a boating lake on our right.

'Enough. Mafia. Racket. Big problem in St Petersburg. Oh, listen. If you have problem here, I have friends.'

'What do you mean?'

He makes kicking movements with his legs.

'You in one of those gangs?'

'No, no – you *know* I am at officers' college. But my friend's cousin, you understand?'

Yes.

A notice: *Do Not Swim – Hazardous To Health*. About 2 dozen people disport jubilantly in the water.

'Bad health problems here?'

He pulls a face of exaggerated disgust, then says – 'No!' and laughs.

'AIDS?'

'What?'

'You know – the sex disease which kills people.'

He brushes my ear with his hand – 'Mosquito.' The unexpectedness and gentleness of the gesture . . .

He appears not to have heard of AIDS. But everyone's heard of AIDS. Maybe it goes by another name in Russia. He should know about these things. Skin cancer too – his complexion would be particularly vulnerable to that. The grassy bank is on an estuary with a view to the Gulf of Finland. He lies full length on his belly, resting the side of his face on his hands, and immediately falls asleep, plump lips in an open pout, chipped tooth showing. He doesn't have that cheekbony Russian look but it's Russian all the same, dreamy and intense and very alive, capable of rapid transformations – in profile quite fierce. He alters from boy to man to boy to child to babe to man to child to boy in the space of a few minutes. After an hour I'm bored watching him sleep and place a foot on his bottom and rock him from side to side. One eye opens and looks up at me. It is absolutely direct and entirely without emotion, an expressionless eye establishing where it is, who I am. Then the personality seeps back into it.

'I sleep . . . Sorry . . . Last night with friends to celebrate the beginning of the holiday. We drink much Royal.'

Royal is pure spirit. If you drink water the following morning, you become drunk again, because spirit forms crystals in the system which are reabsorbed. A mosquito is sitting in the hairs of my bare legs, trying to struggle close enough to stab into the blood supply. The hair is too thick for it but even so – slap! That's the end of that little ambition. I walk over

to bushes for a pee. Dima does the same but something makes him stop
and he returns to the path to wait for me.

'What is Russian for cock?'

'What?'

'You know, this one.' I pat my fly – or what would be the fly if my
shorts had one. The sun is low and pearly light filters through the trees in
level planes of green, yellow and pink. The answer is 'hooey'. The 'h' is
actually the guttural Russian 'x', pronounced like the 'ch' in the Scottish
'loch'. I repeat it several times, putting increasing conviction into the
opening letter. The origin of the phrase 'a load of old hooey': in the
addendum to the Oxford English Dictionary, it says of this word *US slang
1924. Origin unknown*. Well, now they know.

'And the woman's?'

Pizda – emphasis on the second syllable.

I repeat 'Piz-da! Piz-da!'

'Shshshsh!!!' He blushes, put out by the presence of a couple walking
not far ahead of us. The man turns round, ready for an argument,
thinking we're teasing them or worse. But the word has no connotations
for me, is merely a sound. And yet – hooey – pizda – yes, they do have a
sexual vibration. These words usually do.

Tram to Kirovsky Prospekt – tea and rum ba-bas – outside the café a
group of young fascists (dirty hair, black leather jackets) shout at each
other. Dima gives me his phone number (he only had mine before); we
agree to speak in a few days; he descends to the metro, waving 2
semicircles with a fully extended arm before disappearing round a
concrete corner. Shan't get a cab . . . Which direction? I stroll through
quiet, unthreatening streets, walking on the inside of St Petersburg.

Back at the flat Serafima is having a wassail in the kitchen.

'Drink with us!'

They are awash with champanskoye. Plastic corks litter the table which
is perfumed by a vase of lilies-of-the-valley, the scent so agile it can outwit
cigarette smoke, while from the musical apparatus in the Best Room
throbs a selection of funk and soul: Grover Washington, Sade, Ella
Fitzgerald, Joe Cocker.

'Nina lived in New York for a while.'

'Is it possible,' asks Nina, who is glamorously thin in the New York style, 'for women to comb their hair in the street in England?'

'It's possible. But you don't see it.'

'Then it's not possible. In Russia it is possible.'

The third woman, Mrs X, says 'There is a dissonance in our city between the grandeur of the buildings and the meanness of the life lived in them.'

'At the moment we are all reading Bulgakov,' explains Nina.

The 2 men are largely silent. The women are eager to reach out. But the current state of affairs is especially hard on men over 30 – their lives simply stopped with the collapse of their society. This was a great humiliation and has turned them into either crooks or victims or both. Maybe the process began under Communism which took from the man his traditional role as breadwinner and source of enterprise. Everyone became the drudging wife of the State, which was the Universal Male. Testosterone's only outlets were sex, corruption, and the conquest of others . . . Can't get into this now . . . . . I am just trying to work out why the 2 men don't speak, why they sit there paralysed.

Serafima moves on to coffee, bossa-nova-ing through its preparation. 'I drink coffee and sleep very well.' Nina decides to crash here for the night (the law forbids drivers any alcohol at all). Neither of the men, it turns out, was with her – but she has one somewhere. At 3 am I am in bed, on my back, hands behind my head, in a luxurious frame of mind. Italian grand opera at high volume is streaming down over my face from the flat above. The 5 satin roses tremble with delight.

Beginning To Rave. Woken by Ozzie howling to get out of the room. How the hell did he get in? . . . . . . Foaming toothpaste de-furs post-champanskoye tongue . . . At the kitchen table Serafima and Igor are cracking walnuts for a cake.

'The kettle's boiling, John.'

'Thank-you, Miss Jones.'

'Do you want any milk in your tea?'

'Yes, please. Sugar?'

'Thank-you. Do you like biscuits?'

'Yes, I do.'

'Do you want one?'

'Yes, please.'

'Is this tobacco for me?'

'Well, it's certainly not for me!'

An English lesson is on the television. Serafima, attired in a blue mini-kimono which stops less than halfway down her femur, and socks with coloured pompoms pinned to the side, prepares a porridge of rice with currants and walnuts.

'Nina has gone. Burglars broke into her car and took radio. But her husband is a big man. Rouble millionaire.'

'What does he do?'

'I don't know. Many things. I do not like to ask. My husband also rouble millionaire, with beautiful house in the countryside . . . but we break. He love me but I no love him.'

She smiles, not sadly.

'Does he give you money?'

'In our country it is traditional when husband and wife break, the man gives nothing.'

A stranger called BT rings for me. We arrange to meet later at his house. On television a staging of Gounod's *Ave Maria* is relayed from a theatre. The chorus stands in blue light against a background of moving green comets. In the foreground a gymnastic androgyne, in strawberry costume under a strawberry spotlight, writhes among aerial rings and ribbons and slides obliquely through the air with a degree of control to his smooth, impossible movements that is inhuman. Only in the country which produced Nijinsky could such a reptilian robot appear. Serafima is now stuffing nettles into a bowl to make an infusion for her hair. As a child I had watered vinegar poured over my hair after shampooing – forgotten that until this moment. Russia often awakens one to the pre-kitchenroll, pre-plastic bag nostalgia of childhood. Nikita rings about the Gayfest. It's to-night. I'm to meet him at the Astoria Hotel.

BT is an intellectual and lives in the middle of the Petrograd Island. He is thin, with a thin ponytail and thin cotton clothes, and a face not especially thin, a face of bland affability which belies the acrobatic aggression of his mind. He is Francophiliac and we talk in a mixture of English and French.

'I looked in to-day's journal,' he says, 'and discovered there is war in Moldavia, Armenia, Georgia, Azerbaijan, everywhere.'

'It's surprising that Russia wants to be bothered with these places now.'

'Many Russians live there. In future the big problem will be Ukraine.'

'It isn't interesting any more to control people.'

'I agree – and yet, what does one want to be most of all in life? One wants to be contagious! Infecting people – *this* is interesting. But it's not only Russians in these places. The withdrawal of Russians creates wars too. We are surrounded by a hundred Ulsters, a thousand Beiruts! Not pretty prospect. Excuse me, I must telephone.' But the phone is broken. BT is perturbed and pulls on his ponytail. 'This is terrible! 10 minutes ago it worked – now kaput! Without telephone I am without hands! Would you have something against it if I smoke?'

This item of exceptional courtesy (do you object if I smoke in my own home?) one only ever encounters in Russia – where it is not uncommon.

'Aaaaaaaah!!!!! – we must go out – I have to arrange my evening! To meet my friend who has a group called Pop-Mechanika and they will soon do a free concert at the Artillery Museum. What French books do you read?'

'Um – Saint-Simon, Balzac, Baudelaire . . .'

'Good – no Voltaire!'

'Oh yes, before –'

'No, no! Voltaire lived in a clock but we live in a maelstrom. Is that the Balzac of *Le Socrate Chrétien* or the Balzac of *La Comédie Humaine*?'

'The latter.'

'I prefer the former – as a prosodist at least. Yes, Saint-Simon, his story of Peter the Great visiting the child Louis XV and lifting him into the air with great delicacy – and kissing him! As for the other Saint-Simon, the romantic socialist, the contemporary of David – ah! David of *Sappho, Phaon & Cupid* – ridiculous! charming! We also have his *Portrait of an Unknown Young Man*, a more sincere work. Do you know the other David?'

'No.'

'The last master of the Bruges School – there is here his *Virgin Embracing the Dead Christ*. Such tenderness of pain and tears! Don't you agree that French culture is superior to English culture?'

Several streets away he locates an operational telephone but there is a queue for it.

'It's true', I reply, 'that their wallpaper and cuisine are superior to ours. But the English have the best history in the world, don't they?'

'Yes! The most success with the least tyranny!' he says. 'The English have, I think, an inferiority complex about French culture and the French have an inferiority complex about English history.'

'What do the Russians have an inferiority complex about?'

'The Unmysterious! We are terrified of it. The Unmysterious makes us feel fools!'

'But France is dedicated to the Unmysterious.'

'You must remember that if you have an inferiority complex about something it is because you are very impressed by it, are very attracted to it.'

'Don't you find the French taste too static?'

'In what way?' he enquires, pricking.

'They are terrifically good at filling up a flat surface with a clever and formal arrangement. But going into 3 dimensions always produces corners in France.'

'Let me make a note! Do you have a pen?'

'No.'

He ransacks the queue until he finds one.

'Continue.'

'The French have not at all the Italian plasticity or English naturalism,' say I, swelling to the theme. 'Bernini tried to bend the Louvre but the French weren't having it. In architecture the French are masters of the box!'

A tiny car stops at the kerb, farting clouds of exhaust smoke into our faces. A human bundle extricates itself from the passenger seat and the car squits off. If this really is post-industrial meltdown, they will probably return to the cleaner, safer horse.

'If they try again for totalitarian state, there will be civil war!' says BT, giving his ponytail an emphatic tug. 'Nuclear bombs, KGB, torture, concentration camps, insane bureaucracy, midnight arrests, everyone afraid to speak, the lies lies lies lies lies lies lies – young people don't want it back!' He can't be more than 26, 27 himself. 'But do you know? Nostalgia is a very strong emotion in our city. We have a group of artists working on that. Almost kitsch, but talented.'

(e.*g*. Bela: returning to the period before the Revolution.

Guryanov: celebrating the heroic style of Stalinism.

Smelov: who photographs the decaying city. Black and white, not at all kitsch.)

'Let me ring Smelov,' says BT. 'He lives nearby.'

But Smelov isn't in, so we bid adieu to each other, and I take off for the rendezvous with Nikita at the Astoria Hotel. Until recently this was the best hotel in town, government-owned, but it has been overtaken by the Grand Europe. Uniformed thugs hang around the revolving entrance. Anywhere vaguely prosperous in St Petersburg has thugs hanging round it. Whether that's cause or effect is impossible to know. The day has grown more and more and more sweltering and so the air-conditioning smacks deliciously. But it's the wrong entrance. Life at the Astoria is confused by the fact that it has 2 entrances, 2 foyers, 2 sets of bedrooms – and no internal connection between them! – you have to go back out onto the street – Nikita is in Foyer B saying to a middle-aged woman 'When I worked for the BBC Russian Service . . .' Don't recognise him at first – he's in a white Russian peasant blouse with buttons at the side of the neck *and no shades.*

She is from BBC Radio 3. Her Scottish sound recordist turns up, fully rigged with paraphernalia hanging from straps. We walk to the House of Culture. There are many houses of culture. This one is called Lighthouse, another shiplike palace from the 19th century moored to good intentions. The ballroom is a rococo temple of dust: faded swishes of cream and gilt plaster, murky glass chandeliers the size of space stations. An audience packs rows of seats in worn red plush. On stage polemic and pantomime miscegenate: *As Freud said, sexual alternatives free the soul from the factory of life!*

The ballroom is faintingly hot, so short of air that the walls seem to buckle inwards, and I transfer to a room got up like a cave of stalactites. Here the second ponytail of the day says 'Hullo.'

'Can I get a drink somewhere?'

'Follow me.'

But the bar has only champanskoye or vodka and either, in this heat, would be the end.

'Then let us take air,' says Ponytail, and to us there attaches a girl in powderpink velvet suit of capricious design. Her face is pale and sensual and square, with lips of scarlet impasto and jetblack hair cut in the manner of Louise Brooks. We pass a poster: *Same sex love is Nature's answer to overpopulation. It doesn't exclude anything except children.*

Beside the Neva the atmosphere is a little fresher and we descend steps to hold our faces as close to the water as possible.

Ponytail says 'I am at jazz college. Do you like *Alice in Wonderland?*'

'Yes.'

'What style is this book written in?'

'Can an original book have a style? Is it not unique?'

'Is it not absurdist, this book?'

'Surrealist would be better.'

'Russian people much love this book.'

'Is there a good translation?'

'By Nabokov,' says the girl. She explains that we are standing on the Red Navy Embankment which before the Revolution was called the English Embankment – a fashionable address at the time – 'and my name is Bela.'

'You are a painter.'

'How did you know?'

'Telepathy.'

'You can see my paintings if you want. Do you have a light?'

'Where is Wonderland Embankment?' asks Ponytail.

Returning to the House of Culture for Bela's light, we bump into an American from Milwaukee called Don – I met him at the Richard Wilson Arts Centre in North Wales.

'What on earth are you doing here?'

'Distributing condoms,' he replies. 'I've found the word for Russia – engulfing. I've been engulfed.'

'I heard you got married.'

'Maybe I will.'

There is some discomfiture at the door when a group of small-time mafia spivs try to get in on the act. Funny how you can tell this type the world over, that tacky slickness . . . The police refuse them entry. Inside we hit the champanskoye in a gold-and-coloured-glass Moorish-style room of alarming magnificence, a room made for kif. 'And for kife!' says Ponytail. To the Beeb woman I declare it odd that the only media interest in this revolutionary event should be from BBC Radio 3 and she asks 'Can I interview you?'

Her: How do you find St Petersburg?

Me: It reminds me of Palermo.

Her: Really?

Me: No . . No, I only said that to steady myself.

(The Scottish sound recordist confesses the theft of all his dollars by gypsies on Nevsky Prospekt.)

Her: You were a bloody fool to put them in that pouch.

Him: Can I have some of that champanski?

Her: Aren't the mosquitoes awful? But I've got stuff.

Me: You have stuff?

Her: Jungle Jelly.

Me: When do you go back to London?

Her: To-morrow.

Me: Can I have it?

Her: Here. Don't get it in your month. It's awful if you get it in your mouth. Where's Nikita?

Me: Dunno.

(We haven't seen much of him. He's networking in that blouse and – to complete the outfit – black pleated trousers narrow at the ankle.)

Her: He's taking us to a rave afterwards.

Me: Can I come?

Her: Is Monroe here? We want to interview Monroe. Nikita said we could.

Him: I'm going to record some of that boom-boom for background.

The disco has begun to roll in the Cave of Stalactites but the real boom-boom is beyond, in the ballroom, where a skinny painted figure in top hat, gold falsies and army boots croaks out in English over a furious techno beat . . .

> *I am a Soviet queen*
> *From behind the Iron Curtain.*
> *Life is pretty obscene*
> *But of one thing I am certain –*
> *When you're sick of Revolution and find Lenin a bore*
> *You can strut your polyester near Gostiny Dvor*
> *And if you want a heavy hooey that is red and erect*
> *Hang around at midnight on the Nevsky Prospekt!*
> *Hooey-hooey*
> *Hooey-hooey*

Now I'm a liberated queen
From the Russian Republic.
Life's still pretty obscene
And it's making me sick!
Demo-crassy is here! Communism – what was it?
The Iron Curtain's gone and now we're in an Iron Closet!
But if you want a heavy hooey that is red and erect
Hang around at midnight
  – or midday
  – or tea-time
  – any time you like
  – anything you want – on the Nevsky Prospekt!!!!!!
Hooey-hooey
Hooey-hooey
Hooey-hooey!!!

'He must be from London. We should interview him,' says the BBC woman.

'No, it's a Russian girl,' says Bela.

'No, boy from Hamburg,' says Ponytail.

'But the words are English.'

'So?'

'Where's Nikita? We want to interview Katya. He said we could. Where's Katya?'

A pair of uniformed government officials approach Bela and say 'We are not against anything here to-night except smoking. This is a No Smoking building.' She petulantly stubs out her fag. Nikita turns up and we all leave for the next rave, all except Ponytail who has evaporated for ever.

Adjacent to the House of Culture is an army barracks. Soldiers stand outside in loose khaki trousers tucked into soft Cossack boots, jackets with belt outside, and small round caps. Others lie propped in the ground-floor windows, smoking, stripped to the waist, cracking jokes. They say 'Look!' and point upwards: 3 shocking pink flares burst in the sky and hang there like transfigured souls enjoying a conversation. The soldiers laugh.

In the taxi Nikita asks me 'Will you give the driver 150 roubles?'

'But he's agreed to 100.'

'I'm trying to get more money for him.'

'You said it's a short distance.'

'I'm still trying to get more money for him.'

'Is he a friend of yours?'

'Never seen him before.'

'I'm sticking to the deal.'

Using the word 'deal', Nikita explains to the cabbie who shrugs his shoulders and seems quite content. Generally I live not in the dollar but in the rouble system and I hope I'm generous. But I don't like to feel pumped. No one likes to feel pumped because it's unfriendly, it puts you on the outside. Nikita can be uncertain company. He has tasted the West which has made him discontented inside and put him partly on the outside of himself, a figure both fashionable and out of gear, love-hating Russia, love-hating the West.

We pull up outside Dom Kino, the House of Cinema, to which has been fixed a placard: *Oklahoma Dansing*. We hand over roubles and Nikita smoothes the entrée. Invitation reads *Professional Security & Aesthetic Control*.

Loud rap and techno vivace burst through balustraded staircases and fans of green laser bounce off baroque mirrors. Young mafiosi in tracksuits mingle with a more way-out crowd: all are spectral in a green fug laced with perfume and dope. Policemen put booted feet on tables and rest guns in their laps. After a round of beers, we dance. Somebody passes me a joint and mouths 'Hullo.' Seen him before, can't think where. The BBC woman, gyrating in dry ice, yells 'It's at times like this that I *long* for Tamla Motown!'

DJ Groove from Murmansk is in charge of the music, is about 20 years old, wearing a bomber jacket with *Active Physical* across the front.

'Is this how you live?'

'Officially I am at the Conservatoire.'

'Doing what?'

'Studying to be a baritone opera singer.'

'Isn't Murmansk where the nuclear fleet is leaking radioactivity?'

'Little bit. But it's not a problem.'

Suddenly, at 3.30 am, I am alone, the people I came with gone. Trailing lost up an ornate staircase, I notice 2 Africans leaning over the gallery parapet, staring miserably down at the dance-floor. They feel far from home and so all at once do I. A girl with short blonde hair and heavy black maquillage round the eyes talks to a policeman. She moves to take his gun from its holster but he prevents it and they snog. I'm lonely, tired, want to be in bed.

Walking home through shadowy streets in blue light, my nerves start to play up. A knot gathers under the ribs. A car slows beside me, flashing its headlights, and purrs on. Any minute I shall be attacked . . . An overturned phone kiosk blocks the pavement . . . In London a psychic healer said 'If you feel uneasy in Russia, imagine yourself surrounded by white light. White is the colour of protection.' I don't go for this stuff but here I am desperately trying to imagine the white light – no, no, that's wrong! my shirt is too smart, Kenzo, and blazing white! too much attention! . . . Is someone following me? . . . . . .

When finally I reach my bed – unmolested – I fail to sleep, hyped up by the music and the danger.

Serafima is bashing away in the kitchen. My eyes unglue. Sunshine floods saffron across the ceiling. She is tenderising a steak. A soap opera is on television. It's mid-day.

'*Santa Barbara?*'

'No. Different – *The Rich Also Cry.*' It is made in Mexico on what appears to be a single cardboard set and dubbed into Russian by one man.

'Last night I met painters and went to discos.'

'I know many painters. I can introduce you to painters.' Turning her mug of coffee on the oilcloth, she adds 'Most painters are alcoholic.' She is downcast, the brave face, the watery smile, the eyes, I can tell.

Advertisements come on, mostly private businesses giving out their phone numbers, and Tampax. Serafima, again in the thigh-cooling mini-kimono and pompom socks, rouses herself and sashays out of the kitchen. A moment later the thump-thump of Boney M leaps in from the Best Room. Ra-Ra-Rasputin – Lover of the Russian Quin! She reappears in the doorway, snaps her fingers and gives a shoulder shimmy, leans over to adjust a pom on the socks, bending her leg at the knee, and her upside-down face turns to look at me. I laugh, blurting tea down my blue shirt. But she doesn't laugh. Straightening up, smoothing her kimono front, she asks 'Duncan, are you hungry?' and takes various materials from the fridge and pushes back her hair with a sigh. Soon a pile of hot blinis, with homemade blackberry jam and fresh cream, appears on the table.

I decide to ring Dima. Perhaps he can help me do some shopping. A girl answers the phone and passes it to him. We arrange to meet by the Flame on the Field of Mars.

At the appointed hour, crossing the road and taking one of the gravel paths between lilac trees, a sense of repressed panic buzzes within me. There are the usual couples on benches and individuals absorbed in paperback books. He is not here. I shuffle round the memorial. He is still not here . . . He appears out of the blue 35 minutes late. I hurl a packet of cigarettes through the air which he catches, approaching with his head tipped to one side, an eye half closed. 'Sorry,' he says.

'No problem.'

Shopping:–

1. The Philharmonia Hall – 2 tickets for next week's concert, 7 roubles the pair. The cashier explains that the tickets were printed last year and that the prices therefore cannot be increased in line with inflation. So a concert of Prokofiev, Tchaikovsky and Scriabin is all but free. Near the box-office a girl is selling secondhand records. I ask for Balakirev piano music – no luck, and she suggests the Melodiya Shop on Nevsky Prospekt.

2. DLT Department Store, more spacious and less hurried than Gostiny Dvor. Everything clearly marked with a price. Nobody hassles you. If you want something you ask an assistant. Far more pleasant than in the West where you are likely to be pounced on the second you enter a shop. India and the Arab countries are worse still – their merchandising zeal amounts to assault. Ennio said you cannot build a country on the Russian lack of motivation but I cannot see that a society in which the commercial consideration has swallowed up every other, in which you are bludgeoned by sales pitches every waking moment, is a superior place to be. However, they do not stock what I want – a ruled writing pad which is, it seems, a very esoteric item. What the stationery department does stock, in great piles, is the standard lavendery pink Russian loo roll. No shortage of that (another myth punctured).

3. The shop next door to DLT, lately a record shop, is now an antique arcade of various stalls selling china figures, tea-cups, imperial plates, objects easily concealed in the past. There is very little old furniture – that

which wasn't destroyed by Revolutionary ardour was used as fuel in the Siege . . . A mangy dancing bear, tethered to the grass in front of Kazan Cathedral, hops pathetically from one paw to the other, hop, hop, terrified to stop in case something awful happens, hop, hop, hop. Further along on the same side is the Headbanger – not the peasant woman but a well-known beggar who bashes his head against stone rationally rather than emotionally. His bald pate is a mass of blackberry scabs and his trousers are rolled up to expose legs in a state of advanced eruption. Dima says 'He rubs toothpaste in his legs to keep them that way.' A section of the road is being remade and pedestrians scramble round piles of rubble – it is obvious what is going on in this case but quite often in St Petersburg you will come across a heap of mysterious mess in the street, the colour and texture of which defy explication, as though the underworld vomited up something esoteric and left it there.

4. Babylon Shops have sprung up lately, offering a small range of Western goods. Let's go in. The queue is deceptive – they are only spectators. I buy a packet of biscuits. To judge from his face, Dima is absolutely horrified by the price. I feel guilty – we eat them fast, raspberry waffles in silver foil and a box, repulsive in their excess of artificially coloured jam, painful sweetness, and childishly overdone wrappings. Made in the Netherlands. Never again. What junk.

5. The Melodiya Shop is in a sorry condition, the once-mighty Melodiya catalogue reduced to a few new platters – Led Zeppelin, the Beatles, George Michael, Prince. George Michael is playing. Dima does a quick jiggle of his hips. It is fruitless to raise even the subject of Balakirev, let alone his piano music.

'Last night I was at disco with lasers.'

'Expensive?' he asks.

'Yes. But all Russians. And mafia.'

'I hate mafia.'

'You have problem with mafia?'

'Everyone has.'

'What problem?'

'I am bad boy sometimes.'

'Was that your sister who answered the phone?'

'No. My girl.'

'Your girl?'

'Yes.'

'She was visiting?'

'No. I live with her.'

'You live with a girl?'

'Yes. It is my home.'

'How old is she?'

'16.'

I'm taken aback.

'The 2 of you in your own place?'

'It is her grandmother's place.'

'Oh.'

'I live there when I am not at college.'

'Oh.'

'Her grandmother love me.'

'Yes.'

I'm still taken aback. And vaguely annoyed, you know, that he's all fixed up, but well – no mother – he needs this – makes sense – the Navy can be his father – still, I have to reassess him. Boy, child, man? But how? I haven't even assessed him yet. Jammy little bugger. No. That's unfair . . . We have waited 1½ hours just to *hand in* a film for development. 'Collect in 2 weeks,' they say. I'd like to see where he lives . . .

After that we decide simply to walk for a while. Over the Kirovsky Bridge, built in England at the turn of the century but too short – the Russians had to add an extra arch. As you walk across, the great size of the Neva becomes increasingly apparent. Buildings tilt back from each other on opposite banks in accordance with the curvature of the earth. Every 70 feet or so a fisherman stands patiently, hoping to pull out a semi-poisonous sprat with his rod. Very soothing under a pacific blue sky until you look over the parapet and down at the water and see thick muscles of strong currents whipping past the stanchions.

Dima says that not long after the Revolution an English company proposed to clean the Neva free of charge if they could keep everything they found in it, the Soviets refused. In 1917 people threw in jewels and gold, hoping to recover them at a later date. 'I know someone whose father threw in a gold sword! But we have never cleaned the river properly ourselves so – jump in, Dooncan. See what you can find. But be careful. The whole of Mendeleyev's table is in that river!'

At first I don't understand this remark about the table. Dima explains. It continues to escape me. Sometimes language difficulties tie us in knots.

One grasps the wrong end of sticks. Pennies refuse to drop. A cloud of unknowing descends.

'It was joke,' he says in exasperation. 'Joke no good when you must explain . . .'

On the left, crossing the wooden bridge into the Peter and Paul Fortress, is the Physical Fitness Lawn where bodybuilders adopt Tarzan poses and one in particular sits on the grass in striped bathing drawers holding up an inverted bottle of vodka. Prone in the grass beside him, are 2 further empties. Pushing his head forward on his neck, he groggily contemplates the emptiness of the third bottle, unable to accept that for the time being it is ALL OVER vodkawise. He rolls onto his back, kicking his legs in the air from pique. Incidentally, Russians buy vodka in ½ litre bottles with silver caps on them. Even so, this is no way to preserve the body beautiful . . . The Peter and Paul Fortress embraces the eponymous cathedral wherein are entombed the Tsars after requiems at St Isaac's. It is a structure of unusual but beautiful proportions. The dynamo of the building is the spire, the tallest in St Petersburg, which tapers very gradually like a golden needle, drawing all the rest up with it into weightlessness.

Over another wooden bridge . . . past the Naval Museum and the 2 red columns . . . over Palace Bridge . . . to the Triangle where 3 benches have been drawn together under trees beside the river.

Dm: Do you want to visit my home?

Du: Now?

Dm: Yes.

Du: Yes.

Ring Serafima to say I shan't be home for dinner – oh, the tenderised steak – guilty again – but maybe I'm a little bit Russian now, compelled to alter arrangements at short notice. Dima rings home to warn his lot – there is a brief agitated exchange – he's quite sharp and puts down the phone: 'It's OK.'

Admission to the underground railway system is gained by inserting into an automatic gate a brown metal token costing a few kopeks. Once in, you can travel any distance. The escalator dips at a sharp angle and is deep . . . down . . . down . . . Vertical white stick-lamps are planted at regular intervals down the centre, dividing ascending from descending passengers. The lights flick past endlessly like a drip torture, a nervous tic . . . I can't clearly make out the bottom. People are silent and motionless on their descending platforms, sinking down . . . down into a rational insect hell of white light and sinister rumbles. My stomach tightens. Don't like it. At last the bottom slides under our feet and I defer to Dima for directions to the train.

'Come,' he says. And there, gaping at our feet, is another escalator, deeper even than the first. White stick-lamps vanish downwards into vagueness and a hot wind blows up into our faces. I look at him hesitantly and he touches my arm. He is in charge. I am being led. Although we are both standing at the same level on the lip of the escalator and I am taller than he, I have the impression of looking up at him, that he is taller at this moment. Curious how people's height can vary with one's mood. We step onto it and go down yet again . . . down . . . I continue to shrink with every flick of the stick-lamps – flick – flick – flick – and as I shrink, everything is being squeezed out of me and left behind, personality, social reflexes, my whole world squeezed out as we descend, leaving only a tense blankness and warning signals from my body that it doesn't like what I'm doing to it. No one talks. No one is coming up the other side. Down. Down. The rumble of escalators is the only sound and at one's temples a beating of the pulse. I am thankful for the blankness, aware that quickening beyond it is a howling terror which, one hopes, with an effort of concentration, can be kept at bay. Just standing on this escalator, I seem to be using up a huge amount of energy, and this depletion of inner resources abets the shrinkage of my being. But the outer weight on my chest is also considerable, and these 2 effects work in horrible tandem. Down. Down. Dima takes my arm – we trip down the last few steps – run along a gallery – he's heard the train – jump on, very crowded, very hot, but I'm cold – look out of the window at streaking blackness away from compress of faces – lean against Dima – steady myself with his warmth – the journey passes in stupor. The only remark I make is 'Why so deep?' to which he replies 'Because of swamp.' I conceive quivering walls of mud eager to slurp together, oozing and pushing through fissures in the tunnel, ravening to devour us.

Now we are rising again. Escalator rumbling slowly upwards. Too slow. The anxiety becomes almost intolerable in my eagerness to reach the top. Up – up – up – up – up – towards light, air, freedom, life – and at long last – pop! My body reflates and the skin stretches like chewing-gum, my arms visibly extending as I look, shoulders widening, waist thickening. Here we are above ground at the Baltiskaya Station. I am pathetically grateful to the blue and gold sky, so much so that an agoraphobic dizziness steams in my brain and eyes, as the mind, all loosed, takes a few seconds to establish equilibrium after so tight a claustrophobia.

The Obvodny Canal is not the most picturesque conduit in town, but since there is not a corner of Old St Petersburg that is not picturesque, the Obvodny has a charm all its own. The water is sluggish and low, a pale coffee colour, and the inclined concrete banks are littered with junk dried out by the summer's heat. This is a 19th-century manufacturing district of redbrick factories with crenellations like forts, a poor area but attractive, with trees and cobbled streets. There is a brightness to the light and a freshness to the air which says that the sea is not far away.

We walk due west and after about 20 minutes stop at a small block of flats built in the early years of the century, quite plain, frayed round all its edges. The staircase is lit by unglazed openings. At a floor near the top Dima pulls out his key and we enter a narrow hall. He begs me not to remove my shoes but I do and he finds some old slippers. 'Do you want to wash?' He shows me the amenities where I freshen up. The flat is small and clean and packed with brown cardboard boxes of various sizes.

'This is my girl,' he says. She has a charming, startled face and is only a little shorter than he is, with long black wavy hair, blue jeans, a maroon blouse and small pearly ear-rings – and she is dumb with diffidence, some of which rubs off on him – and on me. I present her with bananas which we bought outside the station and, breaking through, she shakes my hand saying 'Valentina.' Behind her in a privy space created by a carved wooden screen sits a thin woman in her 60s, knitting and wearing a crocheted cardigan with violet glass buttons. It is at a funny angle as though pulled quickly on because of company. The woman smiles narrowly, takes a sip from a small glass of vodka on a table beside her, and carries on knitting, sequestered in her corner like an anchorite. This is Agafea, Valentina's grandmother.

Black tea and a dish of sweets in purple wrappers appear on the table. When the sweets are unwrapped the purple from the waxed paper sticks to the pale capsules but they are filled with chewy nut caramel and taste very good. Dima is nervously subdued.

'Have a sweet,' I suggest.

'No. My tooth hurts.'

'For how long?'

'6 months. I had a problem and the dentist did it but he did it wrong and now it hurts.'

'You must go back.'

'Yes . . .' He fades out on the idea in that Russian way and retreats to the bathroom and makes splashing noises. Granny knits on, detached, slightly amused. Valentina clatters in the kitchen. I sip tea and look out of the cracked window – a few cars, broken pavements, a dog, a gang of children, all very familiar, all utterly alien. It transpires that this is a communal flat but that the other people who live here are in the process of moving somewhere else. They are away at present. Whether they will be replaced by new sharers is something I cannot determine. There are times when, despite misunderstanding, despite cluelessness, despite feeling lost, despite curiosity, one must curb the interrogative.

Dima has put on a plain white shirt. I ask 'Would Agafea tell me something about the Siege of Leningrad?' He speaks to her. She takes another sip of vodka, her face empties of all expression, she continues to knit, and says nothing. He shrugs and takes me into another small room. It is his – or their – bedroom, the bed halfway between a single and a double. Dresses and coats hang from the walls. A pile of books and papers in one corner is topped by a volume of Lermontov. He closes the door behind us and opens a flimsy wardrobe – more women's clothes – and a corner for him, a couple of naval uniforms hanging up, a long military overcoat, sailor boots. He puts the boots on the floor, soft ankle boots curving in over the heel at the back, 8 pairs of close-set eyelets, the top around the ankle cut to slope backwards at a slight angle, 2 felt inner soles for winter, altogether very stylish creations, with a handmade Victorian look and surprisingly light. From behind the boots he brings forth a sturdy shoe box. Ah, things are coming out now in Russia! After 75 years – things are coming out. From beneath floorboards, from the back of cupboards and wardrobes, from hidden passages and the choked mute recesses of the soul – things are coming out. It resembles the slow traumatic thaw after an ice age. A few green shoots here and there but the whole vast ground trembling with suppressed energies. Any day it will burst forth into a frantic luxuriance!

The box contains a ball of dull white cloth which he takes out and places carefully on the floor. Kneeling beside it, tongue-tip showing between his lips, Dima slowly peels back the cloth until there is revealed between us an object of uncanny beauty. In that lacklustre room it has unexpectedly arrived from another, more refulgent dimension. Dima gives me a strange look, a mixture of wonder, confusion and despair.

On the floor glimmers a large chunk of crystal, or rather of many crystals locked jaggedly together in an infinity of blues, from a narrow band of ice blue to a mass of opaque dark blue, via sapphire and ultramarine, cobalts and indigos and slivers of purple. 'Look,' he says and lifts it onto the narrow windowsill where it is pierced by a spear of sunlight. The crystal flares into a commotion of iridescence, its essential blues and blades of purple generating a thousand minute rainbows of varying spectra. He turns it, making prismatic detonations of light, smiling distantly, his eyes shiny and moist.

'What is it?'

He swallows and gives a short cough. 'Don't know. I have it from my father. It is the only thing I have from my father.'

'Where did he get it?'

'Don't know. Maybe – did you hear about the Great Meteor? It fell in Siberia before the Revolution. They make famous photographs.'

Yes. I remember – from my sister's encyclopaedia when we were children – an old black and white photograph of pine trees flattened outwards for miles around a cratered centre. Or was the point about the phenomenon that there was no crater commensurate with the effect?

The Tunguska Event. On June 30th 1908 there was a mysterious crash in a remote district of Siberia. Eye-witness reports describe the flight and explosion of a blinding blue light in a cloudless morning sky. There was devastation over an area 80 kilometres in diameter. The sound was heard 1,000 kilometres away. The explosion's air-wave, picked up by instruments in many countries, went twice round the globe. But no pieces of anything were found. Dima's father's explanation to his son was that this was because there was no official expedition to the site until 1927 and in the meantime local people had removed crystals such as this.

'Do you believe it?' I ask.

'Maybe it is silly story. But I want to believe. Does it give you a strange feeling when you look at it?'

'A beautiful feeling.'

'Yes – beautiful feeling. When I am sad . . .'

He doesn't finish the sentence but packs up the box and puts it away behind the boots and rubs the back of his hand across his eyes.

Dima and I eat in the kitchen while Valentina joins Agafea elsewhere. Brown bread and butter, soup with coriander and specks of ham, meat rissoles, a salad of potatoes and peas and chopped onion, and another salad of tomatoes and cucumber. The tomatoes are very red and sweet.

'Excuse me, sorry, I forget!' exclaims Dima and produces a bottle of vodka from the fridge. These ½ litre bottles cost about one US dollar, so this is an expensive dinner for 2 teenagers to produce.

'Look,' he says and picks the tiny squat glass up with his teeth, tilts it back, swallows the contents, and returns the glass to the table, all in one smooth no-hands movement. 'You try.'

I make a half-hearted attempt but get nowhere and polish off the glass in the normal way.

'Not that way!' he protests and refills the glasses. Valentina comes into the kitchen for the butter and takes a sip from Dima's glass, the first intimate gesture I've noticed between them. When she's gone he tries the drinking trick again but drops the glass. It doesn't smash, it bounces, but makes a nasty noise and he looks sheepishly at the doorway but no one disturbs us. 'Stupid Russian boy,' he mutters.

The kitchen is smoky. His cigarettes. For the first time in 13 years I feel an urge to take up smoking again, less from inner agitation than from a sense of fitness. Russia is such a deathtrap that it becomes liberating. In the West, the Land of Possessions, good health becomes a possession to be protected from violation the way you would protect a garden from trespassers. But the Russians are more casual about 'unhealth' in this giant cracked ashtray of St Petersburg. So I take a cigarette and halfway through hand it over to him. The same applies to alcohol. When a place is on the skids you have to be slightly drunk to feel normal. I drink here not spectacularly but significantly more than in London. However, because my system is so tuned up in Petersburg, I hardly feel the effect. Usually. To-night, a moment ago, the room started to rotate. But don't worry. It is going round very slowly.

Valentina comes in and talks to him.

'She say you must sleep here to-night.'

'No, no.'

'Yes, yes. Maybe it is dangerous for you to go back at this time. And if you stay, we like it. She has made bed.'

'Please,' says Valentina; and looking up at the ceiling, iterating carefully from memory, she continues 'Message from Agafea. In Siege,

no birds, no flowers, no grass, no cats, no dogs. All eaten. Good-night.'
And she disappears to sleep in the grandmother's corner.

He takes a bottle and some cheese with holes in it from the fridge.

'Russian cheese?'

'Lithuania.'

'Very good.'

'Try this.'

'What is?' My English has gone completely pidgin. I swallow from the glass he offers – too much! – am gasping! can't speak! Shit! He squeals with laughter, rubbing my back and head.

'Here, water.'

'. . . . .'

'Pepper vodka.'

'. . !!!!!! . . . . .'

'Very good for fr – th –' He is trying to say the English word 'throat'. He cannot pronounce it.

My body is aflush with heat but through the worst and I start to tell him a little of my life – since he never asks about it.

'Have more vodka,' he says. 'Not pepper.' And he raises the little glass to my lips encouragingly like a priest, narrowing his eyes, pouting 'Choot-choot.' Then he looks away, self-absorbed, looking at nothing: what curious thoughts, Dima, pass at these moments over the sky of your skull? He mentions the loss of his mother, grants me a momentary glimpse into his private pain and confusion, then moves on. 'Do you want to play cards?' A focus of greedy intelligence in his eyes. He's got me drunk. Now he'll take me to the cleaners. No thanks. He has a scar above his right eye. So do I.

'In the old days, when everything was secret, people talk easy only with a few friends, in the kitchen, with closed windows and doors.'

'And the tap running or the radio on loud!'

'You have it too in your country?'

'No. It was in a play I saw.'

Valentina, who is sleeping somewhere with Agafea, has made up an extra bed on the bedroom floor. I say I'm happy to sleep down there but it's not so simple. She used the *old* bed sheets for the floor and put *clean* sheets on the bed for me.

'You can share with me if you like.'

'No, no,' he says, 'you will have good sleep.'

His body is trim, lightly muscled, very white except for tanned arms and head.

'Are those sailor's underpants?' I ask.

He laughs. 'Yes. Always long and blue. Are those writer's underpants?'

'They are what writers should be – brief and to the point.'

He is asleep in the floor-bed almost at once, lying on his side with face towards me. The small window is uncurtained but is not disturbing because it is dark outside. But it's not supposed to be dark. What has happened to the sky? It's almost black. Into the hush of the street enters a group of young men, singing a heave-ho song with full-breasted commitment and an almost professional esprit de corps. They are accompanied by a clicking noise. Click-click-click . . . Is there a mouse in the room? Click-click. The clicking grows garrulous, increases in tempo. The choir whoops with delight and rushes away out of earshot. The clicks are now ferocious and coalesce into a roar. A hailstorm is blocking out the world with a thick beaded curtain, creating a cosiness of excitement in here. And out of this clamorous comfort grows an erection – mine – one of those absolute, independent hard-ons like a piece of wood which arise and stand there, with arms folded and foot tapping, as if to say 'Well, here I am, watchya gonna do about it?' But there's really not much I can do right now, so I think I just have to stare this hard-on out. The hail ends as abruptly as it began. The hard-on doesn't. Dima sleeps on undisturbed. Silence . . . . . In the deep silence of the night I hear the playing of an orchestra from the 1930s, a long syncopated swoon of an introduction followed by a voice I recognise on a lovely lifting melody. Al Bowlly is singing *The Very Thought of You*. Don't ask me how. Impossible. 2 distinct realities are intersecting; 2 distinct structures of the universe have blipped into each other; synchronicity is flexing its awesome powers. The song, presumably emanating from a nearby flat, begins. It shimmers ghostlike through its length . . . *living in a kind of daydream . . . you'll never know how slow the moments go till I'm near to you* . . . And finishes. Just like that. Nothing before it. Nothing after it. I want to cry but the emotion is locked dry in my throat. Russia, what are you doing to me? . . . . . God bless you, Dima . . . .

Heaven knows what the time is. I awake feeling weird. With a headache. Dima's bedclothes are tumbled on the floor and he's not here. Can't hear anyone, anything. Pull on clothes – step uneasily out of the room. No one. Go for pee, splash face, brush my teeth with a finger, look into kitchen. No one.

A voice behind says 'Hullo.' It's Valentina. She says Dima has gone out. No sign of granny either. 'Breakfast?' She's looked up the word and memorised it, catching her breath and giggling at her solemn effort at communication.

How Russians make tea: a pot of prostratingly strong tea is brewed. A few lunatics might dive in at this stage but that's not the idea. Only half a cup or less is poured, and the cup then filled with hot water. No milk. Russians generally add sugar. The unemployed gas ring rages upwards, a fury of blue points. Valentina puts a plate of homemade cakes on the table, moving coyly, less withdrawn now, perhaps because we are alone. She is both shy and forward with me, ie. she is flirting. Russians do. They can't help it with foreigners. This rushing together of East and West after so long a separation is not only political and cultural – it is also physical – actual. I'd like to talk to her while he is out, ask her things. She would like to ask me things – I feel her leaning towards me in this way. But we are completely frustrated by language. Strain and a wave of tiredness – I return to lie on the bed, doze off, and when I come round again Dima is in the room reading a piece of paper.

'Excuse me, sorry, I go out. Now I am back.' He doesn't look very happy and becoming aware of that, gives a nervous chip-toothed smile. He uses his smile, hides so much behind it, but sometimes a sadness breaks through, and it does now, a deep sadness gazing at me.

'I had a funny dream,' I say. 'I was in England with my friends and family but it was exactly like Russia and everyone was behaving like Russians. I have a headache, Dima.'

'Wash?'

'Done it.'

'I have an idea,' he says, preparing bread and soup in the kitchen. I look at him suspiciously. 'Let me show you real Russian pub.'

'Oh God.'

'You will like it.'

'Are you sure?'

'No. You will remember it.'

I slap my neck.

'How you know that one?'

'You're not the only Russian I know.'

Valentina, when we say good-bye, looks questioningly into my eyes and presses my hand . . . A heavy, humid day, grey cloud low and oppressive, and the smell of suspense. The air is jellylike, the step slow. Dima takes my arm and pulls me across the road. We enter a courtyard – cross beneath a stairway – another courtyard – down an alley, courtyard, stairway, alley – another courtyard – and each yard is more mournful than the previous, each alley more squalid, penetrating into the amniotic heart of St Petersburg, to the foetus of its dementia and to the ultimate refuge of its sodden souls. He pauses before a door of cracked wood and brown flaked paint, almost off its hinges, and pulls it open with a bravura stance and bids me enter.

A dank fetor of tobacco smoke and stale booze sucks us in. The concrete walls and floor are blotched and split into riverine maps. A single window is so obscured by grime, and by the sticky tape which holds together the star fracture of its glass, as to be almost ineffectual. A solitary lightbulb struggles to illumine dazed faces of indeterminate age in terminal alcoholic entropy. The appearance of a Westerner in this hole creates a stir, albeit minor, as nothing else could.

'Hold onto your money,' whispers Dima.

'Why are you whispering? They don't understand English.'

'Some of us do,' pipes a voice.

Searching for its source I identify a tiny fat figure in brown and yellow clothes, a bumblebee. The powers of his pebble spectacles may be inadequate because he's screwing up his face behind them in an attempt to focus. Or perhaps it's his way of smiling.

'Osip Kokoshkin,' he says extending a hand.

We offer him a drink which he accepts without demur and in the course of an affable conversation learn that he is an adept of psychotronics, as well as a Buddhist – he offers to escort me at a future date of my choosing to the Buddhist Monastery in the north of the city and we exchange telephone numbers. But at the main road Dima and I agree to speak on the phone to-morrow – I give him a quick hug and take a taxi home.

Nina rings. Serafima is out.

'Sorry about your car being burgled.'

'I am very happy. They took only the cassette stereo – they might have taken the car.'

In the evening I visit the Health Club at the Astoria Hotel. The foyer is in a yeasty fermentation of ancient Americans dressed in pale trousers and gaudy jumpers. One of them, going up in the lift, wears a badge marked SDA.

'What do those letters stand for?'

'Seventh Day Adventist.'

'What are you doing here?'

'There's lots of us here. We're needed.'

A new carpet in the upper corridors has '1912' woven all over it, the year the hotel opened. Such institutions now flaunt their pre-Revolutionary credentials. Last week a 1906 edition of the Russian Bible was reprinted with its Doré-esque engravings and red palisade borders. Copies of this high quality product are available at Dom Knigi for 132 roubles.

After a dozen lengths of the small oblong pool (graced by a giant window onto the cityscape at one end) I stretch out in the men's sauna cabin. There's only one other person using the club and he's in here reading a pulp paperback called *Airquake*. I am naked on a white towel, he huddles in a corner in tight red beach shorts. The thought of strapped-down bollocks sweating into clammy nylon swimwear – not appealing. Anyone who wears clothes in a sauna has a psychological problem, pudor in such circumstances carrying with it a sense of traumatised indecency.

'It's my first visit,' he says, 'and a bit of a shock.'

'The sauna?'

'Russia.'

He is American, about 35, staying at the hotel on business.

'Why?'

'I'm on a recruiting drive for my client.'

'No, why a shock? I mean, I agree that it is.'

'The place is falling apart. The fear on people's faces.'

'I don't find the faces more afraid than in London or New York.'

'The youngsters we're targeting for my client are 25 to 30 years old. They include highly qualified doctors who want to become mere salesmen – it's very sad. But there's no sense of urgency. Often they don't even turn up for the interview.'

'The sudden fade – or the sudden switch.'

'Yes. It's weird. But we've had some excellent candidates who speak brilliant English. The education system here is superb. Better than the USA. The courses are longer than in the States. In fact they're the most cultured people I've ever come across, they really know their stuff – but not how to apply it. They haven't a clue about to-morrow . . . It's a bit worrying. We haven't filled all the posts. And my client is due over next week.'

'My God! Do you see? From this cabin window – look – a close-up of St Isaac's. Yes, look, from this angle, come here . . . Who is your client?'

'Oh yes . . . that's so beautiful. Sweat 'n' pray. My client is Tampax Tampons. They have a plant in St Petersburg and another in the Ukraine.'

'Do they sell in Russia?'

'It's quite new here but there's a huge market and the Russian women who've tried them have been really wowed.'

I'm bowled over by this use of the verb 'to wow' and escape into cooler air, go for a swim (in shorts by the way), and ask the assistant for mineral water, but there isn't any, only tea or beer. No weighing machine either. I long to know if I've lost weight – I feel I have, not through lack of food but because of my speeded-up metabolism. Alas the machine I brought to Russia is wildly inaccurate. They try to sell me a massage – 'For you special price. $10.' Under the warm shower I get the horn. Fast – from nothing to everything in 5 seconds. Better wrap the towel round my waist. But no matter what I do, the banana bulge asserts itself through the fabric. Oh what the hell . . . Mr Tampax withdraws a little further into his corner.

'What are they using now?' I ask.

'A piece of rolled-up cotton,' he replies urgently. 'Or external protection. Like America in the 1920s. The tampon, as you know, is an internal device.'

'My landlady says Russia won't improve for 10 years.'

'Do they have that long? I'd guess they've got 3 years at most before the whole lot goes up. We've all got to try and prevent that.'

'I'm going to get a local to take me to a proper Russian steambath – this place is too expensive for regular use. And guess what? They don't have any water to drink.'

'Try the bar downstairs.'

'Right-o, guv'ner.'

'Bin nice talking to ya.'

Cleansed, washed, combed and dressed in clean clothes, I feel thoroughly invigorated and descend to the Bar Angleterre on the ground floor. It is now 10.20 pm. The bar is beginning to fill with women of the night, those blonde stalking felines in dark suits with short skirts, long legs, slanting eyes, a cigarette maybe between glossy lips. Oh, Russian eyes . . So many pairs of eyes in this city touching you inside. It's the eyes that kill you . . . The Bar Angleterre is small and the service confoundedly slow. I am parched, dying, but the barman continues to tot up numbers with a calculator at the far end of the bar.

'They take ages,' says a voice beside me, using the English idiom. It's one in a dark suit with short skirt, by Boss or Lagerfeld, that type, slanting eyes, long straight blonde hair, because in fact they don't all look like that. Several border on the outrageous. The most floozielike among them has a backcombed beehive and a bosom like the bastion of a fortress. Another wears a black dress with too many white lace frills like a waitress from the 1950s at Lyons Corner House. But we do not have here the lycra hams of Berlin or the silicone cartoons of Paris or the junkies of New York or the cockney sparrowhawks of London. On the whole this lot are smart, fine girls.

'Do they always take ages?'

'Not always.'

'Would you like a drink?'

'I'd like another coffee.'

'That all?'

'A coffee would be very nice.'

'I'm not staying at this hotel.'

'Where are you staying?'

'With a Russian family.'

'Ah.'

'Can I ask you a question?'

'Anything.'

'How much do you charge?'

'Oh. Are you interested?'

'No.'

'$100.'

'And if I'm interested?'

'$200.'

'Oh.'

'What are you doing in St Petersburg?'

'I'm a writer.'

'I hate writers.'

'Sorry.'

'They never stop writing.'

'I can't get started.'

'That's an improvement.'

'Why?'

'You are troubled.'

'I'm thinking.'

'The way some of them churn it out . . ugh!'

'Yes, that's repulsive, isn't it.'

'You are sweating.'

'Am I?'

'Yes.'

At last the barman attends to us.

'I was in the sauna.'

'Did you have massage?'

'No. I'd quite like a massage.'

'$50 I will do massage for you. I am no good at money. Some are good at it. Me no.'

'Me no too.'

'This is embarrassing . . . where do you come from?' she asks.

'I only have $30. Nothing complicated,' I reply.

'OK.'

'OK?'

'OK.'

'Hang on . . . I have only $27. Sorry.'

'Oh God, I hate writers!'

'You said that before.'

'Once upon a time I had affair with a writer . . .' She stares down at the coffee, stirring it with a spoon, the memory stinging still. '. . . . OK.'

'OK? You will give a massage for $27?'

'OK.'

'You are sweet to me.'

To leave the Astoria, or indeed any of the other dollar prisons, is to pass through an air-lock of paranoia, propelled onto the streets like a potential

victim, the body clenching against threat, against the 24-hour sunshine
nightmare vibrating around you, quiet at this hour, uncluttered, pensive, as
though the city had drawn in its breath prior to a kiss or an expectoration.

'We can walk. Do not be afraid.'

She is not the first Russian to say that to me. Do I look afraid? Does it
show through so clearly? She is not thin. When I think of 'woman' I do
not think of bones.

We climb a morose staircase on the Moika Embankment to a flat full of
pink light and cuddly toys – bears, rabbits, donkeys, crocodiles, tigers, a
whole zoo of nylon fluff. I must be a bloody fool coming here. They might
rob me or anything – well, no, I'm handing over all my dollars as it is, but
. . . The main room overlooks the canal. Shag-pile rugs cover the floor. A
large square divan against the wall is heaped with cushions and animals.
But it is the heavy aroma of scent which makes me chuckle uneasily – I've
got myself trapped in some preposterous cliché and must somehow see it
through.

'I'm sorry about all this,' she says, indicating the fluffies and sweeping
most of them onto the floor. 'It's not my place.'

'Whose is it?'

'My friend's. She's in Moscow for 3 months – in my flat.'

'You are from Moscow?'

'From St Petersburg. I work in Moscow.'

'Shall I take my clothes off?'

'Do what you like.'

I take the money out of my trouser pocket and put it under an ashtray.
It's mostly in dollar singles. And throw my clothes onto an armchair in
deliberate disarray.

'Are they all singles?' she queries. She's one of those well-to-do
Russians who find single notes an irritation.

I lie face down on the bed and say 'Do my back and shoulders first. You
can use your fingernails a bit.' I really need this.

'Do you want a whisky?' she asks. 'I'm having one.'

She pours it neat into a couple of vodka glasses and carefully removes
her own clothes, placing the suit on a coathanger. I don't think she wants
to do back & shoulders – a fingernail is running up and down the inside
of my thigh. It feels delicious. I am resting the side of my face on my
hands and thinking – we are like 2 people in a commercial. But
the whisky and the slow relentless movement of the fingernail induce

a sloughing-off of self-consciousness. The edges of personality begin to dissolve . . . turn over . . . her eyes are hidden by her hair . . . the breasts move with a slow comfortable rhythm . . . I like breasts – sssssssssslip . . . she's slipped a condom over my cock.

There is a soft click inside, like a muffled gear-change, as I shift into a different aspect of character. This is the secret of the chance encounter: to take a holiday from yourself . . . . . A second before the magnesium flash I hear a kettle whistling in an adjacent flat . . . . . Relaxed now, I keep chuckling. Sex without love has a purity which can lighten the heart. So long as you have love somewhere else. Sex in a loveless life can be a reminder of inner bleakness – though it is much better than nothing at all. It keeps you in shape for love. She is amused by my grin, not resentful of it. Quite often after surprise sex I have this chuckling feeling. It's the silly feeling of success. It can be resented if the other party has mixed feelings. And vice-versa.

'You are in love?' she asks.

'Er . . .'

'But you have not had her.'

'Aha.'

'Is she beautiful?'

'Yes.'

'I think you can have her.'

'How do you know?'

'Of course you can have her.'

She showers.

Then I shower while she tidies the room with fleet accuracy. She helps me button up my shirt, saying 'This is a beautiful shirt.'

'What is your name?'

'Anya.'

'Aren't you afraid of AIDS in this job?'

'Don't be childish. I love my job. I am very careful. And remember – AIDS brings the death principle into our days – which makes us more alive!'

Only a university-educated Russian prostitute could produce a remark like that. Don't believe them when they say the Russians do not have the gift of self-mockery. Giving a kiss on the cheek, a droll look and a wave, she returns with poise and relish to the Astoria.

CHAPTER THREE

There is in St Petersburg an Englishman in his early 30s called Roger. He's been wheeler-dealering around for quite a while and may know something about buildings for bookshops. I ring him at work. Roger suggests a drink at Sadko's.

'What's Sadko's?'

'My God, you don't know Sadko's?'

The only Sadko I know is the title of Russia's first ever symphonic poem, the setting of a sea legend by Rimsky-Korsakov and later developed by him into an opera. Roger's Sadko is a brasserie looking onto Nevsky Prospekt and attached to the Grand Europe Hotel. It has the style of a dollar bar but is in fact a rouble bar, the only place which straddles the divide, not too expensive, and therefore the most fashionable spot in town, enjoyed by tourists, toughs and oddballs.

'I eat there every other night. You can join me to-night between 9 and 10.'

He breaks off for a wrangle with someone in his office – he needs to borrow 50 roubles to get to the bank – the woman won't lend it – he babbles at her in English but employs a very heavy Russian accent by way of compromise – she is defiant – he spells out his quandary to her – suddenly comes back on the line.

'Sorry about this. My secretary's being a pain.'

'How shall I recognise you?'

'Just ask for Rodge. They all know me. I'll be in check trousers and a check cashmere sweater.'

Play Elmore James – *Rollin' and Tumblin'*, *Make My Dreams Come True*, *Blues Before Sunrise* – and boogie absent-mindedly in earphones – switch on TV – stab at the 3 channels – crikey: Trooping the Colour from London: mind-boggling: the colour, the trooping, the spruceness, the buildings standing up, the whole functioning like a dream of Paradise: immediately I become a rampant monarchist. En route to Sadko's: a neurotic Doberman slips its leash and helter-skelters off down Nevsky Prospekt cutting a swathe of scream. Opposite the Grand Europe Hotel a Russian reggae band is into the shudderwobble. The promenade outside the hotel is newly flagstoned and planted with trees, the genteel effect obviated by a constant patrol of armed security guards in khaki-blotch camouflage, crewcuts and shades. A brace of them refuse me entry – do I look like a Russian hoodlum? has writerly chameleonism gone so far? Eventually, after I huff and puff and throw my arms around, they relent, but it's a shock all the same – I thought I was posh.

'Is Rodge here?'

'Who?'

'Rodge. Rodge.'

Blank looks.

'The Englishman Rodge. He eats here every other night.'

No one's heard of him. Shuffle around looking for a check cashmere sweater. Nothing, nothing. So I ask for a beer – 250 roubles – another shock.

'Imported. Swedish,' says the barman.

'I want Russian beer.'

'Only Swedish.'

I flop at a nearby table with the beer which is more expensive than champanskoye. There is an excellent local beer called 'St Petersburg' – why these places have all this imported glop . . . The man on the opposite side of the table is gobbling shashlyk.

'I'm looking for someone called Rodge.'

'That's me.'

'But that sweater's not check.'

'Yes it is.'

'No it isn't.'

'Yes, it's my check cashmere sweater.'

'They wouldn't let me in.'

'There's been trouble.'

'Do I look rough?'

'Next time say you've booked a table.'

'They're a funny lot in here.'

Thugs with inflated money belts, tarts, foreigners, trendies, a couple of rent boys.

'It is so *corrupt*,' says Rodge, chewing his shashlyk sensually. 'And *nasty* with it. Heads in attics, legs in gutters. I was at the Metropol – which is supposed to be the best old-style restaurant – and a torpedo was there – a hit & run guy – just let out of prison, shaven head, spider's web tattoo all over his face –'

'Are you sure he wasn't English? They do things like that in the Portobello Road.'

'– and I'm there with this Swedish girl right, and she took some holiday snaps inside the place, and these heavies from the torpedo table came over, demanded the camera, ripped out the film, handed it back to her. I was in a restaurant once – by myself – I am – this lot came over, demanded my wallet, took out all the money, handed back the wallet. There was nothing I could do – every one of them had a doctorate in GBH.'

Funny thing – I'm more or less fine when I'm with Russians but when I get with the foreign set and the story-swapping starts, that's when paranoia begins to flash.

'You know, some people are getting very rich here. Many old Commies moved into business because they had the contacts. Most of the top ones have external bank accounts. They've siphoned-off gold – lots! Some have sold pictures from the Hermitage.'

He is thrilled to be telling all this in his low South London drone.

'Where were you before?' I ask.

'10 years in Sweden, 1 year in Hong Kong.'

'Quite a difference.'

'You're telling me. The Russians are neurotic as hell.'

'So are the English.'

'Not like the Russians. But what do you expect after 3 generations of Communism?'

'Will you return to England?'

'What for? The way I read it – the Brits have always gone overseas to seek their fortune. There's too much energy in the English for *mere* England.'

'Do you know that man over there?'

It's the banana-seller from my first day out with Leonid.

'Yuri. He's all right – in his twisted way.'

Rodge waves. Yuri joins the table and orders a bottle of champanskoye and 3 glasses.

'I follow you in street,' says Yuri to me. 'After Oklahoma Dansing. But

I do not call – at that time of night you run if someone shouts at you! Do you want to buy a tank?'

'This is the standard joke, isn't it?'

'Yes, it's amusing. Lots of old tank to buy.'

'I'm up to here with tank.'

'Something bigger maybe?'

'Like a nuclear bomb?'

'Bigger. Like a nuclear scientist.'

'They need feeding.'

'OK, how about 25 kg of pure plutonium? It fits in a briefcase.'

'Aren't you afraid they'll blow up the world?'

'Yes.'

'Is he serious, Rodge?'

'How the hell should I know?' replies Rodge.

Nikita shows up with DJ Groove and 2 English girls (Vanessa and Henrietta).

'This is Piccadilly Circus,' says Vanessa (the gushier one), putting another table to the end of ours. 'We were at the Planetarium yesterday – it's finished – creepy – full of bandits – we thought we were going to be abducted and raped! We had to hide in the loo!'

'If anything goes wrong,' says Yuri, 'abortion is simple. 500 roubles. Pop!'

(Information: Russia has the world's highest abortion rate. This is not because they are having more sex but because they are more careless. Can't get contraception, can't afford it, can't be bothered. Russia legalised abortion in 1920, the first country in the world to do so. Then Stalin banned it in 1936. It was legalised again in 1955 under Khrushchev.)

'I was sunbathing next to a doctor on the Neva plage,' says Henrietta (the dour one), 'and asked him how much a sex-change costs, man to woman, they can't really do it the other way can they – can they? – and he said 10,000 roubles.'

'This is the last place I'd have it done!' exclaims Vanessa. 'You might come out as a frog! A divorce is very civilised here – you pay 5,000 roubles and they stamp your passport.'

'Are you medical students?'

'Nah, we're improving our Russian,' says Vanessa. 'Henrietta's having an affair with one. He does all the raves.'

'He's going to do one in a huge swimming-pool,' says Henrietta.

'Such a beautiful language,' I say. 'But the commonest word is "engineer". When anyone tells you what their father does it's always "engineer".'

'Mine is labourer,' says DJ Groove.

'The only problem with the raves,' says Henrietta, 'are the banditi. I get worried about Misha.'

'You can tell them by their muscles, their tracksuits, their flat-top haircuts,' says Vanessa. 'In fact they look like you, Yuri!'

He reddens with pleasure and says 'My neighbour just killed his wife.'

'Oh God,' groans Nikita, 'not now please.'

'My neighbour is alcoholic. He beat her up so badly she went into a coma. Then she came out of it. Then she went back into it. In and out of coma for 2 months. Then she died.'

'I'm going to talk to that rent boy,' says Nikita.

'We've got the Greenpeace Man coming to stay,' says Henrietta dourly.

'They've got a great flat overlooking the Neva.'

'Like a sort of you know chunk of palace.'

'We pay $25 a month each! I like the Russians and everything but I couldn't live with them!' gushes Vanessa.

'I could,' I say. 'I do.'

'He's going to measure the radioactivity.'

'When is the longest day?'

'Midsummer Night.'

'When's that?'

'June 22nd?'

'When's that?'

'Something should happen then.'

'Is anything happening then?'

'What did the rent boy say?'

'There's a free concert to-night in front of the Winter Palace.'

(It will begin at 11 pm. All the summer pop concerts begin late. There is one coming up at the Lenin Stadium, midnight to 6 am.)

'He said he charged $100 and I asked him how he got erections with ugly people.'

'Where's the Scottish Bakery?'

'Near the Baghdad Café.'

'And he said "I always get erections. No problem." '

'The trumpet is the instrument of St Petersburg!'

'Yes – *Lieutenant Kijé.*'

'Come to Bela's party,' implores Nikita, beginning to drool, whine, and lose focus. 'I need a brandy to wake me up.'

'But the soundtrack is Rachmaninov.'

'Go on – buy a nuclear scientist – just for the week-end – he'd love it!'

'Yes, go on – buy one!'

'Business is the new form of expression in Russia, the new art form,' says Yuri.

'Do you want to be rich?'

'Yes, to live well. When people are poor, they are not spiritually free.'

'Are the rich spiritually free?'

'Do you know any good Russian steambaths?' I ask.

(I don't feel comfortable in these foreign ghettos. Alas, most of the Russian cafés close at 8 pm – and they often close for lunch too! But to spend too long in Sadko's is a kind of defeat. It breeds a siege mentality.)

'I go to the baths in Dostoievsky Street,' says Yuri. 'I will take you.'

'Where's everyone going?' asks Nikita.

Palace Square is 75% full and thickly clotted with policemen, many of them simply boys with truncheons. The concert headlines 2 heavy metal bands from Britain. Guitars howl and scrawny plastic-covered crotches stab through red and purple floodlights. Fireworks go up in sunshine. The smoke makes fantastic patterns with a faint spangling in the padded blue sky.

'Who's coming to Bela's party?' asks Nikita.

How does he find it so far? He is excited to be here. Everything is blurred except what is happening right now. Everything in human affairs is organised for maximum inconvenience. Nothing goes according to plan. Every day is a conundrum.

The most surreal city – summer or winter, people cannot keep normal hours. Nature does not permit it. From the very outset the fundamental distinction between day and night is shattered, and it takes at most 3 days to lose completely all internal references. There is nothing to anchor the 24-hour round – his retiring and arising slide helplessly forward. This is quite helpful, enabling him to roll with the punches of surprise or disappointment. He is both spaced-out and alert. Alertness becomes vigilance which can become anxiety which is overfocus. And in the midst of dubiety there may be, expanding from a dot, a great pool of tenderness . . .

Yes, everyone is a misfit; everyone is single – even the married; they are warriors of the day and dreamers of the night. He can offend Russians without intending to. They can offend him without intending to. Clearing it up may be easy, may be messy, may never happen. Minor altercations are quickly forgotten in the pressure or diversion of the present.

He has brought too many thick clothes. His skin is thinner, emotions closer to the surface. Smarting eyes, 2 small tears, or a choking in the throat, come and go quickly. On most days there is a little emotional shudder to get through, often heralded by a sudden loss of the élan vital. He's fine, then out of the blue this heavy feeling sweeps over him, loss of energy like incipient hypoglycaemia, touch of queasiness, break in the façade, release of tension in tears or whatever, recovery, and one continues to trace one's unique trail of slime across the surface of the planet . . . His emotions feel like a pair of bellows, constantly on the go, in & out, up & down, fanning the flame of . . . well, of the soul perhaps? Who knows . . .

No, he's not noticed that Russians laugh less than anyone else. Bergson's Theory of Laughter asserts that it is triggered by witnessing men behaving like machines – in which case Communism must've been hilarious. What triggers laughter? The dysfunction between cause and effect, the discrepancy between expectation and result. In which case this place is pure comedy – which it isn't.

Russia is still closed in upon itself. Communications with the outside world are poor. As a society they preferred – since they could not afford both – to put the First Man into Space rather than give everyone extra shoes. So they are not materialistic. And yet – they are totally hooked on the frippery of Western consumerism, any old bit of crap with I LOVE NYC on it. And yet, if it should be stolen from them, their sense of identity is not disturbed. They like to give and receive presents. But the realm of products, possessions, things is a minefield – they take a less complex pride in the achievements of Russian art, science and sport in which they have excelled. Many of their highly trained minds are now roaring round the rim of despair. Many are hungry for shoes. The English can sympathise with their post-imperial fatigue. And yet – if Britain finds it difficult to grasp quite how it fell from being the dominant world power to funny little island in less than a lifetime, how much greater must be Russian amazement at their fall from superpower to quasi-third-world bankrupt in 5 years flat. The Russians do not however have Britain's strain of post-colonial masochism which takes unto itself the blame for any current awfulness in an ex-colonial territory – the decadence of decency. Russia remains the world's biggest country. Siberia is the silent fact of Russia, the great vacuum sucking on the back of Russian necks. Geographical Russia has no natural edges. It balloons outward and vaporises in a mystifying shapelessness, an unpatrollable eternity. Russian backs are always cold. This sense of exposure marries, paradoxically, with the feeling of being hemmed-in, without the escape provided by a long coastline – which feeling was the reason for the creation of St Petersburg.

The Russians are the most fascinating and upsetting people he has ever encountered. They combine, in a mercurial compound, the capacity for reserve of the northern races with the capacity for expression of the southern races. Surprisingly they don't kiss when they meet. And usually they don't make introductions – if you're with one and he/she bumps into a friend on the street, you will probably not be introduced. And yet – in this land denied luxury, everyone is a sybarite! They know the world of pleasure but do not often experience it. Pleasure: the word is one of the greatest in the English language, the texture and rhythm of it, the sound and appearance and meaning of it. The Russians do not have a word for 'pleasure'. They have a word for 'delight' and another for 'satisfaction' but not one which subsumes both. And yet the entire Russian language is the subsumption of form, meaning and sensuality demonstrated by the English word 'pleasure'.

There is a great deal of smoking but no loose tobacco, no roll-your-own, no pipe smokers. Beards and moustaches are uncommon. Good Russian vodka is the best you can buy, with a slightly oily smoothness which the stomach enjoys. Western vodkas are watery and metallic in comparison. Inflation is supersonic. He bought an English-Russian/Russian-English Dictionary, printed in Moscow in 1991 with 6 roubles stamped on the back of it, for 150 roubles from a stall outside Dom Knigi – none was stocked within the bookshop itself. This dictionary contains 'napalm' but not 'penis'. There are no tourist brochures, no lists of events, no junk mail or flyers. Just you versus the city.

What was so shocking on arrival, the decrepitude of his landlady's living arrangements, is shocking no longer. Compared to most she exists, it is now apparent, in great comfort and privilege. The majority live like troglodytes in the carved-up classical cliffs of the city. The revenge of barbarism over refinement: the horde swarmed into town and camped in ornate chambers. The whole place became an epic squat; and insofar as it proletarianised the imperial city, the Revolution was successful. Flats have been partitioned several times over, with a number of families sharing one bathroom, kitchen, loo. The insides of these quarters are assembled from erratic gleanings into thought-provoking parodies of the Western lifestyle, held together with rusty pins and discoloured tape, and they often possess an imaginative grotto appeal. At first it is bewildering to meet sophisticated first-world people in third-world conditions, and the absence of fine living in Russian society produces a kind of free-fall in visitors from more stratified societies. A country as rich in natural endowments as Russia does not achieve plenary impoverishment by accident – it had to be worked for, persisted in. *And yet* . . . it is difficult for a Westerner not to equate extreme dilapidation with criminality and threat. This gives a frisson to home-visiting – so much culture and amity behind so many intimidating doors!

. . . He cannot develop consistency of action or mood. Underslept, overslept, slept right but feel wrong, slept wrong but feel OK – old rhythms broken – new ones not established – any momentum which gathers soon slips out of gear – everything happening at once, longueurs, bunching up/crossed wires, a quiet stretch . . . But as Sonya predicted, his acceptance of perpetual disquiet and the dynamics of chance is improving – partly from attrition – but perhaps more because this Russian boy called Dima has become the enabling point of reference from which a structure of meaning can be built.

The Day Of The Dacha. I have been thrashing in all this for some time now without an interval, and so when Serafima suggests we visit the dacha of her friends to swim in the lake I eagerly accept. It will be my first trip out of town. Inspired to develop this out-of-town idea, I ring Dima and we arrange to visit Petrodvorets together the day after.

The sun beats furiously on the car roof as Serafima, in tennis clothes with lace trimmings, rattles north on the Helsinki Road. The radio issues repeated warnings. Do Not Drop Matches or Cigarettes in the Countryside. Big Danger of Fire. At first she drives 'like slalom' to avoid potholes but the surface improves and our speed picks up.

'I like to drive fast,' she says with the window down, vegetable whiffs blowing through, clearing out the smell of petrol (most drivers carry cans of petrol – you can't buy it when you need it), 'but I must not.'

'Why not?'

'Because one of my wheels judders.' She doesn't use that word but it's what she means, and she speeds up to demonstrate a teeth-chattering vibration. 'Anyway – 60 kph is maximum by law. Nina had a radar to detect police before they see her but it was stolen too – this radar machine is very popular in our country.'

By local standards Serafima's car is not bad. She has a spider's web windscreen held together with tape and no wipers (these are kept in the boot to avoid theft). Spare parts are difficult to find and prices running away – a new tyre currently costs 6,000 roubles, so most cars are on their last tyres. To the left the sea glitters through birch trees.

'Is the Baltic tideless?'

'You must not swim in. Maybe you will be sick and anyway your skin will get red spots.'

This is because the last big project of the Communists was to build a flood barrier to protect the city 'even though ecological scientists said no, don't do it'. It was an immense undertaking, blocking out the Gulf of Finland by connecting Kronstadt Island to the mainland with 2 long arms. The sluices are not large enough to permit the free flow of sewage which has built up behind, turning the sea around St Petersburg into a poisoned mere.

After about an hour, she swoops into an illegal U-turn, backtracks, turns off the main road, stops at a level-crossing and immediately switches off the engine to conserve petrol. I climb out to await the passing of the train and mosquitoes swarm onto my bare legs but the air is good. A balmy zest rises from the grass and meanders out of the surrounding pine and birch forest.

'Stretch your legs, Serafima.'

'I can't. We are not flat.'

Her handbrake doesn't work.

The long green passenger train trundles slowly by like a soporific dinosaur and we drive inland for a further half hour to a locality criss-crossed by straight lanes. The trees make a close grid of verticals in every direction, anaesthetising anything exceptional by way of landmark. Many small cabins are set in simple gardens and ragged plots of husbandry. These are the dachas. Few dachas are grand. Most are charming and modest and it is not a sign of exceptional influence to have access to one. Some are private, many are government-owned. The Russians, like the English, maintain a powerful bond with the country-side but whereas the English of all classes enjoy the romance of the country gentleman, the Russians enjoy the romance of the peasant. The Tsars wore peasant dress as casual wear. Many Romanovs took peasant lovers. The Empress Elizabeth secretly married one and so did her cousin. The last movement of many Russian symphonies and concertos evokes a peasant festival. So the Russians, like the English, need every so often to see green, to smell earth.

(Other things Russians have in common with the English – fought as allies against Napoleon and Hitler – both refer to 'Europe' as though it were somewhere else – tea – this *homeliness* I feel in Russia must derive in part from its similarity to England in the 50s, the meat & 2 veg culture, the piles-of-sugar-in-the-tea culture, the semolina culture, plus making interiors as busy as possible with cosifying knick-knackery.)

The car has stopped. Serafima is leaning forward indecisively. The car moves again while she peers through the windscreen and snatches rapid glances out of the window to her left. 'We want 217. That's 31 . . 67 . . . 305 . . 311 . . . . . 28 . . .'

The numbers follow no rational sequence but this doesn't bother her. She brakes to speak to a pedestrian with a mountainous black and white dog. We are on the wrong road. She reverses, tries another lane.

'84 . . 6 . . 293 . . 294 – ooops!'

Pothole. We try another lane.

'17 . . . 109 . . . .'

And another.

'There! 217!'

But it's the wrong 217.

Another pedestrian, another chat, over a hump with a bump.

'Ah, now I remember!' she announces triumphantly, taking off in a new direction.

'52 . . . 58 . . 61 . . 60 . . . 217!'

We drive through a broken wooden gate over a lumpy path which fades into a lumpier lawn, lurch to a halt and get out. The car rolls forward a foot or so, settling. Mosquitoes darken my arms, legs and face. This could be a drawback to country life hereabouts.

Mrs X and Mr Y greet us. Nina, her daughter and their mutinous red setter are already inside discussing lunch which involves a visit to the village shop to buy large amounts of cholesterol in various forms. This shop is from the early 20th century – I've never seen anything like it – only about 20 different foodstuffs for sale but every one good, basic country produce. There is not one printed label in the whole of it, except on the bon-bon wrappers.

Cholesterol Lunch.

We wash our hands with lake-water poured over them onto the grass by Mr Y, and sit at a table with a red gingham tablecloth in the porch. The bread is of rye and wheat mixed. The butter farm fresh. The cheese has many holes in it.

'I know this cheese – it's Lithuanian.'

'No. Russian. Why don't you take cream?'

Nina is referring to the tall glasses of cream they are merrily emptying by way of a drink. Too rich for me and I have mineral water which tastes – interesting (there's a reddish deposit of iron at the bottom of each bottle).

'Do not lose weight,' Nina advises. 'I am losing weight. Look.' She stands and shows everyone how much extra space there now is in the waistband of her blue, whitepolkadotted shorts. 'It just goes! I don't know how!' She laughs with satisfaction. Of course she knows how. She's a diet fiend. Mrs X, who has never had sufficient waistband, looks sick. Serafima is unimpressed, knowing she has the better figure, and says 'Nina is molecular biologist' as if this were an explanation, which somehow it is. Ringo hops up and down, trying to participate.

Mr Y drains off his second glass of cream, pours a third, and says 'I shall have a good view of the moon to-night.' Maybe he's an astronomer – I never did grasp his job. A dab of cream adheres to the tip of his nose. Mrs X wipes it off and licks her finger. They are in love in that heavy, low-slung, unspeaking, automatic way. They do not flirt but no space is discernible between them: one being, 2 heads. But he will not come to the lake. Nina throws Ringo a scrap of cheese in a high arc. For once the dog doesn't move but watches it descend through a parabola towards him. It disappears with a snap like that of a shutting handbag. I take another bon-bon.

'You like sweets. My friend likes sweets,' says Mrs X. 'He found a fingernail in a chocolate bar. A fingernail from a big toe.'

'Nevsorov interviewed a man who found a hammer in a loaf of bread,' says Serafima and removes a crumb from her bee-stung lip with the tip of her tongue.

The first lake is about 10 minutes away and crowded. Serafima pouts 'Niet, niet, niet!', refusing to consider any possibility of joining such a plebeian gathering. Another 10 minutes along a mud road, further into the forest, a second lake twinkles up out of the trees and seems quieter. It has a kidney-shaped beach of fine tawny sand which Ringo, in madcap dashes, throws up into sprays. However we are by no means alone. There are the usual week-end families, but most groups are indecipherable – ours for example. Several girls with large breasts are sunbathing topless and young men strut near them in brief clingy swimming trunks of a thin fabric which outlines penises of various sizes – an example of that Russian trick of covering up and revealing simultaneously. As Ringo skids by, the topless girls sit up sharply spitting out sand and Nina shouts 'Ringo! Ringo! Ringo!' The dog returns via a devious route but the moment her attention moves elsewhere he's off and bounds into the water with great fuss, followed by Nina's daughter carrying the inflatable Gold King Kool Lounge water sofa from the USA. Serafima stretches out in a black bikini for serious sunbathing, her belly taut and snappy as rubber, while Mrs X, whose pale legs are joined together all down the middle, not a chink from crotch to heel, goes 'Ah . . ah . . . ah . .'

The boys, having failed to engage the girls with their display of pectorals and genitalia, return to a black and yellow jalopy in trees behind the beach and turn on pop music and open fizzy drinks. I take to the water which is affectionately chill and crisp. It becomes deep quickly but not suddenly. The lake is black-bottomed and the water gold-coloured. Never having swum in gold water before I am reluctant to swallow any and backstroke round and round in a wide circle. Sinking into a sky of flawless, innocent blue, lifting first one arm then the other over my head, and giving little flips with the feet, I hear Nina's urgent voice – Ringo! Ringo! – and turning my head, notice the dog shaking its wet coat all over a harmless old couple. The poor man, who only wants sun and peace after a hard week, is gesticulating at Nina who grabs the animal by the collar and drags it through sand . . . I like it here . . . plop . . . plop . . . To the right, a sleek coppery head travels past – Ringo's – followed by Serafima's yellow one held clear of the water to keep it dry. 'We are going far out,' she says. 'Far out . . . . .'

. . . Serafima is lying on her back behind dark glasses, raising first one leg and pointing the toe, then the other. She says 'We can stay the night if you want to.'

'I'm going to Petrodvorets to-morrow with a friend. I have to be back to-night.'

'It was completely destroyed by the Germans,' says Nina, pinching her waist, seeking out non-existent fat. 'Ringo! Ringo!' The lunatic beast is swerving across the beach at full gallop, shooting sand into lunchboxes and open-mouthed faces. 'In England is it possible to buy white chocolate?' she asks.

'Yes.'

'In Russia – not possible.'

When we leave the beach at 7.30 pm, the sun is still very hot. A short way along the hard mud track, a bank is smoking. The undergrowth and dry lichen can smoulder for days in a spreading black weal, without ever bursting into flame. But it *could* burst into flame and become a forest fire. This one is extensive, about ¼ mile long. It would not be a great task to stamp it out but car after car drives on by.

'Why doesn't the Government put it out?' asks Nina.

'Why don't we put it out?' ask I.

'We go to my sister's house,' says Serafima.

This turns out to be Igor's mother who lives in a small modern block of flats among woodland and allotments. The building is in good condition and the household prosperous with an expensive music system. Tea is served from delicate china, accompanied by small nutty cakes. Nina shows Serafima's sister how much extra space she has in her waistband. On television is a film of *Anna Karenina*. Greta Garbo spins a globe, extends a finger and says to her little boy 'Here we are in St Petersburg!' I can discern the original soundtrack beneath the Russian dub.

The Russians laugh.

'The actor made a joke,' says Mrs X. 'He said "With champagne I love salt cucumber!" But everyone knows this is only with vodka. Did you see Nevsorov last night? All those mutilated babies in Yugoslavia.'

(Information: Nevsorov is the maker of Russia's most popular television programme, *600 Seconds*, on every night at 9.30.)

Serafima fills large bottles with water, and suntanned, rested, refreshed, we return to bluegold St Petersburg. Driving south over the Kirovsky Bridge, with the windows down on a hot sunny evening, is one of the finest things you can do in life – oh yes, it is sweet returning to a home in this city.

'Is the Baltic tideless?'

She does not answer and stares ahead.

The low sun burns orange at its heart and knocks pink ink across the sky.

The Day Of Petrodvorets. Serafima is out. At the appointed hour Dima fails to show up. This is nothing in itself – he is normally late.

I pace the squeaking hall, unable to settle to anything else, growing more and more prickly.

After waiting for 2 hours, I decide to telephone. Someone – I don't know who it is – says 'Hullo'. All Russians use this form when picking up a call.

'Is Dima at home please?'

There is a pause. It seems to last for ever. I know it's not the wrong number. I hear some discussion. My heart races. Then the phone is decisively put down on me. This is a shock – a dark explosion in the head combined with a kick in the guts. I break into a cold sweat. Why the rejection? What has happened? A ball of lead begins to grow in my belly. What is going on?

NIGHTMARE

CHAPTER FOUR

This evening the air is iron-coloured and smells of thunder. I am in a different room now. It is between the Winter Palace and the Marble Palace. My new landlady is called Zoia, round and compact and vigorous, her face dimpled, a paranoid doctor living behind 2 steel doors and many locks, who stands guard with assorted weaponry over sacks of sugar and oats and rice, jars of coffee beans and boxes of tea, a kitchen cabinet of assorted alcoholic drinks and continental perfumes, cupboards of Italian pasta, Danish pork luncheon meat, bottled fruits and juices and jams, ranks of caddies whose contents are edible but unintelligible, or intelligible but inedible, or which enclose mysteries utterly defunct. Plus a fridge stacked with salamis, meat, eggs, cheese, butter, cream, blocks of gelid matter wrapped in white or brown paper. And she doesn't want me bringing any Russians here! Why the hell did I move? There are antlers in the kitchen.

Zoia and her son Boris (who studied painting but now runs a café) sleep in the Big Room where the television is, along with a black upright piano and lots of furry furniture. Thick oriental rugs hang on the walls and several old oil paintings. From the high ceiling a chandelier contraption in the art nouveau style drips with Christmas decorations: fringes of silver lametta, glass baubles in blue, purple, green. A guest from Paris put them up last year and Zoia and Boris are too short to get them down again – which doesn't explain the Christmas cards still propped inside one of the glass-doored cabinets. Most Russians keep totems from the West for special occasions. And quite often these occasions never arrive. So chocolate, perfumes, soap attain to an apotheosis of ossification, no longer products of consumerism but transformed by an endlessly renewed postponement (bordering oxymoronically on indifference) into abiding verities. In Russia all objects aspire to the status of icon, that is to practical uselessness and metaphysical symbolism, and a group of foil-covered Beatles in the cabinet here have acquired the deathly patina of eternity. Are they playing in Paradise? No, they cannot play there! Paradise is barren. There are no possibilities, no becoming, no beyond in Paradise – just a tingling glare of light for ever and ever – it's enough to set your teeth on edge . . . Among the books are several for learning English, including one in 2 volumes entitled *Introduction into Modern American*. I wonder if we shall be able to communicate.

The flat is in Ulitsa Khalturina which until 1917 was known as the Millionaya – Millionaire's Row – the subsequent alteration being in celebration of Mr Khalturin who planted a bomb in the Winter Palace in 1880. I cannot discover whether or not it went off. It is typical of the Russians' lack of false modesty in money matters that 'Millionaya' was not a nickname but the true name.

Despite such superiority (our building has a central sterilisation plant so that water may be drunk directly from the tap), the flat is approached by the most off-putting entrance yet, a sort of sootblack cellar before you come to the lift and the main flight. We are one below the top floor and the Big Room has a south-facing view over rooftops, and even a slice of the Church of Blood – or would do 'if only I could chop down that tree', complains Zoia.

'But there are only 2 trees in your view.'

'I still want to chop it down.'

This is the sort of person she is. Alas, one cannot enter the Church of Blood – it has been closed for restoration these past 20 years.

I have Boris's room, smaller than my previous one but more comfortable, with rugs on the walls, its own telephone, and mosquito grilles. But again no effective curtains. I improvise with hooks, coats, tablecloths – quite a performance every night. On top of the wardrobe a statuette of Lenin tries to speak – and fails. It is made from a greyish metal, another of those inexplicable local alloys. 'But we were never Communist,' Zoia is quick to explain. 'My grandfather was a rich man. My mother lived with us here and when she died I thought – I can live peacefully alone at last. But my son finished his marriage to a very nice woman – he wants children, she not – so he is back here. Are you married?'

'No.' She is the only Russian who has asked.

'My husband was in the medical institute with me – a doctor, a hypnotist, a boxer, a big man. But he drank too much vodka and I said go away and he went to live with a young girl and she left him. We are still good friends. He still loves me.'

I am hearing this often in Russia – he loves me, she loves me, they love me. Russians seem to hunger above all for the assurance of being loved, being cherished. To love, to make the first move, is to risk pain and being taken advantage of. But to *be* loved – this is the ideal, one which they imagine allows them the superior power. But it is an illusory power. If many people are happier to be loved than to love, then . . . *the one who gives wins* . . . or he may founder on the reef of expectation. But either way – he lives higher. The drama is his.

My room is beside the steel front doors – there is no tramping through the flat to reach it – the view, another tarmacadammed well, colonised by cats. After 3 days I am beginning to grasp the technique for opening these front doors – some locks turn this way, some that, all with different keys, one of which, the long brass one, Zoia says is useful for striking people on the head in an emergency. The inside of the inner door is purple, padded and studded like a tart's bedhead in Las Vegas. But the 2 most important features of my new life are:–

1. Zoia goes out to work at the clinic all morning and afternoon, or all afternoon and evening, and Boris is usually at the café until 11 pm. It is a relief therefore not always having to relate to someone when at home. There is time to draw breath, reorientate oneself.

2. I have moved into the very heart of my fantasy of St Petersburg. Each time I step onto the street there is a frisson of enchantment and disbelief. Along on the right is the bridge over the Winter Canal and beyond it the epauletted shoulders of the Winter Palace, sideways on, close up, haveable. At noon each day the cannon of the Peter and Paul Fortress rattle the bedroom windows – it is always a shock but a shock of Ruritanian dalliance. If you walk not into Ulitsa Khalturina but the other way, back through the courtyard, and through another courtyard, you emerge on the Neva Embankment directly opposite the cannon's discharge. I can walk everywhere now – I am at the hub of the wheel – less tiresome for questing feet. But . . . it is less homely here . . . . It was not a pleasure saying good-bye to Serafima and to my first room in Russia with its print of Briullov's *Last Day of Pompeii* (saw the original at the Russian Museum) and little Sergei's painting of the ship at sea. On the day I left her, it was 26 degrees C at 10.15 am. Serafima looked upset but was determined not to show it, playing Black Box so scorchingly loud

that, well, she showed it – bopping round the flat, snapping her fingers, shimmying her shoulders, shaking her bottom, skipping her toes, while I packed.

'I am sad to be leaving Serafima,' I said to Leonid.

'I explained to her', he replied, 'that you are a writer and have certain spiritual needs.'

Sadness had entered in for another reason also. That day of the painful rebuff, when Dima or Valentina or whoever it was put the phone down on me – I could hardly eat. Serafima asked 'Will you not go to Petrodvorets?' How I wished to be alone at that moment. But she perceived my unhappiness and changed the subject, suggesting a cheese something for lunch – I ate in small pulls and stabs, chewing each morsel as though it did not exist, trying to chew it into existence, into appetite, chewing interminably, unsuccessfully, and at last forcing down the foreign gobbet against the will of the body, but forcing it down nonetheless because food in the stomach tethers one to the earth and I felt untethered and at a loss . . . She asked 'Do you want to go to the Artillery Museum?' . . . no, no, no . . . . .

I expected Dima to ring back. He didn't. So I went out for a walk, descending the staircase, stepping over vicious pale-blue broken glass halfway down, in a rage mixed with incomprehension and disappointment . . . After all that business of come to my home, come to the Black Sea, you are my friend, he can't even get it together to ring and cancel our meeting – just doesn't turn up, can't be bothered, it means nothing – can't even be bothered to speak to me – but tells her – yes, it must've been she who answered – that brief crackly hullo was a girl's voice surely – his is quite deep, slightly husky from the cigarettes, a rich expressive voice – and with it he tells her oh I want to sleep, I can't be bothered with that silly Englishman, hang up, Valentina, just put the phone down on him . . .

Many times in a life one may encounter someone who touches us with an adorable and perplexing charm, who cuts the ordinary day with a moment of magic, and almost at once the person has gone, been swept away, sucked back into the crowd. When rarely, through force of circumstance or ingenuity or imagination or daring, one manages to arrest this transience, to jam the conveyor belt of passing events and say no, stop, yes, hullo, and retrieve that person from their fall into the pit of what might have been, and to bring him or her forward into the real, the now, the light, your life, this is . . . important. And it means more still in an alien place where one has little, nothing. And this happened. And as suddenly, it came to naught. I thought the contact meant something. Does anything mean anything here, or is it all fucking quicksand? Is every gesture hollow? How can a person be so full of it one day, and the next – nothing? Is it possible to know someone in this town?

. . . At the Yusupov Palace I could not make myself understood. I was not being allowed to look round the building, that was clear, and I left with a gracious, furious bow from the waist. What's the sport of Russian gentlemen? Huntin', fishin' and shootin' Rasputin! Yes, everything is broken and cracked including the people! It may take you a little time to find the crack in a person but hang on in there – after a few days, a week at the outside, it will appear, the crack, or cracks, a mangled piece of inner-space furniture thrown at *you*. And you are knocked from your pedestal, plunging down the turbulent water of their predicaments.

At the Intourist Head Office (designed by Peter Behrens in the early Brutalist style to house the German Embassy and briefly used for this purpose before the outbreak of the Great War) I enquired 'I want to get out of town for a few days. Are there any country hotels? In Karelia or the Pushkin Hills?'

They looked at me with faces of basalt. We weren't even on the same planet. Do the Pushkin Hills exist? I overheard someone in a bar refer to them and thought they would do. At the Astoria Hotel opposite, where I repeated the request, a woman flipped a ring-file of grey documents and said 'I think . . yes . . here, yes, a camping site on the outskirts of St Petersburg.' She was very proud of this camping site and eager to book me in. He didn't turn up not because he is a free spirit but because he is a distracted spirit. For a moment I thought I wasn't alone here. And for a moment I wasn't. There was a spark. Then it went . . . Oh so rude of him! After leaving the Astoria, I was approached several times by Russians wanting directions, out-of-towners or suburbanites. Was I looking exceptionally Russian myself? Did feeling wretched make me one of the gang? . . . Sudden agitation – went home – maybe he rang – no, nothing. I know he's young. I know that the only way to overcome disappointment is to reseize the initiative. But I didn't have it in me to risk a second rejection just yet. Besides, in a foreign world, you always wonder – am I doing the right thing? did I do the wrong thing? was it something I did?

That was then. And now I have escaped here – uptown – to clearer air –

to a new phase of adventure – and for the first time since my arrival in St Petersburg, clouds have rolled purposefully over the sky like wine barrels, stained clouds from the south in a clanging light, with deeper darker masses following on. Faint shivers of thunder. A storm approaches. It will look better from outside.

A soldier near the barracks in Ul. Khalturina asks for a cigarette – I have some. 'Storm,' I say, pointing up to the louring sky. He pulls a funny face and walks beside me but not so close as to imply we are together. The question hasn't dawned on me before – but men and boys in uniform should not be seen talking with foreigners? The south side of Palace Square swings out into Rossi's bow-shaped curve pinned down by the giant double arch commemorating Russia's victory over Napoleon. This square, the core of tsarist florescence, is carpeted with green bottle glass from the recent pop concert, ground to a powder by trampling and dancing. A horse trots across it, pursued by a little dog with that peculiar Jack Russell temperament, very vivacious but impossible to tell whether it's playfulness or irascibility. The air is close and still, standing to attention with arms at its side. Far away, beyond the golden domes of St Isaac's, distant lightning flashes white and rose, its violence reduced telescopically to a décor over there, nothing really to do with us. And into this amphitheatrical space intrudes the long croon of a saxophone. It is disproportionately loud, which unhinges one's Newtonian assessment of scale, distance, time, gravity. Grandiloquence becomes personal, supple and floating. The disproportion comes from the saxophonist having chosen to play beneath the cyclopean vault of the arch which serves as an amplifier, giving the meditative cadenzas of music a sonority which penetrates to the very marrow as though through warm wax.

The shark grey cloud, with its assegais of lightning, has moved forward, spreading from the west along behind the spire of the Admiralty, writhing into the monstrous shapes of wyvern, centaur and cockatrice. But its leading edge is distinct – and from here on, a cloudless raspberry red sky engorges with an impossible glow the whole north-eastward accumulation of towers, cupolas, pediments, statues, columns, spires, trees and lanterns. For more than 10 minutes, this elemental schizophrenia between the approaching storm to the left and the throbbing red sky to the right holds true, defined by the gadrooned but absolute line of division which crosses the dome of heaven above Palace Square: a spectacle beyond perfection because it is alive, yet perfect in the dynamic balance between its Dionysiac and Apollonian aspects.

Heavy drops of water fall fast, and the spectacle vanishes. The sky collapses with a monsoonlike slap. The soldier and I rush beneath one of the Winter Palace's twirling porches as the rain builds like the ferocious applause which rewards a theatrical triumph. Others run into our refuge, babbling with laughter, but eventually all become quiet and reflective. The water descends with such force that it splashes up off the ground, producing a solid layer of mist to a height of 5 feet: the whole townscape sits on this pale mattress. When the downpour has spent itself, the cloud thins to admit a heartless light in corroded patches. A few umbrellas are opened (always of the collapsible packaway type in Petersburg) and by degrees the world returns to business.

The soldier waves good-bye and I negotiate the puddles. A crocodile of perhaps 40 long-distance runners, springy and soaked, their kit clinging to them as if painted on, sploshes across the Square to a few supportive shouts. Massive drainpipes (as characteristic of this city as are the tall, silver, flowery lamp-posts) open directly onto the pavements, with no drainage channel, so that little rivers constantly whirl across one's path into the gutter of the road. The dust has been washed into soup by the storm. Directly the rainfall ceases, it begins to steam and congeal, encrusting all.

Zoia takes one look at my bedraggled state and demands a change of clothes, warning of pneumonia, muscular spasms, head chill, and joint pains. Later that night, from my bed, I hear the courtyard drip to a halt and the far-off boom of thunder and much closer the hacking cough of a child unable to sleep. At 2 am something explodes outside the window and colours drench the wall in a spasm. And again. And again. A firework display is taking place over the Neva but the height of the courtyard grants me only tantalising squints in a royal blue sky. I love fireworks but to watch them alone always sets off a touch of gnawing despondency. But not to-night. To-night I feel very good. Because:–

Another thing happened when I returned to the flat. Zoia said 'You had a phonecall. Somebody. Dima.'

'Ah . . .' I tried to sound casual but she noticed the jump. I rang him at once.

'Oh. Hullo,' he said with a short nervous laugh.

'I was outside. In the storm.'

'Oh. Very beautiful. But, Dooncan, I am sorry. I must explain about the other day. I have bad problems.' I love it. I am also cynical – what's the little shit after? 'Can I see you now?' he asks.

'No. To-morrow. Come here at 2 pm. How did you get this number?'

'From your before number. She give me.'

'I was going to call you anyway.'

Zoia looks uneasy – I'm making this call from the Big Room – my bed telephone is very scratchy – and she doesn't miss a thing. For example, as I make a note of the time – 2 pm (but would I forget?) – she sees I am left-handed.

'I was too!' she declares, delighted that we have this in common. 'But during the war I moved from Leningrad and lived with my grandfather and if he saw me eating with the left hand he hit me on the head with a spoon, buff! buff! I soon learned to use the other hand!' She is overcome with laughter at the memory. (Because she was in Leningrad for part of the war she has special privileges: free public transport, no prescription charges, ticket concessions etc.)

We watch *600 Seconds* while Zoia cracks filberts with her teeth – she bares them at me and points at them with a finger, saying 'Only wiv teeth!'

'Nevsorov is a neo-fascist?'

'Yes. Not educated but big talent. His father was head of the KGB in Lithuania during a period of nasty repression.'

Judging by the wet way she stares at the screen she finds him sexy. He does have the possessed look of the poet-thug, and his television manner is characterised by a brilliantly self-conscious disregard for the occasion. He is always in close-up and closes his eyes, or turns away nervously, or goes into a quick swoon, or squirms inside his leather jacket, as though on his first date with a new girl.

Zoia produces from under her bed a metal swivel disc which you stand on and rotate, twisting and exercising the spine. She makes me do it, knees going one way, shoulders the other. Zoia proclaims the glories of massage, banya and keep-fit, whereupon I am made to lie on the floor and perform complex movements to improve my posture. We are in the middle of this when Boris returns earlier than expected, laden with goodies.

Boris is short and round like his mother but much darker, of Mediterranean colouring. He is extremely good-natured, with a wide, warm smile of white teeth and none of his mother's 'side'. From a capacious blue and purple sports bag emerges a rainbow of bottled liqueurs, followed by lumps of anonymous foodstuff and a soda syphon, designed in the 60s 'James Bond' style of sophistication, which takes bomblike metal cartridges. He does not succeed in making it work but promises to do so. Boris loves to eat – eat – eat – and before long, plates of cheese, gherkins, salami and bottled sturgeon appear on the coffee table. He asks 'You want snack?', handing me a giant Georgian cognac.

The expansive mood is upon him and he visits the large wardrobe beside the television set and brings forth a collection of Communist badges, manufactured from an exceptionally light metal and embossed with enamel and glass in vivid colours, hundreds and hundreds of them (the Communists had a badge for everything) pinned to sponge pages, interleaved with plastic sheets, and held in ring binders. Absorbed in these for less than a minute, I am beseeched to consider further Soviet memorabilia excavated from the wardrobe, all characterised by triumphalism and the engines of war – birthday cards embellished with battleships, bookmarks printed with artillery, writing paper wreathed in nuclear warheads, the pathological militarisation of even the most innocent human artefacts, beautifully designed. Killing and conquest – they were never allowed to forget it – what a narrow escape we had! The Red army 'bible' is pressed into my hands (a Communist homily for each day of the year) followed by every child's first schoolbook, a reading primer with a large picture of Lenin at the front. Presumably this was supposed to be someone's idea of a kindly uncle but in fact he looks like a child molester, eyes narrowed like those of a predatory feline, and about the mouth the beginnings of a lecherous leer.

Trying to register this welter of scarcely sane and, one hopes, moribund material is not easy, and is made more difficult by the behaviour of Zoia who, not to be outdone (Zoia is never to be outdone, it transpires), fumbles under a pile of blankets and holds up a splay of Tsarist banknotes to attract attention, elbows Boris aside and dumps them in my lap. He counters with his collection of stamps from Cuba, Czechoslovakia, Hungary, Mongolia, Poland, Vietnam, the USSR, huge multicoloured images of flora and fauna, technology, space and agriculture, architecture and sport, successfully hooking my perusal. Momentarily stumped,

Zoia quivers and rallies and produces a box of old postcards, easing him
out with her hip and almost tipping them over me. Meanwhile I attempt
appreciative noises. 'Wonderful . . . oh yes . . . this is beautiful . . . you
have got a lot . . . that's big . . . mmm . . . .' But one is beginning to be
overwhelmed. Regardless of that, the battle between mother and son is now
joined in earnest. He brings out his secret weapon – the coin collection in a
case with draw trays – puts it on the table between the salami and sturgeon
and directs me to its marvels. I lean across but am at once pulled back by
Zoia insisting I appreciate her gold Tsarist buttons! There's booty all over
the floor, my lap, the coffee table, among plates of food, but still the great
wardrobe continues to vomit out treasures. Playing cards of runic character
from Boris. Silver bracelet charms from Zoia. Antique watch from Boris. A
sort of heathen metal belt from Zoia. They have been seized by a passion to
expose their *things*. They are both collectors by nature but few fellow
Russians could be trusted to gloat upon the hoard. In the foreign lodger
however they have at last the chance *to display without risk* what has been so
painstakingly acquired. The opportunity is irresistible and it all comes out in
a frenzy. Boris does observe the basic proprieties but Zoia, squabbish and
highly energetic, is absolutely without compunction in pushing him aside. I
have gloated to a glut but goodness knows where it would have ended, had
not Boris's restraint given way. 'Mama – no!' he exclaims.

There is a silence. All movement stops. She has done the unpardonable
– exposed his student drawings and paintings to public view. He is not
ashamed of them. Quite the reverse. He is ashamed of his failure to live up
to them in subsequent life. The memory of what might've been, of what
was supposed to be . . . Slowly, lingeringly, as parts of it are re-examined
with sharply focused eyes, the hoard is packed away again, the wardrobe
doors closed, and the key turned. Mother and son are reunited now on the
sofa, both cracking filberts with their teeth.

Next day I land in the middle of a distressing situation with which I am not
equipped to deal. But first there is brunch and an ill-omened meeting
with Zoia's friend from upstairs, Lydia the Psychiatrist.

Brunch: bowl of curds covered with bottled blackcurrants and
smetana. Bread and cheese. Pot of tea.

'This cheese is good. Lithuanian or Russian?'

'Estonian. French people', says Zoia, who this morning is attired in cinnamon dungarees with 'Joy' on the back, 'have a strong coffee at breakfast and immediately afterwards a big cup of tea!'

'Do they?'

'Yes, I know it. Because a French woman stayed here.'

(Memorandum to self: one must always resist the temptation to generalise about a nation from a brief experience of only 1 or 2 of its members.)

Shower, shave, fresh clothes – I use up whites so quickly. The doorbell rings. It's a couple of minutes after 1 pm. Zoia brings into the kitchen a skinny woman in her late 50s with thick steely hair (cut short), wearing a pine green tracksuit. Her eyes are a faded blue, not piercing but calculating, and their mobile orbs stand out from the grey lines of the surrounding face. Lydia is Zoia's best friend and clearly wants to look me over, size me up, so Zoia says 'Bring tea into Big Room' and we troop through the damask curtains into the Big Room which is awash with sunshine and fiercely hot.

'Zoia is a good hostess,' says Lydia.

I want to correct her use of English but know it would be tactless to open with a reprimand however gentle: 'Oh yes, and a very good cook.'

'I teach her recipes. Have you visited the palaces?'

'Yelagin. Wonderful.'

'Pushkin is better,' she says with a sour sniff.

I see. It's going to be like this, is it?

'I don't think they are in competition,' I reply.

Zoia goes out, Lydia sniffs again – and lights a cigarette. 'My husband liked women to smoke,' she says. 'He bought me an expensive cigarette-holder to smoke with. But one day he gave this cigarette-holder to a beautiful woman in front of my very eyes! I said I will never smoke again, never! And I kept to my promise.'

'But you are smoking now.'

'He left me. Which I felt released me from all that. Do you want one?'

'I gave up.'

'There's a lot of nonsense talked about how it is bad for the health.'

Zoia returns with a plate of biscuits shaped like letters of the Russian alphabet, a dish of brandy butter, knives, plates, triangular paper napkins in a glass.

Lydia says 'They think Russians do not have enough food. Look in the streets! There is hardly a thin one to be seen!'

'We have brandy butter at Christmas in England.'

'We have when we want,' she replies.

Zoia says 'When people ask if I do sport I say yes, every day – boxing, running, carrying heavy weights – all this to get food! I have very good connection for meat but he is far away. In Russia everything is done through connections. Not only now. But before too. It was always so. Otherwise nothing could happen.'

I recall a reference and tell them: 'Catherine the Great said "In Russia nothing happens without money." '

'Not true!' counters Lydia. 'But it's expensive, good beef!' She is walking round the room, restless, choleric. 'My income is 1,000 roubles a week.'

'So is mine,' echoes Zoia.

'And I have 1,000 patients to look after.'

'I have a few more than that,' says Zoia to me.

Lydia spits smoke and says 'You are general practitioner. Most of mine are schizophrenic. But! many patients tell me they feel better just for seeing my smile.'

She gives a smile at this, her first, but its curative properties elude me. There is something elasticated and tense about it, in that one is aware of a counterforce compelling its contraction. I start to sweat.

'I haven't been paid for 2 months,' says Zoia.

'Neither have I,' responds Lydia.

They are not really speaking in dialogue but both addressing me directly, and they chorus in unison 'The Government says there will not be any money until 6 weeks' time.' All of which is not by way of gaining cheap sympathy – Zoia, I know, hates sympathy and works hard to prove that she doesn't require any – but more from a need to expunge their astonishment at what has happened to them. Lydia is the more rancorous. Beside her, Zoia – who normally strikes me as a tough character – is downright demure. My main thought however is that Dima will be turning up at any second.

L: I used to go to restaurants twice a week – now never!

Z: I used to belong to an aerobics club – now I cannot afford it!

L: I worked hard for a good pension – now it's worth nothing – a few cigarettes a week!

Z: I never had much money in my life and I have always been happy.

D: Do you seriously mean cigarettes *aren't* bad for the health?

L: Of course they are bad! But there is still a lot of nonsense talked about it. Do doctors in England make love with their patients?

D: Yes.

L: And in our country also.

D: In England they can be prosecuted for that.

L: The English are mad.

Z: From Leonid I receive $5 a day for you.

(I have never probed this side of things, having agreed and paid for everything in London [£12 per day, bed, breakfast, dinner] and cannot judge if her share is considered reasonable. But since she's chosen to toss it into the conversation at this particular stage, it has an air of complaint.)

L: Everything was better before! Gorbachev destroyed our country! Then he disappeared . . .

D: My impression was that it unavoidably collapsed from rottenness.

L: Your impression! You know nothing! Listen – Peter the Great dragged Russia into the 18th century. Stalin dragged it into the 20th. Who will drag it into the 21st?

(Which sends a shiver down my spine. Actually Lydia doesn't so much converse as hit volleys. Zoia's remarks often contain an implicit chastisement of me but in Lydia this quality moves from surliness to sheer aggression, yielding nothing in the interests of sociability. I can see why Soviet psychiatry has such a vile reputation, was an agent of persecution. Lydia was trained by the totalitarian system to countenance a very limited range of certainties and her attitude is directed not towards understanding but towards carnivorousness – the objective was to devour the patient. The falseness of these certainties is now largely exposed and her response is despair and vituperation. Here comes another volley.)

L: Hah! To-day on television our President will speak about the Constitution!

D: Will he change it?

L: They always are changing it but since we can never remember what the Constitution is, it doesn't matter. Your trouser button is undone.

D: I always leave the bottom fly button undone. Edward VII did it with waistcoats. I do it with flies. It's my one fashion invention.

Z: What sign are you?

D: What?

L: She wants to know what astrological sign are you.

D: Libra.

Z: I knew it!

D: I should've made you guess.

Z: I already said Libra to myself.

D: We'll never know now, will we?

Z: I can always tell.

D: You are doctors, you can't believe astrology is a guide to people!

Z & L: Oh, astrology is very true!

L: You want balance and you won't find it in Russia, ha!

D: But –

L: He is very argumentative.

D: But –

L: Give me your hand.

D: What?

Z: Give her your hand.

D: Why?

L: Relax, nobody will hurt you – give it!

D: [So abrasive – they keep shouting across me] God, not palmistry as well.

Z: She is very good.

D: You are suppose to be a psychiatrist, Lydia.

L: Of course. Give it to me! Come on . . . thank-you . . . yes . . . . oh!

D: What?

Z: What?

L: Ah!

D: What, what?

L: . . . . You will live many years . . . you will have much love . . . . . and much pain. [One of her quick curative smiles here.]

D: Thank-you.

L: I've not finished . . . 2 children I see . . . . . and illness – when you are 60, 65 . . . .

D: What about my books?

L: I don't see any books.

D: Why not?

L: Sorry – no books! Maybe you will turn to something else, such as agriculture.

D: It probably says landscape gardening.

L: Probably . . . Do you have cirrhosis of the liver?

D: No.

L: You will.

D: Oh good.

L: Not good! Tell him, Zoia, that cirrhosis of –

D: It was a joke.

Z: Do not joke about the liver.

D: Or the pancreas.

Z: Why not the pancreas?

L: Pay attention! I see . . . . a big house –

D: My castle.

L: You have a castle?

D: Very big.

L: Zoia didn't tell me.

Z: He didn't tell me.

D: Over 100 rooms.

Z: You have a photograph of this castle? I should very much like to see it. English castles are –

L: Zoia! . . . Yes, I see a big house but –

Z: What?

L: I should not tell him.

D: Tell me.

L: Your castle – on fire!

D: Good. I'll get the insurance!

L: But –

The doorbell has rung and, saying it is for me, I excuse myself: 4 eyebrows arch in surprise. Dima is only 20 minutes late – I can't face a full introduction number and take him into my room by the front door.

'I ran,' he says. 'Feel here. It's wet.'

I feel the back of his neck which is hot and damp, and rub it and say 'No problem' and give it a kiss.

'At my college we must be out of bed at 7 every day, so when it is holiday I like to sleep late. This is my' – he picks up the dictionary – 'luxury. Then afterwards I must rush to do many things. Always I am running.'

'I don't believe it.'

'But now I cannot sleep at night. Do you have good days?'

'Oh yes.'

'I am sorry about the last time, the telephone going down. It was my girl. She did not understand the situation.'

He smiles anxiously.

'That's OK. Can we visit the Naval Museum? You must know all about that. What's the matter?' He is sniffing.

'Block here.'

'Sick?'

'No, no, no. I often have.' He means sinus.

'Try this.'

I hand him a small bottle of Mackenzie's Anti-Catarrh Smelling Salts and he takes an enormous sniff, letting out a cry as his head knocks back as though kicked.

'I should've warned you.' But I deliberately didn't and howl with laughter. It isn't dangerous but always gives them a terrific jolt. He blinks at me with red eyes. As we leave, Zoia comes down the corridor and sees his back going out of the door. 'Bye,' I say. She grunts petulantly.

Vertigo. In Palace Square a gypsy family of immaculate filthiness, as though they all have just crept out of a coal shed, are besieging an Intourist busload of Danes or Germans or Swedes, that sort. Fruitlessly. These ragamuffins are too far gone in Breughel to elicit alms. With matted hair and calloused feet they disconcert the sightseers who, though well-disposed and probably kind, are out of their depth – the scrubbed child-prodigy-violinist on the corner will do much better.

'Are the gypsies a problem?'

'No, they are only beggars,' says Dima. 'The men from the south, the black men, are very problem, very mafia in St Petersburg – if I had a machine-gun I'd kill them all!'

Struck by the vehement tone I look at him but he is looking elsewhere, moving along with his scuffing skip . . . The Naval Museum, in one of the city's most famous buildings (the Old Stock Exchange), is closed to-day. He has another idea. We walk round the bend to the Museum of Anthropology which, among the artefact displays of eskimos and maharajahs, houses Peter the Great's collection of curiosities – the lavatories, situated by the entrance, make a frightful stink as overture. Dima insists on buying the tickets and heads straight for the Samurai warriors dressed to kill.

'You like this? I like this. Over here is the knife for hara-kiri.' But he's twisting about; this isn't what he's looking for; and he speaks to an attendant. 'It's that way.'

We descend into a circular space beneath the central lantern and confront a dumbfounding array of monstrosities. Pickled embryos of calf, lamb and dog; gadgets and samples of primitive dentistry; a calf with 2 heads, less attractively patterned than the one at the Hereford Museum, but more complete in body. Greatest interest however is excited by the cabinets of pickled human foetuses, whole babies, and baby parts, all of whose flesh has assumed the creamy texture of bleached chamois leather.

The whole babies, after gutting, have been sewn up with black thread like crazy cushions. Many are malformed – eye in forehead, Siamese twins side by side, Siamese twins back to back. One squat figure is embracing itself as if shivering, staring out at the spectators (mostly enthralled and jostling schoolchildren) with a bewildered intensity in blind eyes. Others resemble infantile buddhas adrift in nirvana.

Of the parts, here are several tiny severed ears arranged in a bouquet; there a free-floating nose and mouth with teeth; babies' brain, hand, arm, foot, cleverly combined; a hand clutching an ear; or several legs and an ear just so; all suggestive of the Japanese tradition of flower arranging. Indeed Dima says these jars were often valued as ornaments, conversation pieces, in 18th century drawing-rooms.

A number of the little loves' faces are distorted into expressions of distress by being squished painfully against the glass. Some are horrifically asleep. Others look happier – one says 'How do you do?' with bleary eyes; one gurgles up at us playfully, its features magnified by refraction through the preserving fluid. Dima keeps looking at me out of the corner of his eye, lifting his eyebrows, checking my reactions. He is in a bubbly humour. We laugh. One can't help laughing.

'After that I feel hungry,' I say.

You do not pass out of the museum as you came in. To be sure, the place of entry and the place of exit are the same. But what one has witnessed turns the tang of urine, pettishly scorned on arrival, into a philosophical idea: we pass as water on this planet, and our smell is the very last of us to go. When finally our smell has gone from the world, we are mere bones – or in jars.

Dima is walking along, eyes on the ground; neither of us is talking; abruptly he looks up and round about, then suddenly directs his eyes at mine with a soft pounce and holds them on me for several seconds, uttering not a word: a total and unaggressive directness. This is one of the things he sometimes does.

St Isaac's balloons ahead, the cross mounted on an anchor at its apex (anchors and tritons are everywhere in St Petersburg). This is the almightiest cathedral in the city, with Samsonic columns to prove it outside, and within an opulence of malachite and lapis lazuli and harlequinades of coloured glass. The building is less forbidding than Kazan Cathedral in Nevsky Prospekt, but both concoctions of rock weigh heavily on the ground and the down-pressure has been exacerbated by the Soviets having taken out any spiritual uplift. There are plans to return these prodigies to liturgical use and their interiors, at present dead ballrooms belonging to no one, would benefit from a mirage-like complexity of icons, candlelight and incense smoke.

'Let's go up,' says Dima. We buy another ticket and climb the spiral staircase to the drum, overtaking an enormously fat woman plodding at measured pace with 2 children. They are from the countryside and all 3 in their best clothes. The mother's saccharine features are painted red and powdered white, masking iron powers. Her red shoes have a strap across the instep barely holding in blancmanges of feet wrapped in white ankle socks – the feet spill out of the delicate tip-tap shoes threatening to split them with every step. The children lag behind, absorbed by something. She pauses, does not turn round, but through a lipsticked mouth emits a terrifying bass growl, summoning the errant offspring to her side.

We emerge at the great tourist view, available in 360 degrees. How galvanising to be above it all again, but this time at the centre, removed yet not estranged, able to read it, to relate one part to another. The city below is settled in a great stillness. I dash from point to point, grasping vast blocks of stillness which can be fitted together for the first time into an image of the whole, detached, tranquillised, susceptible to more than provisional or partial examination. There is a complementary ease across my back and shoulders and air moves naturally into the lungs, my whole being permeable to oxygen. While we stand up here, St Petersburg comes softly to a stop.

The city was premeditated and is often said to have a rational lay-out. There are rational elements of course but, given that they were in a position to command everything, the surprise is how irrational it is, how organic and unforced. From our vantage the city becomes an abstract, without relinquishing its humanity which is transformed into the frivolities of toytown. Childhood associations of play are invoked alongside the adult gratification of being in control: its grandeur shrinks to delight and all grandeur is transferred to ourselves, emperors of space. Now we and the sky are companions, smiling down at the town. The experience is fraught with danger of course, the sensation of gravity pulling at our heels, wanting to annihilate the space between us and the earth, to magnetise us back to our proper place. To claim kinship with the sky is perhaps asking for trouble.

Dima lights a cigarette.

'Dooncan.'

'Yes.'

'I must say something.'

'Yes.'

'I have big problem.'

'Yes?'

'I don't know what to do.'

'What is it?'

'I cannot sleep.'

'What is it?'

'I must give money.'

'Why?'

'The racket. Very bad here.'

'But why you?'

'Too big story.'

'Tell me.'

'I have not the words.'

'How much money?'

'$300.'

'What?'

'$300.'

'Yes . . . I heard.'

I'm taken aback by the amount. In fact I'm knocked sideways – it's a staggering sum for a Russian boy – an annual income indeed for many Russians. What the hell has he been involved in?

We start to walk beneath the soaring colonnade of the drum, the city spinning below in a slow cyclorama under a vast blue sky pranked with small white clouds: briefly fixed, briefly intelligible, St Petersburg is moving again. But there's more.

'I have to midnight to find the money. They came for my girl but she not home so they take grandmother.'

'What . . . ?'

'I go crazy. I don't know what to do.'

'And if you can't find the money?'

'They say they take my girl. Do bad thing to her.'

'You must send her away!'

'I can't. She is too frightened. It may not happen.'

'Can you go to the police?'

'No!'

'I don't have this money.' It's true. I have enough to last my stay, that's all.

'I am not asking you for money.' His eyes go glaucous, fade out in non-expression.

'Of course you're asking me for money.'

'I only want to talk to someone about it.'

$50 I could give but $300 . . . He seemed jolly enough in the museum, giggling at the pickle jars. Now this . . .

'It's a shock,' I tell him. 'I don't understand.'

He can't reply – he's tongue-tied. I feel with a conviction in my stomach that there's something here that doesn't fit. Besides, even if I had the money, would it be wise to pay mafia demands, just like that, without having a clue as to what it's really about?

The whole life has gone out of the day. Back at the flat, when he pulls out a cigarette, I say 'Let me light it', take a drag and hand it across. 'You want something to eat?'

'I can't eat,' he says, looking down at the floor.

'You have tension.'

'Yes.'

'Let me massage your shoulders.'

'No.'

'Where did they take the grandmother? Will they hurt her?'

'I don't know.'

He is grinding his teeth, staring nervously ahead at the door, his face hot and red. Tears brim in his eyes but do not spill over.

'Silence . . .' I murmur.

'I must go! Good-bye!'

And he's flown, leaving behind cigarettes and plastic lighter. I'm very disturbed, having been made responsible for someone else's peace of mind, perhaps for someone else's life, and shuffle distractedly into the kitchen. Zoia saw him leave and I say 'That was my friend . . .' but she's decidedly put out.

'I make your dinner. Ragoût of pig.'

'Pig.'

'Schwein.' (She visited Germany.)

'Yes, pork.'

'Pig.'

'Yes, pig.'

While I'm eating she remains standing and says 'You must not bring strange people here.'

'I don't.'

'I do not know him. I see only the back of his head. He hides his face from me.'

'He's not hiding his face from you.'

'You are an educated man. You have a castle –'

'That was a joke.'

'Joke? But I am surprised you bring in people from the street.'

'I do not! Why do you say that?'

For God's sake . . .

'There are many banditi in this town – often with nice clothes. They will try to take something of you.' I flinch. She's hit the raw. 'Whenever I go out, I take gas gun.'

'Have you used it?'

'Not yet. And don't use the lift with strangers. A man was attacked and robbed in our lift. I was stopped in the street outside here by boys with knife. But you can bring your foreign friends.'

Silly old houri . . . No, there is sense in what she says. But I cannot live in a prison. I cannot suspect every person. Besides, my own flat is in a raffish part of London – one isn't so green. Sullenly I consume the pig ragoût and retire to the bedroom, taking out one of Dima's Camels and smoking it. What is the best thing to do?

Boris returns from work. He catches the atmosphere at once and brings me a glass of his best Georgian cognac with a mollifying smile.

'Georgian cognac I like number one. But Winston Churchill preferred Armenian cognac. Duncan, the news is on television – you want?'

'No thanks, Boris. I'm enjoying this book.'

The pages of *Martin Chuzzlewit* flick over, but I remain absolutely here and they remain absolutely there – no possibility of the 2 streaming together. The television is very loud. Why do they turn it up so loud? At the same time I can hear them cracking filberts with their teeth. This must be the filbert season.

An art nouveau chandelier in copper, glass and beads, hangs above the bed. 4 glass shades descend in pearly twists. Dust and dead insects have collected in the nipplelike nub of each. They throw a custard yellow light onto the ceiling. 2 men are arguing flamboyantly in the courtyard. Dogs join in. Glass smashes violently. One pair of footsteps walks away with steady self-possession. Silence.

Where could I find the money?

Should I give him the money?

Will I give him the money?

(insomnia)

The Scented Villain. To-day my mind has a serrated edge, precise but uncomfortable. This afternoon Yuri the Banana-Seller will be at the Dostoievsky Street Baths. This morning Leonid comes over at my request to help clear the air with Zoia. She tells him that Dima looked like a streetboy and had dirty shoes – this is naughty of her because he is always spotless. Anyway, she must understand that I do *not* invite bad people here but that it would be appreciated if she'd stop pumping paranoia into me because it's making life here impossible and poisoning my attitude to other Russians. She steals the show by producing 2 tickets to the ballet, saying 'Take a friend' but I say 'No, we shall go together.' Peace is declared. I move to kiss her cheek but she pushes me away, in embarrassment not animosity, and leaves for the clinic.

Leonid changes money – he is convenient, although there is now little difference between official and unofficial rates – and speaks of the Pototskis, an old noble couple it would be interesting to visit.

Alone in the flat, I count all my money, retreating into the security of wealth, sorting the coloured wads of cash, the various denominations of roubles and dollars held by elastic bands, fingering and lingering over the piles of furry notes with a delicious sense almost of sin. Yes, I could give Dima his $300. But it would leave me short in a difficult foreign land – and I cannot take the risk. Oh, the corrupting influence of money! When am I being generous and when am I being mean? There is no way to judge. One takes off at Heathrow poor and lands at St Petersburg rich: it's a trick of the system – but it's true.

Pack towel, shampoo etc in plastic carrier bag, and leave to meet Yuri. It's warm outside but the wind is up, blowing dust in the face. A road-sweeping van aggravates this with tawny clouds as it comes round the bend of the green and pink Imperial Stables. The extremity of the Stables terminates in an apsidal structure supported by 2 massive Doric columns. A drunk is peeing in the scooped space behind the columns, his vodka-sharpened urine streaming across the path, and having peed he sways zombishly with his fat yellow Slav prick hanging out.

Nevsky Prospekt is even busier than usual this afternoon and the wind changes, becoming chill, the sunlight brittle and cold. A child passes haughtily through the throng on stilts and as I walk I start to cry. The serrated edge dissolves in a hot tight mixed-up emotional wetness smudging the dusty eyes. I hate Russia! Pop into the church near the Vladimirskaya Market – hundreds of flickering tapers and a sussuration of headscarved women crossing themselves. In a corner sits a crone. There's no crone like a Russian crone – this one is swathed in dark blue sheets from which emerge 2 wry little hands and a tiny brown face weathered but refined like a carved walnut. She is eating a lunch of bread and salt: plucks a small piece of bread, adds a pinch of salt, carries to mouth, chews and swallows, a slow manoeuvre repeated again and again in exactly the same way. She is not to be pitied in the concentration of her figure, in the honed elegance of her frugality. There are few men in the church – a young soldier leans against a pillar looking down at the parquet floor, blinking now and again, alert, thinking, trying to work something out. I light a candle.

Nearer to the market itself, hawkers line the streets, arranging merchandise on pavement cloths, cardboard boxes, low walls. A woman offers single shoes; another, a gallimaufry of zips; another, 2 paperbacks;

another, a lone champagne flute erect upon an outspread handkerchief. A man offers radio parts and a lightbulb; another, some lengths of electric cable, a bottle of Pepsi, a jam jar lid; another, a single fretsaw blade; another, pieces of metal – 'What are they for?' I ask. He shrugs his shoulders: 'I don't know. Whatever you like.'

The entrance to the Dostoievsky Street Baths is via an oblique slit – a mere gap in the brickwork – and Yuri is playing fruit machines on the ground floor. 'I always win,' he says, 'but to-day – nothing!' There are 2 sections for men in this building – the Lux on an upper floor and the General above that. Yuri wants to go Lux – he says the General is full of old drunks.

'Nevsky Prospekt was very busy.'

'Yes, they closed the Metro', he replies, 'while they search down there for a madman with a machine-gun.'

'There are lots of guns in this town?'

'More than enough!'

The attendant gives us each a white sheet and we undress and hang up clothes in a private cabin.

'I like that,' I say, referring to a spider's web tattoo over Yuri's left breast. Slavs are not usually hirsute, and he is very blond besides, so it shows up clearly, his well-developed pectoral muscle giving the image a 3-D quality. After a shower we enter the Russian Steam Room. There is a cavity covered by 2 metal doors, above a fire, for slopping in water with a pan on a long stick. Next to it a wooden staircase leads up to a platform where one sits in scalding heat, but never hot enough for some Russians who raise the temperature as far as they can with more pans of water and afflict each other with bunches of birch or oak leaves. Yuri slaps himself all over and has a go at me. The platform is carpeted with broken leaves which sweeten the air but the heat is overpowering and I must go down. It is afternoon and quiet, only 2 other men in the Lux, not quite what one was expecting. I thought the Russian banya was a huge Auschwitz-like installation, rows of showers disappearing into a hot mist – he says it's like that in the General section above.

The cold tank absorbs me with its ruthless razors – half a dozen corrective circuits followed by the Finnish sauna, less hot than the Russian. In our private cabin afterwards, Yuri orders beer which comes in ½ litre bottles. It has an elusive undertaste, spicy, redolent, but of what? aniseed? not quite. Feeling in his jacket pocket for cigarettes he alters his voice and says 'Let me show you something' and turns to face me, naked, tattooed, yellow hair dripping, brandishing a squat pistol.

'Are you mad?!!!'

He waves it in the air, pulling a silly clown's face with tongue lolling out, and says 'Not only madmen have guns in our city.'

I shouldn't be surprised by the amount of firearms around the place – Communism was a military culture armed to the teeth. But a weapon so close . . . He lets me handle it. It's warm.

'I must cut my nails,' I say, switching the subject. 'They grow so fast here. My entire system has speeded up. Always hungry, always eating, always thirsty, always drinking, but I stay lean and muscular. See these 3 fingers? Eczema on them – this one in particular was quite bad. But it's all gone.'

Oh that eczema! Never had it in my life before but about 18 months ago a few bubbles appeared on the tip of the middle finger of my *right* hand. Very mild, not itchy, didn't go to the doctor. It jumped onto the index finger, still in mild form. I bought a book called *Eczema* and studied it, became convinced I had AIDS – had an AIDS test – nothing. Chemists suggested sundry creams, which brought no assuagement, and the problem grumbled on for months becoming uncomfortable only occasionally. Then a few unassuming bubbles appeared on the index finger of the *left* hand, hardly more than an annoyance at first, but suddenly flaring from the insolent into the wicked – a pulsating tower of pus and ginger crusts – down to the middle knuckle, awfully painful, and grotesque to behold (I have kept photographs with which to terrorise the unwary).

Definitely time for the doctor, and the night before was filled with intemperate self-diagnosis from *Eczema* and *Black's Medical Dictionary*. The trouble with self-diagnosis is that you can't come to any conclusion – the symptoms seem to fit them all, according to mood. Scabies? Shingles? Dermatitis? Psoriasis? Impetigo or the hives? One grew ever more exotic – shingly ptiriasis? Herpetic eczema? – this was the really dangerous one, conceivably fatal, so of course one finally opted for that. The doctor referred me to an Etonian dermatologist of august standing in Harley Street who said on the phone 'If you think it's herpetic eczema, please come over immediately!'

In his consulting-room, soundproofed with plush, he confided in a low reassuring voice 'So you've gone in for self-diagnosis. People should do more of it. Now where is my eye-glass?' He groped about the room, found it in a pewter tankard full of broken pencils, screwed it into his eye, contemplated my little tower of gleaming poisons, and announced at a suddenly much higher pitch 'But your self-diagnosis is wrong!'

'It's not hermetic eczema?'

'Hermetic possibly. Herpetic no.' And the consultant, alone in triumph upon the wilder shores of dermatology, raised his eye-glass to me and averred 'If I am not mistaken, it's acropustulosis. And there's no cure!'

I ogled the ulcerating digit and moaned 'Oooooh, I shan't be very popular.'

'You'll be extreeeeeeemely popular with dermatologists – I've seen only 2 cases of acropustulosis in my entire career! We have to be certain,' he said, as though confirming a win on the National Lottery. 'I'll take swabs of the pus and test it. Meanwhile a course of tetracycline. It sometimes works a bit – anyway it's the only possibility.'

But his euphoria was short-lived. It wasn't acropustulosis after all – but simple eczema infected with *2 sorts* of germ. The tetracycline cured the infection and briefly calmed the eczema. I spurned the use of cortisone cream which the consultant offered, having read in *Eczema* of its long-term perils, and went instead for tar cream which the Victorians used. This is very sticky and had no effect whatsoever. The eczema returned aggressively on the Côte d'Azur and I thought – screw the holistic approach – this gore on my left finger is ruining my writing life, and on any finger is ruining my sexual life – so let's go cortisone. Which worked well but no cortisone cream may be used indefinitely. When the cream stopped, the eczema returned. Mason & Black have suppressed eczema by hypnosis – perhaps I should've tried that. Which was the position on the eve of my departure for Russia – hence my luggage contained pairs of plastic gloves, Permitabs, tar cream, cortisone cream, tetracycline, the whole kit – and I haven't used any of it. Within a few days of my arrival the eczema subsided, as though the body now had more important things to think about. Gone! Pshoo! Oh, I love Russia!

Yuri says 'I also had eczema which went away.'

'Mine was going under the fingernail.'

'Mine went under the fingernail.'

'Did you lose it?'

'No, you don't lose it. It was this fingernail.'

'Looks fine.'

'Yes, it's fine now.'

'It went away without explanation?'

'Yes. No. I used to go to church.'

'Which one?'

'The Salvation Army.'

'Why not the Russian Orthodox?'

'Because we were cut off from this tradition and have lost the understanding of it. But the Salvation Army is easy to understand. But I left it. And when I left the Salvation Army, that was when my eczema left me. Now I visit gym and come to banya and I am in very good shape.'

'This beer is terribly strong.'

'Yes, it's Russian. You want more?'

'I don't want to get drunk. I have to go out to dinner to-night.'

'Where?'

'The Italian Consulate.'

'You know them?'

'Not yet.'

'Maybe they want to buy blankets. We have very good blankets next week. You want blankets?'

'Don't think so.'

'We have 4,000 blankets.'

In a corridor Yuri greets a friend but doesn't introduce us even though our 3 cocks are only inches away from each other. The friend has a scar round his throat in a red crescent-shaped line and a nervous habit of giving side-glances without moving his head.

In the Finnish Room I ask 'Was he in a fight?'

'Didn't you see how perfect it was? Tracheotomy. He was stung in the throat by 2 bees.'

One bee I've heard of – 2 bees is Russia.

'And how did you get this scar here?' I point to the corner of his mouth.

'Oh, don't,' he replies. 'A woman.'

'I have a friend who says he's in trouble. He asks me for a lot of money. He says if he can't find this money his girlfriend will be kidnapped and hurt. The bandits have taken the grandmother somewhere. Do you think it's true?'

'How can I say? Could be true. Could be a trick. You want me to find out?'

'No.'

'It would be easy. I know many people.'
'I don't want to spy on my friend.'
'You know him a long time?'
'No.'
'You have big money to give to any Russian who asks?'
'No.'
'It could be true. These things happen.'
'At 17?'
'17 can be very old in our country.'
'Maybe I'll borrow the money . . .'
'Find out more first. And take care, my friend.'

He splashes an astringent cologne over his body, stretches out on the bunk, closes his eyes, inhales and exhales slowly. On the way home I buy chocolates for Zoia as a peace offering.

The Return Of Camilla de Martino. An English friend, Joan Wyndham, said 'Do look up my chum Camilla. I believe she gets frightfully . . . something in St Petersburg. She says she has to dress up all the time otherwise the Italian servants won't respect her.'

Camilla has been away. Now she's back.

Heavy dark cloud nudges the northern purlieus and a hot nagging wind disturbs glutinous air. I pass the Yusupov Palace, the Palace of Pain. The Italian Consulate is opposite the Conservatoire, near the Maryinsky Theatre, not far from Ennio's flat (this district between the cathedrals of St Isaac and St Nicholas, the sailor's church, is one of the most subtle and seductive in the city). Zoia cooked a superb dinner and now I'm going for another, late, 10 pm (the Martinos went to a concert at the Smolny). Yes, it's time to introduce oneself to the diplomatic set. Recent days have unnerved me. Jane Rayne said 'Sometimes things go wrong in Russia and it's vital to know people of influence. That doesn't sound very nice but you'll understand immediately when you get there.'

No sentry in the guard booth – press the appropriate button, identify myself and am admitted – up the staircase – the consular flat is large, light, crammed with modern paintings, and its highly polished comfort is a shock – the smell of polish alone sends one's mind dancing – it seems years since . . . but no original features have survived behind the building's pretty pink façade.

Camilla is middle-aged with pale groggy eyes. Although she was obviously a beautiful English rose, she has not acquired the pinched look of one who clings too fearfully to youth through diet and constant exercise. There is a careless quality to her. In fact she is decidedly spaced-out. Have I used that adjective before? It's a useful one – very precise in its identification of the imprecise. Camilla blinks in an emphatic way as though trying to clear hallucinations.

'Where are you living?'

'Ulitsa Khalturina.'

'I don't know it,' she says, flopping onto the sofa in a floaty summer 2-piece. This is extraordinary – like the wife of an ambassador in London not knowing of Park Lane. Her husband, noticeably shorter than herself, enters in English country clothes: corduroy trousers, tweed jacket, brown brogues, windowpane shirt, knitted tie, waistcoat: an attractive and unlikely apparition, 'il stile inglese' done (as the Italians do do it) by the book. I wonder if he is related to Ernesto de Martino, the writer on magic, but forget to ask. She calls him John-Ludovico.

Du: I can't always understand the Russians.

Ca: We shouldn't light the candles. The light outside . . .

JL: Sometimes they don't turn up and you never discover why.

Du: Sometimes all the rules change, without warning.

JL: Constantly.

Du: People you thought you knew, you don't know.

JL: Certainly.

Du: Don't you find it winds you up?

JL: But fascinating.

Du: Gets the blood moving! St Petersburg is sinister.

Ca: Do you think so? I do too.

JL: Excuse me. [The consul withdraws.]

Du: Will he eat with us?

Ca: Are you sure you won't have a glass of wine?

Du: Yes please.

Ca: Perhaps he's gone to measure his blood pressure.

Du: Does he have high blood pressure?

Ca: No.

Du: Low?

Ca: It's normal.

Du: So is mine. Or was.

Ca: I used to sculpt.

Du: I've never sculpted.

Ca: Now I'm writing the libretto to a ballet.

(There is a pecular atmosphere in this flat. It isn't only the surprise of coming across a smart Anglo-Italian hybrid in the middle of fin de millénaire St Petersburg. It's more – like people marooned, or trapped in a lighthouse in the midst of stormy seas. And yet it has that quality – simultaneously jagged and, yes, spaced-out – which I now recognise to be quintessentially of this city. Enter the son Jasper: drooping waves parted in the centre, interesting spectacles, check jacket, grey flannels, slip-on shoes, the Milan yuppie look par excellence – except that later I discover there's not a drop of Italian in him. He is Camilla's son by an earlier husband who was the son of Sir Someone Brown of Aston Martin Lagonda fame.)

Ja: I was kicked out of Harrow.

Du: Where did you go next?

Ja: Gordonstoun.

Du: That's a name I've not heard for a long time.

Ja: Now I'm studying Law at the University of Buckingham.

Du: Where's that?

Ja: Buckinghamshire.

Du: Isn't Law rather boring?

Ja: Intensely boring.

Ca: I can't see a thing.

Du: I can't sleep.

Ca: Neither can I. And I'm lethargic anyway. It's a full-time job keeping up with John-Ludovico.

Du: Why were you kicked out of Harrow?

Ja: For spending a night in London.

(2 Russians arrive, a self-possessed blonde beauty in films, and a frizzy-mopped male composer called Valera. They are both silent. He is writing the score to Camilla's libretto. John-Ludovico re-enters.)

JL: Do you know? Statues of Lenin are still being cast because they were ordered and paid for 2 or 3 years ago. Now of course they're not wanted so they just pile up at the factory.

Du: Is everything all right?

JL: What do you mean?

(The handsome, Roman-nosed cook, Carmine, in white T-shirt and blue & white cook's trousers, summons us to the table with unlit candles, and serves. First course: tagliatelle with herbs and parmesan cheese.)

JL: Red wine?

Du: Mineral water?

Ca: We're a bit low on mineral water. We haven't got any.

(Second course: chicken with green beans. 'Oh fave, fave, fa-a-a-a- ave!' they all chant.)

Ca: Carmine is brilliant.

Du: Who is the most suspicious person in St Petersburg after my landlady?

Ca: Who?

Du: The British Consul.

JL: The British Consul General. They have given her higher rank – but no consulate!

Du: She's working from a room in the Astoria and said to me 'I'm not allowed to speak to writers without getting clearance from the Foreign Office.' The British can be so snotty, can't they, so *ungame.*' She's Scottish.

Ca: She's very harassed.

Du: At the House of Friendship they told me that the British Government has requested for the Consulate a restored building in running order.

JL: No such building exists in St Petersburg.

Du: You have to do it all yourself.

JL: She is the first British Consul here since 1938 – and no staff.

Du: She said 'Hullo, I'm the British Consul General, and the driver, and everything in between.' I hear she is much liked.

(Pudding [same word in Russian – 'pudding' – the influence of English nannies in Tsarist times]: strawberries. Followed by a bowl of fruit.)

Du: Is the mafia a problem?

Ca: There is only mafia here. Isn't that true, John-Ludovico?

JL: . . . . .

Du: Yellow cherries! Where are they from?

JL: The South.

Valera, dragging a hand through his frizz, suddenly speaks. 'I prefer the dodecaphonic system in composition but Camilla wants something more commercial.' He goes into the drawing-room and puts on a tape. Carmine stands in the kitchen doorway, smiling at the party, flexing his arm muscles beneath tanned skin. The yellow cherries are soft and sweet on the tongue . . .

'What is that music?'

'Don't light the candles. The light outside is so . . .'

'Too loud. You know it's too loud.'

'I can't see a thing.'

'Shall we move?'

'It's too dark. Nobody could see a thing.'

'Do Russians find it sinister?'

'What's he doing? It's getting louder.'

'Shall we move?'

'Someone stop it.'

'Come and look out of the window . . .'

'Oh strawberries – you can get everything here.'

'The ballet, quite simple really, it's about –'

'In the market. If you have the dosh.'

'It's about bull-fighting.'

'The loot!'

'Do you know about bull-fighting then?'

'Shall I light the candles?'

'This is my second dinner.'

'I love that word.'

'Dinner?'

'Loot.'

'Where is . . .'

'Carmine?'

'Shall we move? Out of the window?'

Camilla blinks, trying and failing to dispel that something in the air.

'We're hoping for Istanbul next year . . . . .'

More Shocks. VV rings to say he's discovered an outstanding masseur near the Moscow Station. We can go to-day. I tell VV to call at the flat after lunch.

Kitty Bigsby, an American friend living in London, rings to say she's arrived at the Hotel Moskva at the far end of Nevsky Prospekt, with several relations from Florida and her toy-boy Tone from Lowestoft in Suffolk.

'I've a shock for you,' she says over the phone in her frenetic way. 'Are you sitting down?'

Squibs burst in my chest. I sit.

'It's about your flat.'

'It's burnt down!'

'Why do you say that?' she asks.

'A woman read my hand.'

'Actually, it's the opposite. It was flooded.'

'Hell!' I'm on my feet.

'Firemen had to break the window to enter.'

'My locks were too good! Are the books all right?'

'It's all OK. Jill went round and took care of everything.'

'Oh really?' So Jill came up trumps.

'I want to see you, I want to see you!' she wails.

'Yes, yes, so do I! After my massage. There are 2 tickets for the Philharmonia to-night – can you come with me?'

'Yes! You're obviously having a great time.'

'No, it's more than that.'

I nervously ring Dima. I'm so worried about him. But he's not at home. Further information is vouchsafed in Russian but it is incomprehensible to me – I don't even know who it is at the other end of the line.

Sonya rings. At last she has cornered the man on the Sports Committee who will get back to her about a visit to the Dynamo, St Petersburg's most illustrious club for gymnasts.

'I shall make the arrangements,' she purrs.

'Be sure to give me a few days' warning.' Russians often don't and are then downcast if you cannot comply.

'You are always so busy. I think you are having an affair with a Russian woman.'

'Do you?'

'I know about these affairs. They can be very *ardent*.'

VV arrives punctually. I say 'Cor blimey, guv'ner, spot on!' He replies 'Blow me down, squire, er . . . er . . .' and gets stuck. I put him in the bedroom while I quickly rustle up a pot of tea but it's not quick enough because when I go back he's red-faced and discombobulated. Zoia darted in like a harpy while I was preparing a tray, crudely reviled him – I heard words – and ran away before I returned – what's wrong with her? She's round the fucking bend.

'What did she say?' I ask.

'Doesn't matter – but is she mad?'

'Let's get out. I'll speak to her later. God, I need this massage.'

Poor VV – one of the most trustworthy and helpful of all the Russians I've met – and he has to suffer this. She's never even seen him before. We are distracted from the latest embarrassment by 2 Buddhist monks crossing the Gribovedova Canal by the Church of Blood, banging their drums, and a music student with long hair and an ancient cello-case on his back. He walks ahead of us down the hot dusty street, past rubbish bins on fire from cigarettes thoughtlessly dropped in. Nobody, including ourselves, bothers to extinguish these smouldering or flaming buckets – faces – worn in – worn out – a harelip badly sewn . . . We enter a liver-red block housing a variety of ablutionary amenities. 'Up the apples and pears!' And climb to an unmarked door flush with the concrete wall and knock. Silence. Knock. Silence. VV shakes his mop of hair and gets hot. Knock. Silence. 'He knows we're coming,' reassures VV, bashing the door with the applied fury of a Kung Fu master. Eventually, footsteps patter within, locks slide back, a young man of about 20 appears in the doorway, slim, with dark hair, and grey widely spaced eyes of shining innocence: Pavel the Paratrooper who speaks no English.

We traverse a maze of saunas, sitting-rooms, showers, offices, beauty parlour, small plunge, large plunge, very large plunge, cosy nooks with sofas and lamps (most windows are blinded), doors half open onto dripping sepulchral darkness, all absolutely deserted. Leaving shoes in a passage and donning blue plastic slippers, I am ushered into a chamber with large mirrors and easy chairs covered in a smooth black synthetic. A shower and sauna lead off and these I use before entering the massage room. VV interprets – no, there's nothing physiologically wrong with me, yes, a general massage please – and withdraws. I relinquish my sheet and lie naked on the table. Pavel rewraps me in a complex system of white cotton – I feel like one being prepared for Egyptian burial, or a valuable dinner service prior to transit. Then, to background music by a Russian impersonator of David Bowie, he unwraps a part of me, smooths on a little oil, and administers strenuous massage as good as any I've had, before fastidiously wrapping it up again and unwrapping the next part. At no point are my genitalia permitted exposure to the light, as though cock and balls possess Gorgon powers. He is so serious that I ask him to massage my hooey, which causes a splutter between a laugh and a cough – he blushes, says 'Niet,' and develops an exceptional interest in my right arm. One hour later, Pavel's rhythmically investigative disentanglement has bequeathed my body to a lustrous elation.

'Why is it deserted?' I ask VV.

'It isn't in the evenings.'

'Next time I'll come alone.' I have booked a course of 10, so that Pavel can really get to grips with my knots.

The Hotel Moskva is a modern tourist hotel of great size opposite the Alexander Nevsky Monastery. Shady characters hang about the seedy foyer. We take a lift and upon emerging discover Kitty's room directly across the landing with the door wide open to exhibit a suppurating anarchy, VV's second mindfreak of the afternoon. Horizontal surfaces and the face of the television set are smeared with peanut butter and jam. A kingsize bag of custard creams, ruptured, spills its broken innards between litres of Scotch towards something which was once a jam jar and is now a deadly amalgam of strawberry preserve and glass chips. A couple of other jam jars, heavily fouled but intact, stand beside it. Coffee, popcorn, spaghetti, ballpoint pens etc, in varying degrees of torture, escape from fallen carrier bags. Several slimy malt loaves slip from their wrappers across a debris of torn bread, crushed crackers, dirty plastic knives – a couple of these knives have been snapped by an over-eager pressure. Loose chunks of Emmental cheese betray teethmarks and are blotched with jam. A few more Emmentals perspire in polythene. Pumpernickel sweats in cellophane. 6 plastic jars of peanut butter, each one 12 inches high and 3 of them broken into and gouged out of, ornament the desk by the window like a set of sticky Ming vases. Kitty *will* travel with food in soft nylon luggage bags and so the contents always suffer – then she begins to eat it in a helpless panic on arrival. The food bag itself lies in the bath, silently expiring in oversweetened ordure.

This combination of obscenity and naïveté takes the wind out of my sails for a moment, even as we embrace, even though it is wonderful to see her.

'You mustn't leave the door open! All this stuff!'

'Most of it's for you!' she says with her unfailing magnanimity as I lift a bit of bitten, bejammed Emmental between finger and thumb. In the same spirit she immediately draws in, and draws out, VV who has been struck dumb.

'Tone got his bag stolen at Arrivals,' she says.

'It looked like rubbish,' says Tone.

'Was it locked?'

'No.'

Tone is reclining sheepishly on one of the beds, wearing a selection of Kitty's less feminine clothes. They both are underslept and slightly haggard from whisky.

Kitty's gentle-giant Florida nephew, David, enters from the next room, leaving the door wide open.

'David, it's asking for trouble,' I say.

'Should I close my own door as well?'

'You've left your room unattended with the door wide open?'

'Have you seen what Kitty's done to the carpet?' he asks.

Mary Madison Mayo enters, clanking with parures of costume jewelry, dressed for Longchamps via Harrods. 'Hi, Duncan! Jimmy and I are going shopping. Oh, what a lovely-looking person,' she says, advancing on little VV with her huge red-lipped Texan smile. VV, having been introduced to everyone, has withdrawn to a corner chair where he resembles a child engrossed in a pantomime.

Tone pops downstairs to look for chocolate – they've gone through all theirs – and Kitty says 'He said our first bonk in Russia was the best he'd had in ages.'

'Yes, it's something they put in the air.'

Jimmy, one of Kitty's Florida cousins, enters dressed for golf at Palm Beach. He acquires a slow other-worldly smile, switches on the television set, and gazes at the images through their filigree of peanut butter and jam. He's left the door open too.

'I was telling Kitty, you really must sort of you know try to close your doors. Don't you think, VV?'

VV nods vigorously.

'I haven't slept very well,' says Jimmy. 'Why don't the Russians have proper curtains?'

'Why don't they, VV?' I ask.

VV cogitates awhile, then shrugs his shoulders.

'VV is an expert in Cockney slang so – um . . .' It is quite difficult to connect. I try to explain the weirdness but it's not what they want to hear. Kitty says she'll try to snooze before coming to my flat prior to the concert and she presses 2 large carrier bags of provisions onto me. Outside I hand one of them to VV who says 'It was so interesting hearing you all speak

English together – in that fast way of people who know each other well.'

He takes the tube to his Kung Fu class. I walk back. Trying to straddle these 2 worlds has placed me under an unusual strain – the switch from Russian Adventure to Knightsbridge Cocktails – I couldn't make it – and didn't want to. Nonetheless one does want to be friendly with friends. The charged intensity of living here: how to explain to these holiday-makers from the West? If they see anything other than pure joy in my eyes, they'll think something is wrong. That's the Western disease – yagoddabehappy! – and it grows more virulent the further West you go, until by the time California's reached, they're trepanning and lobotomising themselves to gormless death. Halfway down Nevsky Prospekt, outside the posh food shop beneath the Comedy Theatre, a swing band of about 15 members (lots of brass) are polishing off Broadway show tunes with joyous panache. Lump in throat, tears in eyes . . . yes, go for happiness if you can! . . According to a news report there are 40,000 Jehovah's Witnesses in town for a rally, a Biblical plague indeed, and the Prospekt is clogged with them. So many religions suddenly on the streets of Russia, peddling their clashing recipes for happiness to many bewildered souls each of whom searches for that miraculous being who, with a glance, can cancel the inner abyss.

A shout – turn round – it's Jo 'n' Leonid.

'You look great, you look Russian!' says Jo.

The compliment is cheering but I caught my face in a mirror at the massage place and for an instant didn't recognise it – haunted, drawn.

'One book I read was *Exterminator!*' says Jo.

'Good Lord. William Burroughs.'

'Yes, but I never heard of him. A beautiful book I like – *Three Men in a Boat.*'

'Jerome K. Jerome is very popular in our country,' says Leonid, brightening a shade. 'Price control on petrol was lifted a few days ago. Prices will go through the roof.'

'I thought they'd already gone through the roof.'

'So they go through another roof. There are endless roofs. Have you seen the Pototskis?'

'I'll ring them.'

'They are expecting your call.'

'How did you come across *Exterminator!*?'

'It was the only book we had in the Pamirs,' says Jo.

'Is everything fine with your hostess now?' asks Leonid.

'No. She insulted another of my friends to-day. To his face. Really viciously. For no reason at all.'

'She thinks you are not careful of danger.'

'No. That's not quite it, actually. You shouldn't use that word.'

'What word?'

'Hostess.'

'Is it not the feminine form of "host"?'

'Yes, but it means something a bit different – you should use "landlady".'

Jo 'n' Leonid look at each other aghast: 'Hostess – what means?'

'It means a woman in a nightclub who makes herself available to men.'

'Oh,' says Jo with relief. 'Nice.'

At the end of Nevsky Prospekt I rest by the large fountain in the Gorky Gardens. The Fountain Boys try to sell me souvenirs but I buy only 2 packets of postcards. If you sit down anywhere for more than 10 minutes, you will see something either very loving or very unpleasant between people. This afternoon, sitting by the fountain, along with many St Petersburgers, a few tourists, and a number of uniformed personnel from the Naval Academy, I see a young man beat up a short middle-aged drunk. It begins in burlesque fashion with the young man pulling the drunk's nose, dancing round him, kicking him up the bum, and so forth. Then I realise to my horror that a serious assault is taking place. What the origin of all this is I do not know but the drunk, incapable of self-defence, is being violently slapped and punched. He totters sideways, collapses onto one knee, staggers to his feet, and is knocked again. The young fiend is in a growing fever of sadism, a hard grin gripping his face. He really gets to work. At the climax of the attack, he several times rams the drunk's head against the pink granite plinth of Lermontov's statue. My throat closes up. I am paralysed. What can I do? I prickle with horror, shaken not only by the event but also by my cowardice, my inability to move, to help, to interfere. While it takes place, the attacker's friends joke among themselves, swaggering, not really looking at what he's doing. But when the thug finally walks off with one of them, the remainder turn very serious, contaminated – like all of us – by the event. An old lady crosses to the crumpled, bleeding drunk and comforts him with gentle dabs of her handkerchief.

You know, a few heads turned but not one of us round the fountain – maybe 50 or 60 people – altered our postures. On the contrary, our immobility increased. We froze. The uniformed personnel from the Naval Academy, including high-ranking officers, continued to talk to their companions, looking away from the assault, but one saw from the almost imperceptible stiffening of backs and the exaggerated absorption in each other's conversation, that they knew exactly what was taking place. In a collective failure of nerve, everyone wanted to be invisible, to be somewhere else . . . I feel like slime inside. Do they feel like slime inside? In this way – by doing nothing – the brutality of Russia contaminates you. In this way – by accepting the situation, by deciding to 'understand' why it is for example that people feel entitled just not to turn up when they have arranged a meeting with you, by deciding to 'understand' why it is that people should be allowed to treat each other disrespectfully, thoughtlessly, horribly – in this way, the possibility of a humane world retreats further and further into the night . . . . . Of course people are being beaten up the world over the entire time. But I have never before seen it done with such infamous, almost philandering pleasure, with no other objective than the assault itself, with such confidence that there would not be the slightest intrusion from private citizen or public officer, done so brazenly, in the afternoon sunshine, in such a non-violent setting – before indeed a readymade audience sitting on a circle of benches. Even the mugging of tourists by children in Palermo, awful though it was to witness, was at least a purposive act and over very quickly . . . *Oh everybody everywhere, be warned – be vigilant – the thugs and fiends of the world are always ready to take over!* . . . And throughout this episode, there could be heard jaunty 18th century music: on the edge of the Gorky Gardens a clarinet and flute duetting an inadvertent accompaniment.

I should like to take a taxi to the airport and depart. But I cannot. And soon find myself inside the Astoria Hotel going up in a lift to the Business Centre from which I shall presently telephone my parents to tell them I'm well, St Petersburg is great, the people are wonderful.

My mother explodes with astonished delight: 'We've been so worried!'

'But I told you. It's impossible to phone out – you have to book the call 4 days in advance.'

'Is that what you're doing now?'

'No. I'm phoning on the satellite connection – it's $9 per minute so I can't talk long.'

'Well, Peter came round yesterday and we tried together but it was always engaged.'

'You can usually get a line on the fifth or sixth dial. I'm having an incredible time. The Russians are wonderful. I've moved to a doctor's flat and have a new number – have you got a pen?'

She writes it down and asks 'What's the weather like?'

'Boiling.'

'Daddy and I went to Queen's last week – it was 106 on the court. To-night Bud and Chrissie are coming to stay for Ascot Week.'

'We saw Trooping the Colour on telly here. My flat in London was flooded. Can you check it's OK?'

'We've spoken to Jill. Everything's under control. Don't worry. Oh darling, I shall be thinking about you all day.'

For 3′ 46″ I pay $35.96. Turning out again onto the Russian street I have never before felt so far from home. England has continuity and tolerance. The English are outraged by cruelty and injustice. The English have been free longer than any other nationality. England has a highly evolved network of charity and mutual help. English history is deficient in atrocities. England has country lanes with old inns and an easy welcome. England has had the world's most extensive and least brutal empire. England has a palace in every corner of every shire, its original pictures and furniture complete and undisturbed, set in an arcadian park. England has absorbed African and Asian and remained itself. England has won all the wars. England has a secondhand bookshop and several antique shops and tearooms in every small market town. The English can laugh at themselves as well as others and are surprised to find this practice not universal. O Inventor (circa 1800) of the modern city, of the modern world! And yet – O Keeper of Courtesies! O Kingdom of enchantment, of stone circles and white horses! . . . . . . I forgot to tell my mother that Kitty has arrived. I have forgotten about the concert this evening – must rush back to the flat.

There is no one at home. On the bed a message reads *Telephone Osip Kokoshkin* (the bloke I met with Dima in that pub) followed by his number. When I do so, he lifts the receiver directly the ringing tone begins, which throws me.

'Oh, Mr Kokoshkin – you're in.'

'I'm always in.'

'I saw a man beaten up to-day.'

'I am sorry. But it could have been much worse. Things are getting very bad here. Let me tell you, Armageddon will be no later than 2012. My friend did a hypnotic progression – which is the opposite of a hypnotic regression – and discovered only 5% of the present population living at that date. There will be a collapse of the ecology, beginning in Africa, and the world will be consumed by negative energy. It has already begun. We can see it in AIDS and other developments. Look, I propose an interesting idea. We visit the Buddhist Monastery and afterwards row on the lake. I like rowing. Research has shown that the Monastery here is one of the few places on the planet where this 5% will be.'

'Research?'

'Very thorough research.'

When Kitty arrives I say 'Your peanut butter is terribly sweet – I can taste only sugar.' Although I eat tinned, bottled, and dried food, as well as fresh food, I don't eat processed food. My taste-buds have improved on the Russians' essentially home-prepared diet and become sensitive to and disparaging of excess sugar, salt, preservatives etc.

Kitty says 'Mary and Jimmy on their shopping spree were surrounded by gypsies trying to pick their pockets. Then a gang of teenage boys started on them too.'

'Did it turn nasty?'

'No. Mary said it was very odd – like a sport or something. She lost an ear-ring.'

The Philharmonia Hall is an inflated shoe-box (the best shape for orchestral acoustics) in off-white, gold and red. It is supported by a giant Corinthian order in double row with bowed balustrades between the plinths, and gallery above. The chairs are white and gold with red seats and the hall is lit by foaming cut crystal of a magnificence exceptional even in this, *the* city of chandeliers.

The first half of the programme is Prokofiev's *Romeo and Juliet* suite, and Tchaikovsky's *Variations for Violin and Orchestra* starring the latest child genius hereabouts, Ilya Konovalov. During the interval we saunter 'the loop' in the crush hall, a circulating parade which you may join and leave as you wish – like a caucus race. Kitty says that a boy sitting near us with his parents was weeping through much of the Tchaikovsky. The second half is Scriabin's *Poem of Ecstasy* – of which it was said that when first played in London to highly strung Edwardian ladies at the Queen's Hall, there wasn't a dry seat in the house . . . the Tsaritsa lays out the Tarot cards on an ebony table in the Winter Palace while outside the snow falls softly and ceaselessly through the night. She longs for Rasputin but he is gambling in a casino over the bridge and does not come . . . . . It is a performance both brilliant and withering. The score, with leaping trumpets, is brought to the highest pitch of neurotic irresolution.

(Scriabin was Rachmaninov's class-mate and if this were a film the second half of the concert would have been Rachmaninov's First Piano Concerto. And later this night I do play it on my personal tape-recorder, in a favourite interpretation – Vladimir Ashkenazy with André Previn conducting the London Symphony Orchestra: only *they*, crucially, have the opening right – tense and magisterial and shocking. Everyone else snatches at it, takes it too fast, as does Ashkenazy in his later, creamier, less impassioned recording with the Concertgebouw under Haitink. One of the worst offenders of this 'snatching' was Rachmaninov himself. In the third movement however Richter's recording with the Radio Symphony Orchestra of the USSR eclipses all rivals by best bringing out its prescient, Gershwinesque jazz syncopations. The piano concertos of Rachmaninov: music cannot be more *glamorous* than this.)

The audience applauds Scriabin furiously – bang – bang – bang – bang – Kitty enjoys this manner of applause, calling it 'the heartbeat'. And afterwards we perambulate the city's tracts of moulting stucco beside still water and along wide and silent avenues. The sky is overcast, foreboding.

She says 'You look dreadful.'

'I know . . . I saw someone attacked to-day.'

'Oh God, I've seen that in New York.'

'I'd probably look dreadful anyway . . . There was nothing I could do.'

'Perhaps it would've been like trying to interfere in a family fight – they say that's one of the most dangerous things to do because they *all* turn on you. Don't feel bad about it.'

'I do.'

'But don't.'

'I do though.'

Palace Square is sealed by a lid of grey. We continue to the Triangle.

'I was originally going to the concert with someone else.'

'Who?'

'But he . . probably he doesn't like classical music anyway. Something happened. We got on really well – then it went all funny.'

'What sort of funny?'

'I don't know.'

She hugs me.

Food. My objective to-day is to try and recover from yesterday. In the kitchen Boris, redfaced and puffed, is wrestling with a sealed milk churn. The lid is stuck fast and after many minutes of battle he sits down laughing and resorts to a tin-opener: inside are tens of thousands of aluminium bottletops which he proceeds to count. Zoia rocks with laughter too. She is preparing blinis.

There are many types in the family of blini – this is the little light breakfast one (eggs, sugar, milk, flour) served with butter and blackcurrants-in-syrup. They are sometimes eaten with honey and cream or raspberry jam and smetana. I say how delicious are her jams which is the cue for another demonstration – out they come, strawberry, cherry, raspberry, blackcurrant, honey from the farm, honey from the shop, something brown and sticky which Zoia has 'forgotten what is', crash, crash, crash, down onto the breakfast table, eviscerating the kitchen cabinet in an outburst of prodigality.

The butter is superb, such as you now find in England only on Devon farms. When they have it, Petersburgers down huge amounts of butter, cheese, meat. I hesitantly speculate that there might possibly be too much fat in the diet? (I have a touch of acidosis.)

'After food with fat you must drink hot tea,' says Zoia, 'then there is no problem. I am telling you this as a doctor.'

'But the cholesterol is high.'

'Cholesterol is not bad for you. Meat makes you strong.'

2,000 calories per day are required to survive in a condition of total repose. Here I never come within spitting distance of total repose – and to try is to fidget – so I am grateful for the extra protein. But she is always urging me on to greater excesses. While I drink tea she asks if I want coffee. While I am eating blinis she asks if I want porridge. While I am eating porridge she asks if I want bread, butter and cheese. While I am drinking vodka, Boris asks if I want Georgian cognac. While I'm drinking Georgian cognac, he asks if I want Azerbaijan cognac. On the one hand I am learning to tame the exuberance of their generosity, while on the other Zoia is discovering that to maintain a full-time job in addition to providing for the needs of a lodger is not as easy as she thought.

'3 years ago a bottle of Georgian wine 2 roubles – very good with beef and paprika. Now you can't find it at all. Oh, the Georgian people were the best in the Soviet Union. They love you and they *say* they love you!'

I eat alone. My food is prepared and served to me separately in the kitchen. If I bring home biscuits, bananas, chocolate etc and leave them on show, Zoia and Boris wouldn't dream of touching them. If I say 'Please eat some if you want,' they still don't. I have to say 'For you! For you!' whereupon the articles will vanish – eaten or hidden.

Zoia makes crumbly cakes, very tasty, rippled with fruit and dvorok (curds). She makes much of her own jam, with sugar but without boiling, 'so they keep vitamins', and she bottles a blackcurrant juice with no sugar and says it is excellent mixed with fresh milk, creating a natural yoghurt.

She regularly buys spinach, carrots, potatoes, spring onions, remarking how important it is to have fresh vegetables every day. The taste is usually very good, the appearance not always. Zoia makes a salad dressing which isn't bad, but she puts sugar and water into it (I have yet to create French dressing but have brought the ingredients with me). And once she served me fried chicken with fluffy white rice and before I could stop her she'd poured a panful of chicken fat all over the rice.

The main problem however was that Zoia kept knocking me up for breakfast. This drove me crazy and I told her so – and told her so. She seems finally to have understood and now, if leaving early for work, will cover the porridge on top of the stove.

I am drinking tea from my customary cup and saucer – cobalt blue painted with gold stars (the cobalt blue church domes of Petersburg once had gold stars painted all over them, but no more) – and say 'Zoia, you must not insult my friends without reason. The young man who came yesterday is not a bad boy. He is one of the best students of English at the University. Especially recommended by the Literary Director of the Maly Drama Theatre.'

'You are a foreigner and the Russians will descend on you like *flies*!'

But it's a sulky reluctant morning and neither of us has the energy at present for another row. Besides, maybe it's not all Zoia – I think Lydia is a terrible stirrer behind the scenes.

'Come,' she says appeasingly, 'I show you.' And we trot into the Big Room where she turns on the television and inserts a video tape. 'Boris Wedding.' Oh God. Boris has gone to work, otherwise he'd surely not permit this.

'My sister's wedding video is over 3 hours long.'

'No, no, 20 minutes only,' she assures me with an unctuous twist of her mouth.

'My sister's is as long as Cecil B. de Mille's *The Ten Commandments*.'

'No, 20 minutes all.'

'You have to set aside a whole day to experience her video and make eating arrangements, like for Wagner at Bayreuth. She had an engagement party, 2 weddings – one in the register office, one in the church, 4 wedding receptions. But it's not all on the video.'

Zoia looks lost. 'Boris 20 minutes.' She clings to this concept.

'But much of it is.'

The sound is painfully loud. Boris's marriage to an older, pretty woman is like a register office wedding anywhere in the world – bleak room, flowers, awful piped music, people in dreadful clothes. The wedding breakfast is better: champanskoye and cartwheel plates of red and black caviar on bread.

'That's my husband. He look like Karl Marx.' The man is feeding a large dog with scraps from the table. 'Do you have dogs at English weddings? That man there plays piccolo in orchestra. He was never married. Do you want to be married?'

'No.'

'You do not want to be faithful.'

'Yes – the impulse to fidelity is very strong in me. But so is the impulse to infidelity.'

Kitty rings to say that she's booked the Metropol Restaurant for to-morrow evening. 'What are you doing to-day?'

'I hardly slept a wink. I want to do nothing. Is that awful?'

'No. I feel shattered too. Mary and Jimmy got mugged again.'

Phone rings – it's Katya. She's going to Moscow for a few days. Phone rings again – Dima! Instant resurrection!

'Dooncan, it is very bad – can I visit you?'

'No. The woman is here. She doesn't like it.' I'm taking these calls in the Big Room and Zoia, ostensibly rotating on the swivel disc, is all ears. 'We can meet at the Flame. 2 o'clock.'

Is he desperate? Will he mug me with a knife or a gun or a canister of paralysing gas? No, no, no, get a grip on yourself. Nonetheless I'm terribly twitchy and have to leave the flat before the appointed hour.

Sunshine falls on buildings across the Neva. And behind them deep purple and greenish clouds, scrolled with silver and grey, rise like massed ostrich feathers. A breeze chills the hands and face in petulant gusts, and when a shiver passes down my back, I decide to kill time in the Marble Palace. Until recently this was the Lenin Museum but Lenin was never once inside the building. Now all his memorabilia have been removed – whereto no one can say – and the Marble Palace has become a gallery for Tsarist portraits.

The 18th Century:–
Not a pretty bunch.
Catherine I: resembles a gross drunken gypsy. Peter the Great's second wife and a one-time Lithuanian laundry-maid.
Elizabeth Petrovna: Mae West. Daughter of Peter and Catherine.
Peter III: hideous jellyfish. Assassinated.
Catherine the Great: wife of Peter III. Hockey mistress in Torelli's official portrait. Torelli's other, with the Empress striding into the centre like a randy prize-winning cow amid swirls of drapes, leaves and cupids under a cerulean sky, is the finest picture in the Museum, energetic but harmonious, and most beautifully coloured in pastel shades.
Pavel: pugface. Assassinated.

The 19th century:–
Considerable improvement in looks.
Alexander I: abolished nostril-slitting as a punishment.
Nicholas I: looks exactly like the superb shit he was. His terrifying eyes of pewter have not been exactly rendered in paint – they are bluer here. The colour of a person's eyes is important but often difficult to recall because either we do not look directly at the eyes or if we do, we look through them to the soul. One may also be distracted by being unable to focus on both eyes simultaneously – one flickers from one to the other. Only a softer focus, which means slightly out of focus, allows us to take in both eyes at once, as in love when there is that melting congress of the eyes. Nobody knows the colour of Napoleon's eyes. Dima said 'My eyes are blue. But they go green when I am angry.'
Alexander II: degeneration creeping in? He looks alarmed, as though expecting a swagger stick up his jack any second. Emancipated the serfs some years before Lincoln did the same in America: both men were assassinated.
Alexander III: tough – yet looks perilously dreamy-eyed and unrealistic.
Mary Fyodorovna: she was wife of, well, actually there were 2 of them – the Dowager Empress Mary Fyodorovna, wife of Tsar Pavel, mother of Nicholas I, died 1828; and the Dowager Empress Mary Fyodorovna, wife of Alexander III, mother of Nicholas II, died 1928.

Not sure which one this portrait represents but in her pearls, curls, jewels, and massive headdress of gold cloth and feathers, she's ready for anything, Ascot or the Firing Squad. There was a third empress, Mary Alexandrovna, wife of Alexander II, in whose honour the Maryinsky Theatre was named.

Nicholas II: has a translucent, far-away look (not quite as vapid as the Duke of Windsor's but almost). The dreaminess becomes wateriness, so that Nicholas II's son could not even clot his blood: both assassinated.

A woman is following me round the rooms, closely examining the bases of pillars, the corners of picture frames, things like that. It's not certain she's 'all there'. She is of medium height, Duchess of Windsor thin, in black shirt and trousers, any age over 50, sporting a henna-red wig in a bread roll round her head and sunglasses with glowing cherry red lenses. Is she an agent from the constellation of Cassiopeia? She moves to the music of Webern. Is it time to leave? Not quite. I cannot find a likeness of Ivan VI who was deposed at 1 year old in 1741 and assassinated in gaol in 1764, a particularly unkind variation on the theme. Nervous.

Time to go – through the gates towards the Field of Mars. The nights are light in St Petersburg's summer but darkness can come in the afternoon. The sky is boiling lead, pregnant and pendulous. Its swollen teats seem to brush the steeples and domes of the city in a rolling horizontal slide. The imminence is uncanny, physically felt, one's brain a conduit between the sky and the stomach.

Dima, with his head jutting forwards on his neck, paces up and down by the Flame. He is not late to-day – this means a problem.

'Here, you left these.' I return his cigarettes and lighter and he starts to puff, avoiding eye contact. My mind jumps recalcitrantly, taking in only shards of him. The effort of appearing normal makes a tremble in the thighs – I don't feel normal – I haven't felt normal since the moment I landed in this bloody town.

'So what's happening now?'

He looks up, frowning, grinding teeth again which causes a muscular movement at the base of his cheeks. 'Not good,' is all he can say.

'Let's walk.'

'Sky very beautiful. Storm.'

'Yes.'

'They take my girl.'

'Oh no.'

'She go to different place – like you say. But they find her.'

'And grandmother?'

'She is OK now but she is unhappy.'

'I'm not surprised. Where did they take Valentina?'

'I don't know.'

'Wasn't granny enough?' This is becoming ludicrous – Living Hell starring the Marx Brothers. 'And why you? Are you in business with them?'

'No, no, no.'

'So?'

'They think I am easy.'

None of it makes sense. He is omitting the vital ingredient – his own part in it. Then the tone goes wrong again. He says 'I hoped the 3 of us to go to the Crimea together,' which sounds less like desperation than a play on my emotions. 'Can you help me? I have until midnight when they do something bad. I find $100 myself. I need only $200 now.'

Passing the Russian Museum, we step into the road to avoid Tokyo's Watch Tower Bible and Tract Society evacuating tourist coaches. A great black weight hangs in the sky, the deluge barely held aloft.

'You had until midnight last time,' I say.

He is silent, shifty.

'Dima, I don't have all these dollars.'

'How much you have?'

I blush fast and go cold – the awful directness of his question. But I am learning not merely to be shocked in this city but also to bounce back from shock. Anxiety hardens into an instinct for survival which says that I shouldn't become known as the foreign fool who hands over hundreds of dollars upon request for reasons which are not explained to him, for purposes he cannot trust.

'For Christ's sake, Dima, I'm not paying mafia money! If Valentina has been taken you must go to the police!'

He looks at me defiantly: 'Police no good.'

'Then speak to your uncle.'

'I cannot!'

'Why not? What's going on, Dima?'

Sweat beads his temples. He is silent.

Oh Lord . . . and there are so many misunderstandings through language. His English is not as strong as I assume and he often pretends to know what I'm saying when he doesn't, so that misunderstandings ride on the back of others . . .

At this point a roar breaks across the city, very loud and increasing in volume. Hail is pouring from above, hitting us, rattling spitefully round our feet – sudden lawns of white combustion extend everywhere. We dash to a grand portico assembled from caryatids and gryphons and rusticated pillars, bulges of soft stucco flesh and splays of gripping claws. It is enclosed by sheets of falling ice, deafening, bouncing like smashed marble, cracking against the city's windowpanes. Across the darkness lightning makes violent modulations of light, and thunder augments the din.

'Funny weather for the time of year . . .'

'No,' he says, half smiling, but understanding too my use of the word. 'Weather always funny in St Petersburg. Do you have yellow rain in London?'

'No.'

'We do. And when the . . .' – he means 'puddles' – 'dry up, there is yellow powder. Not always. But often. You must use an umbrella or hat when it rains here. People who do not lose their hair.'

Is he acting? Is he making a joke at a moment like this? He goes to light a cigarette. I do it for him, take 3 quick drags, hand it over. None of it makes sense.

'Why can't you speak to your uncle?'

'He doesn't understand me! Only you understand me.'

'Do I?' I am distraught and my forbearance fails. 'After a few meetings you ask me for a lot of money, a *lot*, but I don't understand your story because you won't explain it honestly to me. Understand you? For God's sake, I don't *know* you!'

The moment I've said it I regret it. He looks as though he's been struck across the face. I try to make amends by adding 'I want to know you – but I don't . . .'

His response is immediate: 'I'm sorry, I'm sorry!', having almost to shout it above the noise. 'Excuse me, excuse me, I'm sorry! Good-bye!' He runs into the storm. I'm close to panic, close to tears, move forward and hail knocks me about the head and shoulders.

'Dima!'

He keeps running and quickly vanishes in the screaming descent of ice.

CHAPTER FIVE

The humidity is high. I am not in good shape for the Metropol Restaurant and prop myself up in smart clothes – charcoal flannel suit, burgundy waistcoat, silk tie, white shirt, silver cufflinks. There may not be another chance for the full bit. I look surreally up-market, not only because the place is full of crooks in tracksuits but also because the American party has decided to 'go casual' (Tone, who has not recovered his bag, is in a unisex outfit). To-morrow they leave on the train for Moscow and to-day appear far more interesting than when they arrived – gone is the gush of 'Let's party!' and it's been replaced by an air of intelligence having been uncomfortably aroused.

'Are you closing your bedroom doors now?'

'Yes, yes, yes!' They certainly are.

The dining-room is like a school hall, with fawn pillars, a stage at one end, and at the other a balcony with private dining booths. It's about half full, composed of small groups, except for one blond hunk dining ostentatiously alone near the stage. He looks like a capo. The waiters are shabby in short-sleeved nylon shirts and humourlessly polite. There is a set dinner. We order champagne, vodka, and mineral water.

The table, white with napery, is already covered in hors d'oeuvres (red & black caviar, smoked salmon, crab, cold meats, tomato & cucumber salad, celery leaves) on the Metropol china (white with purple monogram and gold trim).

David, the gentle-giant nephew, says 'I went shopping with Mary and Jimmy to-day down Nevsky and Jimmy was in a cap and blazer with a red hankie in the breast-pocket as if he was off to the country club and they kept stopping every few yards to take a photo with the dangling camera and he was wearing a fat money belt which said "I've loadsa money!" I know the mafia types wear them but for a tourist, well, and Mary was done up in rings and a gold necklace and big dangly ear-rings and –'

'I don't see why I should drop my standards,' says Mary.

'– and going on in her southern drawl with "Where can we find caviar? Is that a shop?" and every few minutes they were set upon by gypsies, really dirty, especially the little ones, and Jimmy kept saying "What despicable children! What disgusting brats!" and pushed them off, not too worried, continuing to shop, and a group of Russian boys tried to mug them but Mary said "Stop it!" and the gypsies again –'

'It happens every time we go out,' says Mary. 'I think I'd miss it.'

'– and outside one of the shops was an old beggar woman on her knees and she started to paw Jimmy's shoes and he said "Grovel a bit more and I'll think about it" and the woman was genuflecting and pawing his feet like crazy –'

Jimmy is smiling his smile-which-is-not-a-smile (he is always on the verge of a joke, and sometimes cracks them, yet is not a joky person) and says 'Well, I was getting very upset with all the attacks. We could hardly move in any direction.'

'– and I said I'd had enough and wanted to go back and went back and slept,' says David.

A band goes into action onstage.

'Do you know what Kitty did?' asks Mary. 'She went round the market with a jar of peanut butter, trying to trade it for an icon. And another thing – I've been having really weird dreams in this city.'

We all have.

They've given us one of the best tables. Be careful not to ask for one of the best tables – which are considered to be those nearest the stage, adjacent to the loudspeakers. Oompah-oompah pop music is under way, gutsy and trivial, with a strong element of Russian or Jewish folk music in the progression of minor chords. There are 2 front singers – a woman with a deep voice in fringed lamé and a man with a falsetto voice in a cream suit. The main course arrives: chicken Kiev, redcurrants and mushrooms in pastry cups.

'What about the black riots in Los Angeles?' I shout.

'Troublemakers!' ripostes Jimmy. 'They take drugs, steal, kill people, and then blame white society. By world standards they are not poor.'

Compared to most Russians, the LA rioters looked well-off.

'Dance with me!' yells Kitty.

'I don't feel like dancing.'

'But you must – we've danced in so many strange places.'

I like to dance but this evening the mood doesn't stir me and in Russia one is not obliged to fake emotion. The Americans take turns to spin each other on the floor among a handful of wildly jigging locals.

A girl in a black mini-dress pauses at our table with a basket of long-stemmed red roses. I buy one each for Mary and Kitty. They stand them in the empty champagne bottles and we order more champagne.

'How did Catherine the Great die?'

'I always thought it was getting screwed by a horse,' volunteers Mary.

'Could that be one of those myths which circulate at school? Like the prodigious length of Errol Flynn's penis.'

'Errol's *was* quite large,' says Mary. 'But Humphrey Bogart was the Hollywood salami. Lauren Bacall had good taste.'

'That was before they allowed black actors in,' says Kitty.

'I read somewhere that Catherine died on the loo. Like Evelyn Waugh.'

'How do you prefer it? On top or underneath?'

'Both.'

'I don't like it sideways.'

'Yes, it's sort of irritating sideways.'

'I like it standing.'

'Upside down's good.'

'Whether it's good or bad doesn't depend on the position but on the third factor, the excitement factor.'

'That's tautology.'

'No, it isn't.'

'What's tautology? I haven't tried it that way.'

. . . Sometimes one is aggressive, sometimes receptive. Lying on the back is less hard work – and leaves the arms free. To relax thus and be drawn out can be more genitally intense because the thwarted movement of the loins compresses the explosion. More genitally intense – but less generally satisfying, because to move the loins is to enact the drama, to release the sensations outwards, and the sense of fulfilment is greater . . . but bad sex can sometimes be better than good sex – more seditious . . . Normality we quickly forget, but events which take an unfamiliar path create unease and excoriate the memory, developing character . . . and then there's sex which simply goes wrong or doesn't go at all, which is a disaster or utterly risible – from this you can learn most of all, even a certain self-questioning. Sex is very democratic. Through it, we enter the pool of individualised sameness . . . 'Oh, go on – dance!' implores a voice

. . . Why are we so attracted to the bad? Even as we protest, our attention is helplessly, magnetically drawn to it. Because the bad creates friction and thereby teaches us more than the good. The good we can only accept. But from the bad we may be able to forge our own virtue . . . Sex which is love, yes, of course, this is central. But sex without love is not invalid: the brief encounter has the beauty of a firework, and like the firework becomes a metaphor which makes us thoughtful: the brief encounter is an escape from time and reminds us, before the walls of commitment, habit, familiarity close in again, that we live in a condition of infinite possibility . . . In Russia you feel the eroticism of a society at the edge, a society of infinite possibilities . . . A sense of dissatisfaction is not enough. It is important to have a crack to the core of one's being, like a thin slice out of a cake. Only then can the heart be reached by new elements. Only then can one grow internally . . . . . . the freezing of the Fountain crowd during the attack on the drunk – since it was absolute, a truly collective act embracing all classes of people including military officers, it must have had an instinctive purpose: to isolate and contain the violence – because these things get out of hand so easily. . . . . Sex, when it happens, is always different from one's projection of it, from the fantasy which repeatedly plays before it is achieved. This is because it is 2, not 1 . . . Emotional involvement needs physical earthing into confidence and hence the release of the heart into action . . . . A voice enquires 'Do you think there will be a military takeover?' . . . I don't think . . I am rambling within, adrift at the table. Come on. Snap back into it. What's this coming towards us?

The pudding arrives: vanilla ice-cream with red jam and chocolate flakes. And the flower girl returns, presenting Kitty with 5 more red roses. From the blond hunk dining alone! He is looking away and refuses to turn in her direction, so Kitty goes over to thank him. Despite radiating importance, the man is very tense, cannot smile, is embarrassed by his own chivalric gesture. Who is he? Perhaps he owns the place. No, that doesn't quite fit. Kitty asks him to dance, and reluctantly he obliges, unable to communicate his feelings, but acquits himself well once on the floor.

'Do you think there will be a military takeover?' reiterates Jimmy.

The idea of anything taking over this volatile mess is implausible. Tone has been working quietly through the alcohol. He betrays no jealousy of the dancing couple and smiles at them beatifically, perhaps because he's a computer genius.

'The hunk wouldn't look at me,' says Kitty, back at the table. 'How is your friend?' she asks me, excited, with a high colour. We all have a high colour.

'I haven't the faintest idea,' I reply, 'and neither has he.' I can't get into it. Electric quicksand.

The bill arrives. $165 for 6. Very steep. We fumble flushingly in our pockets for extra cash. There's a group sense of having been 'done' but how to question the bill? There are no menus or prices anywhere and the place is packed with affiliated muscle. On the way out a man offers to change 150 roubles to the dollar. Hugs, kisses, good-byes.

'Ring me from Moscow. George II died on the loo too.'

Zoia and Lydia are in the Big Room. Doesn't Lydia have any clothes other than her pine green tracksuit? Usually they'd be playing cards or chequers with the television on but to-night they are sitting silently in the room as though waiting for an overdue train. Betrayed by a dislocation behind their eyes, they are startled by my smartness, but only for a few seconds: recovery is adroit: and both are determined to make not the slightest comment on it. They concentrate their intentions on the bill.

'The Metropol must be expensive now. Is it expensive now? I have not been for a long time,' says Zoia.

'Yes, it's expensive.'

'Oh, it's expensive now, is it?'

'Mmm.'

'*Very* expensive?'

'Probably.'

Lydia, exasperated, volleys 'How much?!'

They are delighted when I tell them and feed each other's laughter.

'If you were with Russians they would charge maximum $70,' says Zoia.

'You made the restaurant a present of $100!' thwacks Lydia.

I stand skittishly on the swivel disc, twist this way and that way. The blond hunk . . . the roses . . . was he softening us up for the sting? See how I've been corrupted. The doubting of another's motives is the seed of corruption in human relationships. Generations of police statehood have sown the seed of doubt in Russian hearts and those who come here soon catch it. Mutual trust is difficult to establish. You cannot easily know what the bottom-line motives of Russians are – but worse, they do not know them themselves. Everyone inhabits a scenario of manifold knavery and cluelessness, never trusting appearances, always expecting the worst. The tiny germ of doubt sends the whole of Russian society toppling into fog, fantasy, despair. The tiny germ of doubt is all that is necessary to rot the world. . . . . I wash and go to bed, worrying about Dima. At midnight the telephone rings – Von, an old friend in London – she sounds odd.

'I've been trying to get through for ages and ages.'

'Usually you get through on the 6th or 7th dial. I can't phone out.'

'It's about Jill. You remember she rang you just after you arrived?'

'Yes. 2.30 in the morning. Pissed. Waking everyone up.'

'Well, after she put the phone down on you, she tried to commit suicide. Took every pill in the house and was found 24 hours later on the floor covered in black vomit. She's been in hospital. Her legs aren't working properly yet. She says she's coming to see you in St Petersburg.'

'What? Please tell her St Petersburg is no place for a woman with no legs. *Please* tell her that.'

Arpeggios of pity do not sound in my heart. Anger does. That's all it needs – Jill doing a suicide number. Something finally lets go inside me. Fuck the lot of them! For the first time in weeks, I fall asleep like a stone.

To-day is the day that I've arranged to meet Osip Kokoshkin. Zoia has gone to work but Boris, who came in late, is still asleep on the sofa in the Big Room. The cover has slipped off him, exposing large buttocks to the warm morning air. Zoia has, as usual, left porridge in a bowl in a pan of warm water and one has only to re-steam it. Her porridge is always delicious and I add several dollops of homemade raspberry jam. While I'm eating and gazing absently at the clutter of condiments on the table, Boris enters and bids good morning, whereupon my nose begins to bleed. Because of the raspberry jam, it is not at first evident that drops of blood are falling sluggishly into the porridge. But it speeds up. Laughing, I tilt back the head, grope loo-wards along the corridor, tilt head forward and let it drip. Often as a boy I had nosebleeds, and once every year or 18 months since, so they don't disturb me. If the blood wants to come out, let it out. Always the head is clearer afterwards.

Eventually it clots, I clean up and return to finish breakfast. Boris has thrown away the bloodied porridge and offers to replace it with stuff he's

pounding up in a pan. 'Best Russian gryechka.' Buckwheat? Not mad
about it as a porridge substitute – maybe there are more seductive ways of
preparing the stuff. Boris borrows several tapes to copy – early Rolling
Stones, Jimi Hendrix, Beat This: the Hits of Rhythm King.

Osip said he would be waiting at 4 pm by the monument to Pushkin on
the platform of the Chyernaya Ryechka tube station. It is a considerable
distance but time is plentiful and I walk up Petrogradsky Island,
currently the most notorious mafia district in Petersburg but it looks like
any other. The heat sucks at my feet. The First Rachmaninov Concerto
begins to play. A pressure in the breast forces emotion to rise into the
head, sliding up behind the eyes like a screen which interferes with
vision. The eyes are glazed and watery by turns, the mind purblind but
fretful. Battling along Kirovsky Prospekt. . . . . The eyes fill with tears,
but the eyes are open only the width of a line of teardrops coalescing. This
line of soft diamonds is held in place by the eyelashes and quivers in
concordance to the music, as though shimmering clusters of piano notes
are inside the very tears, causing them to tremble and refract the light.
They spill when my eyes close briefly – open again – refill.

The station is hemmed by assorted booths and a colourful fruit market.
I descend into the stomach of the earth, retrieve Osip, and bring him
blinking to the surface in his World Peace T-shirt. Outside the sun seems
twice as hot. He indicates a nearby gothick house undergoing restoration,
a casino before the Revolution where Rasputin came to play the tables.

'Layla told me that you helped to have the name of the city changed
back.'

'No, no, the opposite!' he protests. ' "Leningrad" has a more beautiful
sound – blue, green – whereas "St Petersburg" is black and red.'

'My preference is the reverse, based not on colour but on temperature.
Leningrad is a cold idea, St Petersburg a warm one. I should not have
come here if it'd still been Leningrad.'

Names are important. Aleister Crowley changed his from Edward
Alexander Crowley because he said that to become famous one should
have a name which is a dactyl followed by a spondee.

We take a crowded tram and stand. Sitting below us is a tattooed drunk
who gurgles greenly at his wife. She tries to dissociate herself by looking
out of the window while his head lolls over her breasts mumbling drivel.
With every jolt of the tram he seems likely to tip a stomachful of
undigested vodka down her cleavage.

We arrive at the most northerly Buddhist temple in the world, a single tapering block of dark stone set in a bleak garden beside a public lavatory. It is a yellow hat temple of the Tibetan school, founded in 1915 and closed by Stalin in 1938; at the time of its reopening in 1990 it was in use as a laboratory for the Zoological Institute, and before that as a radio station. 15 monks and novices are attached to it, all oriental from Tuva and Buryat on the Russian border with Mongolia. No European Russian monks yet, but they would be welcome.

A handful of bony novices greet Osip with benign mindlessness – the Great Void is easier for some than for others. The interior is mostly taken up by one large chamber filled with shrines, flags and flowers. In front of the chief shrine or altar, 2 monks in their early 20s (and of more athletic build than the rest) are prostrating themselves in an unusual manner. They hold beads between their palms above their heads, collapse onto the knees, shoot forward upon the belly, face down with the hands stretching ahead into a full extension; then reverse the procedure, shooting backwards, up onto the knees, and so to the original erect stance. The cycle is carried out in one smooth strophe repeated endlessly – they do not cease while we are here – assisted by a sliding mat beneath them. All the while they hold fast to the beads whose rattling accompaniment probably helps maintain the flowing rhythm of this very gymnastic form of self-abasement.

Contemplating them, Osip says 'I am told that a crystal of star energy was brought here by the founder and buried in the foundations.'

'You were told what?' My mind has flashed to Dima's swaddled treasure at the back of his wardrobe.

'This is a fragment of the crystal from Orion,' continues Osip prosaically (he doesn't speak of these things in a portentous rubato), 'and its existence has been confirmed.'

'Confirmed?'

'Many people in meditation have located the crystal chip with their inner vision. Under the floor there.' He extends a pudgy finger. 'I have not seen it myself. But I have made mental contact with it.'

I slap my arm. 'Lots of mosquitoes in here.'

'They bite only on acupuncture points.'

'Nonsense.'

'Ha! But maybe they could be trained to do so.'

By the exit a Mongolian peasant in traditional felt and padded clothes is telling his beads. We bid adieu to the monks and walk off towards the public loo.

'How do you find St Petersburg?' he asks.

'I must have a pee.'

'It is one of the 4 mystic cities. The others are Prague, London, I forget the 4th,' he says, following me in.

'What is your particular field, Osip?'

'Psychotronics – the translation of traditional wisdom into new technological world.'

'You don't go in for tarot, séances, all that?'

'No, no – this is the old magic, worn out, ineffective. The headquarters of psychotronic research is in Prague. But look, next week I am going to Tallin in Estonia before they close the border. I propose that you accompany me.' The stereophonic echo of urine wanes.

'I can't.' We walk towards the road.

'The Earth is now taking the eco-problem into its own hands. It sees that man will destroy it and wants to be rid of humans the way an animal wants to be rid of parasites, vermin. AIDS, which is the beginning of it, is caused by a shift in the Earth's axis. Let us take this tram.'

We alight by the bridge onto Yelagin Island and approach the boating lake in the Park of Culture and Rest. The hire fee for a boat is small but there is in addition a 100 rouble deposit.

Osip takes the oars with pugilistic relish. A little way out he stops and hands me from his bag an article to read.

It concerns the development of inner-space creative technology, the insertion of wisdom into the Infosphere (defined as 'morphic blueprint' for the Noosphere): an alliance of meditation and computers to generate morphic resonance in the Noospheric Mind in order to deflect non-violently the rush towards eco-catastrophe by accelerating the necessary jump in human psychological evolution. He says that this work, in which everyone can have an honourable and productive role, will solve among other things the world unemployment problem and Third World debt.

'A good idea?' he asks.

'Hang on. I've not finished.'

He chuckles and plashes awhile, reading the cuppa soup packets I've given him.

D: Will it solve the overpopulation problem?

O: Yes, because behaviour will be governed by long-term intelligence.

Too-many-people is the result of biological anxiety of a planet trapped in outdated industrial-economic machine. I have sent this article to many places, including the Pentagon Meditation Club and the Emperor of Japan. I studied under Dr Sergeyev who used to be captain of a nuclear submarine. He was very famous – there is a lot about him in that book *Psychic Discoveries Behind The Iron Curtain*. I am not in it because I worked with him after the book is published. He was head of the Department of Psychical Research in the Military and I was involved in research to increase the efficiency of submarine crews during emergencies through increased telepathic connections.

D: It seems there are 2 great stimuli to the increase of telepathic connections. The first is Fear. Very effective so long as it doesn't spill over into panic. The second is Love. Is love permitted in the Russian Military?

O: In a way, yes. When any group is isolated on a collective and perhaps dangerous task, love always springs up. There was a clash between the Military, where I worked, and the KGB. The KGB wanted a monopoly of psychotronic research. The KGB were mostly Jewish, the Military not. So in 1975 the KGB tried to annihilate me with an overdose of LSD to make me mad. But I got out of the system thank God and now my task is to turn this military psycho-technology into methods for self-perfection. St Petersburg is cradle of revolution. Hexagram 49 of *I Ching* says Revolution, and the image is fire in lake. And here we have Lake Ladago which in ancient Finn saga they say fire fell in this lake, maybe UFO. And St Petersburg is situated on longitude 30 which is the greatest extension of dry land on the planet north-south and it also crosses the Great Pyramid – and the greatest extent of dry land east-west is latitude 30. These are geographical facts. Look it up! The Great Pyramid is at the 30/30 intersection, connecting it to the cosmos. This system has positive branches in Japan and California, negative branches in St Petersburg and South Africa. Great Pyramid was a programming device created by extraterrestrials. Something will happen in St Petersburg, something absolutely unexpected. Lenin was right – it produces revolutions like a hen laying eggs. The 1917 Revolution was wrong – Jewish material revolution – it was weak. Next revolution will be focused by Buddhist Temple, absolutely efficient and non-violent. Violence happens when change in outer world is not synchronised with change in inner world.

D: And in the meantime?

O: The military will take over here. The democrats, once they make money, leave Russia. Only the military will be left. If they don't take over, the country will collapse.

D: Hasn't it collapsed already?

O: Oh, this is nothing to what *can* happen! But the military will keep more quiet about their takeover. It is stupid to try and develop capitalism in Russia – from Russia come cleansing spiritual fires!

D: Are you saying Russians can never be free? That they must always be the victims of some awful cleansing spiritual fire?

O: No. As you well know, capitalism and freedom are not the same things. Perestroika was essential. Previous social structure was inverted pyramid – the spiritually degraded were on top. Every sort of inspiration or initiative was ruthlessly suppressed. Creativity was forbidden. So something had to break. But perestroika was also clever trick of KGB. Because now everyone hates the democrats who have been very stupid, grabbing all the money and showing off. The KGB could never have achieved this with old repressive methods.

D: Capitalism and democracy are not the same either. What are the KGB doing now?

O: Training psychics. They are intelligent and have learned from previous mistakes. Russia is empty now. The old red world gone. So a new religion can be born here. The West is conformist and materialist and has nothing to offer.

(An electric blue dragonfly skims the lake in angles and curves. Young people with beautiful bodies disport themselves on the banks in minimal bathing costumes: cream bodies, perfectly made, in the afternoon light which has been softened by a thin sheet of cloud. Osip buzzes and hums with contentment, guiding the boat with the minimum of fuss.)

O: Why can't you come to Tallin?

D: I'm involved here.

O: The real reason I'm going is to do some meditation at the site of the UFO which is hidden underground there. I want to leave Russia eventually – before the military takeover. I have many enemies. I want to go to China. Initiates are travelling round the world seeking places which will be safe from engulfment by negative energy beginning of the next century.

D: Where are these safe places?

O: Secret! Do you want the mafia to take possession of them? But the safest place will be in Mongolia. The military takeover will begin with mutinies in nuclear submarines which will fire off nuclear bombs and the Government will use this as an excuse to declare a state of emergency. The bombs will explode 20 miles up. Nobody will be harmed. It will be psychological shock. They already wrote about this in the newspaper here. But these things are in fact decided by the UFO government outside Earth, although the military conspirators do not realise it.

D: Have you seen a UFO in action?

O: No, but I am in mental contact.

D: What is this thing at Tallin?

O: It has been there several thousand years and was found by dowsers. Then the KGB took over and removed part of its drive mechanism to a secret laboratory in Moscow.

At this point we are bumped by another boat and Osip greets its occupants (an elfin-faced young man with straight red hair and spectacles, accompanied by 2 girls) whom he knows. They converse at length. Eventually Osip breaks off to apologise and explain 'It is a theological dispute.' They carry on for another 20 minutes during which one of the girls reads a short extract from a text on a yellow sheet of paper. Finally I am introduced to the 2 girls who speak no English and to the elf who is a trainee Russian Orthodox priest. His English is fluent and on the strength of this I ask him to accompany me to Petrodvorets at some later date and he agrees. The 2 boats divorce and Osip rows to the pontoon where we recover the deposit. At the edge of the park are a drunken couple. The man is on the ground hammering the woman's left foot with his fist. He is sobbing. She is sobbing. He stops hammering and starts to kiss her feet, gradually climbing and sobbing and kissing up her legs, abject, contrite, suppliant, wheedling, while she gibbers and wavers jellylike in a slurry of emotions. When at last the man has staggered to his feet and they are face to face, eye to eye, the sight of each other's soul provokes a revulsion, they start to fight again, hatred spits everywhere, and they have to be constrained by another couple who are with them; whereupon the man collapses, via remorse and self-laceration, once more onto his knees and tips over sideways at her feet, hammering and kissing them, and the process begins all over again.

'Osip, what will happen to St Petersburg?'

'It will crumble away. These mystic cities collapse under the weight of their own mystic powers. Anyway the ozone layer is very thin up here. Nature did not intend man to live so far north.'

He chuckles, his face a stack of horizontal creases.

Arriving back home, I feel both lifted and emptied by the afternoon, curiously wan in the head. Zoia is in the Big Room with her niece, and sitting side by side on the sofa are 2 plain but scrubbed teenage Mormon missionaries. They wear black ties, white shirts, and bizarre fixed smiles. Despite this, they turn out to be sweet. Zoia's niece is in a skintight lime-green dress and is very pretty with warm, luminous, marine-blue eyes. She is likewise smiling but her smile grows naturally out of the whole disposition of her body, the smile is alive, mobile, not an educated thing. How many Mormons in St Petersburg? 250 says Mormon Smile One, taller, vaguer. 500 corrects Mormon Smile Two, younger, smaller, sharper, and the boss.

I say 'If all the world's religions have brought the planet to this pretty pass, the answer is obviously not in religion as we know it.'

Zoia says 'Your dinner is in the kitchen. Ragoût of smoked beef and beans. American dried beans.'

Ring Mira Apraxin who is my neighbour round the corner now, and I suggest a drink at Sadko's.

Mira looks stunning in a tight, very short silk dress of blue, purple and silver flowers, with a neat little black jacket over the top. But her face is drained.

'I had upset stomach. Twice,' she says.

Thankfully I've had no problems of that kind.

The armed guards once again don't want to let me into Sadko's, despite Mira's outfit, so I say we've booked and they let us in. Hubbub. We're given the last table. It is against the window onto Nevsky Prospekt – too close for comfort. At the next table a couple of young street traders are paying their bill with wads and wads of blue rouble notes.

Ordering shashlyk, she says 'I didn't know about this place. I like it in here. I feel normal suddenly. How is St Petersburg for you?'

'Very sexy.'

'You are the first person I hear say that!'

'It can't be true.'

'Love yes. Money yes. Sex no.'

'Oh, I don't mean promiscuous – you have to be a bit careful about that because it *means so much.*'

'Then you are talking about love, not sex,' she says, masticating contentedly.

'That too of course – I'm not separating them. But this is still the sexiest town I've ever been in.'

A white stretched Cadillac with smoked windows slides to a halt on the street outside. Nothing like it has ever before been seen in this city. No one enters or leaves it. The limousine simply stops there, breathing crime and corruption, sleaze raised to the Nth power, ridiculous and terrifying.

'I'm very confused,' I say, sipping beer, watching her eat.

'Everyone is confused. Especially the Russians.'

'I have a young Russian friend – should I bring him here?'

'No. Don't remind him of the difference.'

'I don't know what direction to take, so I must follow my heart. Do you know Katya? She manages a punk group.'

'I am not interested in this. They are just middle-class boys,' she snorts. 'A guitar costs a huge amount of money. Most people here are afraid to rebel – life is only survival.'

'Bohemian rebellion is always middle-class, isn't it? Don't let's get sidetracked by that. I don't give a damn about the Tam Tam Club either.'

Right now I don't give a damn about anything much and inside I am flattening out to a vast plain receding to infinity in every direction, therefore there is no such thing as direction. Like many horses' hooves a long way off, the premonitory subterranean rumbles of a great panic . . . . .

'They said on television' – my voice cracks – 'that in the area affected by Chernobyl the cancer rates are currently 22 times what they were before.'

She gags on her shashlyk, eyes bulbous. I knew she'd be impressed. Over there Rodge is sitting with an English girl.

'The thing I miss most is chocolate,' says the English girl. 'Every few days I have to make a pilgrimage to the dollar shop.'

The thing I miss is packets of salted peanuts. And occasionally it would be nice to snap the fingers and be in a London nightclub – just for an hour – with the beautiful black boys and girls jumping, away from all this churned-up whiteness –

'A Russian woman coming home from the West', says Rodge, 'filled in her currency declaration at Customs to the effect that, you know, she was bringing $5,000 cash into the country. She was "marked" by the Customs man. A few days later a gang arrived, kicked down the door, beat her up until she handed over the money. A friend of mine saw some blokes openly checking their guns in that club at the Astoria.'

Sadko's feels creepy. I'm grogging out, want to escape. I'm very very tired. Why was I so angry with Jill? Am I being cruel to Dina?

'Rodge, would you bring a Russian friend here?'

'Not all of them, no. You mean someone special?'

'Yes.'

'Of course I would.'

'I prefer the more Russian places,' I say.

'Do you know the Baghdad Café?' asks the English girl. 'You'd like it. Uzbeki food. Order plov and manti.'

Staring into space with the eyes pouring out into nothingness . . . city of horizontals . . . insomnia is horizontal . . . eternity is horizontal . . . timelessness is horizontal . . . sleep is vertical . . . death is vertical . . . tipping down . . . down . . . on a downer, on a downer . . . . .

'Duncan, wake up! You sleep!'

That's right. Hasn't she seen how tired his face has become? Of course not. She sees only what she wants to see. He wants to sleep. He just – wants to – sleep.

'Wake up! Wake up!'

'Go away! I sleep when I want to sleep! Not your decision!'

The reproof stalls her but only for a second.

'Are you ill? I want to give you your curds!'

Hasn't this already been sorted out? Hasn't he told her so *many* times? *Russians respond to firmness* he'd read in a manual of attitudes, so he climbs from his bed like an early amphibian . . . and opens the door.

'Can you not understand tiredness? I am not ill! It is 11 am not the end of the world! Zoia, don't *ever* do this again!'

She quails before his seriousness. His heart was thumping all night, trapped in a magnetic field of wonder and worry. The boy Dima, the girl Valentina. What is their life? How do they together speak of him? What nefarious plots do they hatch? And over what do they disagree and become angry with each other? He cannot imagine their life when he is not with them – they disappear into smoke. Oh, the fatigue of a summerlong daylight tension which never breaks. No relief from it. Down . . . down . . . but *not away* from the light which is generalised, uniform, infinite in every direction. Always the light, smirking behind the clouds, behind the thunder, under the carpet. He is trying to swim. You cannot swim for ever unless you are a shark and it's horrible being a shark. Eventually, if you cannot swim for ever, if you cannot find land, you will drown . . . . . Phonecalls from England. He thought he'd welcome them but he is raw and cannot communicate naked. They do not understand. They think he is on some kind of holiday. They phone in from an outlandish normality and he is aghast. He cannot put on an act and yet must put on something in order to communicate at all. To talk naked over the phone would shock the other party. They would worry afterwards, without the means for setting their worries to rest. It is interesting down here . . . funniosities moving in dark blue depths . . . he doesn't want to swim up to the brittle surface . . .

Not that he'd prefer they didn't phone. No, no, no. At a level other than that of convenience, these calls are vital stabs in the chest. Yesterday he went to shake hands with a man and had to switch hands quickly because the man's right hand was missing.

It is not the violence and deprivation – it is the relentless seediness which gets to you in the end . . . and this retreat into the concept of the absurd to explain their world – how hateful! Absurdity is the cry of the impotent. Life is *soaked* with meaning – to toss it all into the dustbin of the absurd – no, never! THERE IS A MEANING TO ALL THIS SOMEWHERE . . . . . . I can't get the fucking Rachmaninov out of my head. The First bloody Concerto. It's like meningitis, hurting, stop, go away – music is so powerful. Joshua demolished the walls of Jericho with music; Amphion built the walls of Thebes with music. Split the cranium upwards with a diamond-tipped arrow! RELEASE THE SOUND . . . shshsshshsh-shshshshshshshshshshshshshshshshshshshshoo–o–o–o–o–o–o–o–o–o–o–o–o–o–o–f–f–f–f–f–f–f–f–f–ffffff . . .

He'll never get back to sleep now. He rises. He has no appetite but eats a breakfast. A cannon booms from the Fortress, shaking the windows.

On her way out she asks 'For your dinner, do you want meat or fish?'

'Fish would be very nice, Zoia, thank-you.'

A queasiness undermines him, as though all active liquids have turned to stagnant brackish water. The pent-up fatigue of 6 weeks doing this place breaks through, dissolving the flesh into a torpid vapour, the limbs becoming vague attenuations of mist, not even that. Perimeters and parameters have gone. Every one . . . which is not to say that he has encountered no trustworthy people here – he has. People do try very often, but that alone is not enough because the *context*, through no fault of the individual, is not trustworthy. The boy Dima is exceptionally vulnerable to context. . . .

The throat tightens. He is in the Land of Nihilists with Eloquent Eyes! . . . which is also the land of bicyclists pedalling frantically in mid-air with round scared eyes, always in mid-air, every one – oh, so heavy and oppressive the weather to-day . . . . .

Nikita said 'Some days, for no reason, I lose all energy. It is partly the climate but mostly our way of life.' Enervation – spleen – angst – loss of aura – lying athwart the bed, he surrenders to a sluggish stream of cheerless reflections . . . languishing athwart . . . lying athwart . . . . . lying . . . lying . . . lying . . . lying begins as expediency and ends by destroying any possibility of happiness which is clarity (contentment is clarity minus threat). Happiness is not knowledge which is always partial. Truth is not a collection of facts. Truth is a motive, the attempt to be true. People do try very often . . . and yet truthfulness is not among the 3 theological virtues (faith, hope, charity); nor among the 4 cardinal virtues (justice, fortitude, temperance, prudence). Truth is the opposite of faith, the opposite of trust. Truth and trust see-saw on the fulcrum of rapport . . . the constant shattering of rapport – so upsetting –

Do these people have no centre, no core of being from which to radiate coherent, significant acts? Communism must have been the attempt to deal with Russian incoherence by mechanical means. And now there is no arena of social consensus in which even modest 'truths' can resonate. Igor Kon: 'Thinking one thing, saying another, and doing something else, has become common for us in all areas of life . . .' The best you can hope for is poetic truth, the vagabond's truth . . .

Disbelief has to be learned and is difficult when young because one's experience of duplicity, the simultaneous operation of contrary forms of reality, is negligible – or rather, one's realisation of it is. But the experience of duplicity grows, and the yearning for truth and trust grows alongside it: to struggle and wriggle finally beyond the ulterior motive.

The boy Dima says he has a ghetto-blaster and can copy tapes. Why does he not sell that to raise money? Maybe he does not in fact possess a ghetto-blaster and was saying so only for effect. This is an example of how facts unglue themselves. The only way to know if he has a ghetto-blaster is to see it and even then it might have been borrowed for the occasion, or be a shared object, or . . . No wonder that mental disturbance blows like a fine acidic mist through the people here – now you see it, now you don't – faintly glimmering behind a conversation – now flaring into naked fear or aggression or thickening into a turbid gloom of irrational clots.

Truth is essential to intimacy, though it may be emotional, not verbal truth. Intimacy is not essential to truth because truth can be cold, intimacy never. Absolute truth is unknowable in life – yet there is a great difference between a man trying to be honest and a man trying to deceive. Truth is not conformity to the objective but to the subjective, ie. a man lies when he believes that what he says is untrue.

Dear Jill. How dare she try to kill herself? What it is – she wants someone to look after her. We all do. But finally there can never be anyone. Finally we must look after others.

Dishonesty exposes a person's inner world – desires, dreams, fears, fantasies – more accurately than honesty. But when the line between fact and fantasy in another's life is entirely lost to us, one loses all interest in them because what they have to say has no significance.

Lying has an evolutionary function. The act of creation demands a leap beyond the actual – and a whipping of reality to catch up. In a world of unmitigated truth there can be no invention, only preconception, ie. the world could not come into being. Yet to pursue untruth, as opposed to truth, is impossible for the creator: his creations will evanesce in the making, either by collapse or evaporation.

Truth exists in the natural world; lying is only in the realm of the mind, the transcendental world: the art of fabulation is a steely business.

Certain statements of a religious, occult, poetic or metaphysical kind can be both true and not true. This is because language is sequential but reality is simultaneous.

If everyone always told the truth, society would be at the mercy of the first man who discovered lying. Lying prevents us from being gullible.

A lie can lift another's soul – withholding a cruel truth, paying an unjustified compliment – because the soul is very susceptible to opinion.

We all lie. To mature is the process by which the human being acquires the confidence to lie less and less.

The Russian language may assist lying. The great length of many of its words means that utterance cannot keep abreast of thought. One would tend to be thinking of something else while speaking. Concision however is no guarantee of veracity.

When you do not know what to believe, you become a paladin of solitude . . . the horrors of Eastern Europe, which begins at the Rhine, have no equivalent in Western Europe . . . do the Russians take pleasure in painful emotions? Why else do they curry them so?

Misgivings.

Skulduggery.

. . . and cogitation has now brought him to a stop, immured in a quag of morbid anfractuosities. Seeking with serpentine probes and a frown, verification of the simplest things, and failing to find it, he turns in on himself in a disconsolate coil, in a saturnine trance, swaying down to the music, snapped at by djinns, coiling down . . . down . . . down into the hot round basket, and the snake-charmer, now musicless, now silent, flips the lid and fastens it on him with a peg through a loop: the Within.

THE WITHIN

Do not be afraid . . . I am afraid . . . I cannot rest . . . It is not normal for me to be trapped at the lowest pitch in a basket . . . Painful now . . . Am I his enemy? One is permitted to lie to and cheat an enemy – to kill also . . . Dima has initiative and naïveté. The combination is always attractive to others and dangerous to the possessor; with few exceptions, foxiness is defeated by stupidity and a life runs and splinters on the rocks . . . I'm sorry. Excuse me, excuse me. Good-bye . . . Breathe deeply. Bestir yourself. Climb out of the circle of Your You . . . Let a little fire mount the spine . . . I go into the kitchen and make a cup of tea. Which isn't enough. Do stretching exercises in the Big Room. Swivel on the disc.

I want to believe him. But he doesn't make it easy. How did I become so involved? Never in my life before have I been so *immediately* and thoroughly subverted by charm. A playful, rejuvenating, warm-hearted mysterious, charm. I feel guilty not believing him. And he fills me with anxiety – I once said 'Every time we meet I know it could be for the last time.'

'Why do you say that?' he asked.

'I *feel* it.'

Dima is in real trouble and has no one else to turn to. Dima is a nasty piece of work who will come and get me with a band of hooligans. How is it possible to entertain 2 such contrary interpretations of character? Neither or both may be true. What has he already gone through in life? I have no inkling of that. On the radio is a sonata by Roslavets.

If Dima speaks the truth, it's bad news because it means he's caught up in a tough crowd. And if he succeeds in exacting the money, he'll think I'm a soft touch – or worse, *they* will – and there will be no end to it. If he has created a problem for himself with criminals, I anyway cannot solve it for him. Only he can – because this is really not a money problem but a way-of-life problem.

I'll give him what money I can before I leave – but when he isn't expecting it. That's what made me snap – 'How much you have?' I want to be generous but not have my generosity belittled by outrageous demands.

Perhaps it is both true and not true. Perhaps the girl has been detained for, say, $50 but Dima thought he'd up the figure while he was about it. Perhaps he arranged the kidnap himself! Or perhaps *she* did . . . Yes, perhaps she's behind it all, the designer of some perfidy, or demanding more and more from him if he wishes to keep her and his home . . . Or perhaps the abduction has been only threatened. Perhaps he is a brilliant actor, which is very possible, growing up in institutions.

'For God's sake, I don't *know* you!'

. . . felt bad about that. Lost my temper. Nonetheless it's true – I don't know him. And losing one's temper occasionally – it can bring you closer to people, can't it? They glimpse the fury which completes the whole. Oh hell . . . How do 2 people know when they know each other? I have the sick feeling which comes from being close to a person and yet sensing one doesn't know them at all. In order to know you I must find the key to you. Sometimes I have the key, only to find you've changed the lock. The obvious key, material gain, does *not* fit, funnily enough. Not-understanding is the interior vacuum which must be eradicated. And so you see, my response to Masha the Sculptress has altered – as she perhaps knew it would, always knowing more about it than I did. Yes – now I want to understand. I hunger to understand. You are the ultimate conundrum, the personification of that daily puzzle which is St Petersburg. And so I am hooked on you as I am hooked on it.

. . . But it's not only Dima. Others too. One suddenly falls out of the other side of a person one thinks one's grasped. Tracks which seemed to become roads vanish into unrecognisable terrain. People who came close are suddenly far away, lost, blinking at you across the tundra as though, yes, perhaps we met once, when was that? when *was* that? Then the head turns aside, looks down to where a little animal is playing, and she kneels and laughs lightly, engrossed in the creature, and you are nowhere, you are looking at her but she does not see you, you do not exist for her, and she abstracts herself under your very eyes, becomes an exhibit in a museum or at a fairground, out of time, out of life, and even if you look right into her eyes, right in, the person you knew is not there, *is not there*, and what you knew is reduced to a detached mote flying away down the tube of memory, whistling away into the void – gone – gone – is nowhere . . . and there remains only the echoless godless universe of desolation . . . . . . Acknowledge that this, my first attempt at knowing a Russian, has failed. Try to cry. It's good to give way. But it doesn't happen. Everything is there but the tears, they don't come. I try but they don't come. I shall not telephone him. He can telephone me when he is ready. If he wants to. I feel awful, just awful . . .

. . . I mean to organise things: boat trips on Lake Ladago, more concerts at the Philharmonia, a ballet at the Maryinsky, a visit to the remnants of the Royal Library at the Zubov Institute (Marisha von Moltke said the remnants were there). But little comes of it. All my windows have turned to mirrors, trapping me within myself. I have shrivelled entirely into the first person singular – which is very ignominious! One thing I hate about all this is having to use the word 'I' so much. It's because we are at the point where honesty and egotism are indistinguishable. Let's quit that mingy state. Come. Slink with me along crumbly streets, dragging our tribulations, the sun hot on our backs, en route to Pavel for a massage – he's been a saviour – scuffing along the back streets because the throng of Nevsky Prospekt is insupportable to-day – roads ripple, split, disgorge their offal – past the Oklahoma Dansing sign – that was a long time ago – the first 'O' and the 'lah' have fallen down – they'll take the rest down soon – the pavements are cratered – we stumble – luckily our ankles are not sprained!

'*Don't bother to wrap me up.* It's so hot.'

To-day Pavel the Paratrooper's massage is even more zealous than usual.

'What sort of massage is this?'

'Thailand.'

'Have you been there?'

'No. My master has.'

'Where have you been?'

'I finished army last month.'

'This is not Thai massage.'

'Why not?'

'In Thailand they massage hooey.'

He introduces Kirill who also does massage, though he's not been here before. Kirill speaks more English and says 'Pavel wants to know if you have any problems with your back.' We've been through all that.

Afterwards Pavel presents me with 2 Soviet flags, a book of photographs, a tasty snack of caviar tartlets and meringues, and a strange brown drink called kvass, the nature of which neither of them can explain. Hope it isn't one of those new-wave psycho-active health bombs served in London nightclubs which promise a mental and physical explosion. More explosions I don't need. But his generosity is very moving.

In the sunlight of the Big Room window, Zoia sews new bedcovers of printed chintz from Pakistan. I show her my Soviet flags. She says 'Not true flag. I have true flag, better flag.' A rummage in the wardrobe produces a gigantic Commie banner daubed with Stalinist peasants and a bright yellow fringe all round. But she fails to destroy my gift – I prefer mine – and inspired by Pavel's tartlets, I decide to open a tin of red caviar I left in the fridge.

'It *must* be eaten with bread *and* butter,' she insists, 'and use a spoon for the caviar. And red caviar, you *must* wash it.' Into the impacted marmalade-y eggs Zoia gently stirs 2 tablespoonsful of warm water which turns milky white, absorbing the salt and Lord knows what else, and is then poured away. This improves the taste of the caviar enormously. Boris arrives home with a new variety of cartridge for the James Bond soda syphon – it splutters gallantly but still isn't right – the water tastes foul – and from now on the syphon will stand in a corner of the kitchen with other failed gadgets.

A few days ago I decided to perform my French dressing. It wasn't easy choosing the moment because if one tries to do anything in the food line Zoia imagines it's because she has in some particular failed. When I announced my intention of making the salad dressing, her face went quite peculiar for an instant before adopting its blank mode. Italian olive oil, champagne vinegar, strong English mustard, juicy garlic, salt: the mixture thickened perfectly which it doesn't always do. But she wouldn't even look at it. She had to be forced to have a taste, against her will, and said 'Very good' in a curt, dismissive voice as though it were horse piss, adding 'Olive oil not good for salad. Good for face.' Later Lydia came down from upstairs and Zoia withdrew with her into the Big Room, taking the rest of the salad and dressing. I overheard her explain that I'd made it, heard them cooing with delight, eating with relish – which made me happy – but it was disheartening that not one jot of their pleasure did they transfer back to me. I was absolutely excluded from any direct credit.

Russia is too big to be normal. Russians can be so weird with a foreigner, can be very insecure with him and can consequently overwhelm or be paralysed by him. Traditionally they are divided in their attitude to the West, hostile to that which disconcerts them so, but desiring it too. Foreigners feel vulnerable here but can seem aggressive to Russians. Russians are vulnerable yet can seem aggressive to foreigners. All this mutual vulnerability and latent aggression crackles in the air.

Guarded and circumspect, initially, is how they are not only with foreigners but with anyone they don't know. This means they miss nothing, forget nothing. All signals are picked up and recorded – you can be certain of that, though they say nothing, though they feign indifference. Therefore there is much unspoken communication in Russia: with the body, eyes, psyche: telepathy is powerful.

Yes, dinner to-night is fish. Fresh salmon, poached, succulent, pink. And a salad of celery leaves, brilliant green and tasting spicy, packed with Vitamin C she says. While I eat, a constant screaming noise comes through from the Big Room, rather worrying until deciphered as a TV documentary on the Beatles.

Slug vodka in the bedroom in the strange hot city which doesn't know its own name – St Petersburg, Petersburg, Peter, Petrograd, Leningrad . . . Want to brush my teeth and go to bed but Boris is an age in the bathroom to-night, the bathroom with its stickers of cats and dogs on blue tiles. At 1 am he explains that the sink unit has fallen apart – he is in there with the components on the floor trying to reassemble them . . . in the kitchen I see my first and last Russian cockroach picking its way delicately and furtively over an unwashed plate while through the window comes that noise of a young person's hacking cough in a nearby flat . . . At 2 am Gregorian chants throb through the air in swelling waves of soul – yet more soul – all this soul raking my breast like pneumonia, making my temples ache – earplugtime – let's keep this soul at bay – I don't want any more SOUL! Please, *just one night of superficiality*, that's all I ask. Can't sleep of course. The diamond at braincentre won't die. Katya's words squeak out from a corner of the ceiling – somehow it always lets you down . . . You need infinite patience here. But life is short. How infinite is infinity? There comes a time when you've simply exhausted yourself . . . But no. No, no, I shall *not* be dragged down by Slav melancholy . . . I intend to *know* you . . . night-time sunshine . . . the longest, fullest, lowest day empties through a white hole . . . snap!

CHAPTER SIX

Meet Maxim (the trainee Orthodox priest) at 11 am by the Hermitage Pontoon for the hydrofoil to Petrodvorets. Boris and I leave the flat and Zoia says 'Duncan, more clothe. Very cold.' As we enter the lift, she calls down from the top of the stairs 'Duncan, back!', squaring her shoulders with a cheeky smile. Such a bossy little hippopotamus but I love this side of her. I wish more people would tell me to stand up straight.

Outside the sky is zinc and the wind is indeed cold and fierce, blowing up-river from the Gulf, and I'm glad of the extra jumper. Oh cold wind, blow all you want, dislodging gravel and sometimes quite substantial items from buildings, exhilarating the blood! Suddenly there's Anya, the Astoria girl, striding along Palace Embankment. Her left arm is in plaster! I call out but she turns a corner and I don't run after her. A faint drizzle comes and goes. Maxim is standing by the pontoon in a dappled suit. He grins elvishly, sending heat into his red hair and gold-rimmed spectacles. A large party of Jehovah's Witnesses swamp the pontoon and I say 'You can always tell Jehovah's Witnesses by their feet.'

'I know someone who is a Nazi,' he counters. 'He goes round measuring the width of people's skulls with a pair of compasses to see if they are racially OK.'

'Osip says you want to become a priest.'

'Yes, but from the seminary in New York, not from the debased tradition that stayed in Russia. It is not possible to solve the material problems here. You have to have something else – belief in God, or even stamp-collecting. Russians have become like animals! They are eating each other now. Russia is a huge concentration camp.'

Strong stuff. Should be an interesting day. The chain across the gangplank is unhooked and we file aboard the hydrofoil. Its interior is like a spaceship and it gathers speed very quickly, banging into the wind-whipped waves of the Neva.

Maxim asks 'How did you meet Osip?'

'Through a contact in London.'

'Did you know he has a piece of paper saying he's insane?'

'No, I didn't.'

'Does it surprise you?'

'Its significance would depend on who issued it.'

'That's right. My father has one too. They can be very useful.'

'How old are you?'

'Almost 18.'

Oh please, not another 17-year-old. 'Where do you live.'

'With my wife's parents.'

Has he made a mistake in his English? No, he hasn't. They do begin early here (this is the 4th 17-year-old-boy-living-with-a-girl that I've encountered. In Commie days, people married young because there was hardly anything to do and because it was the only chance of getting away from parents. For the moment, the tradition carries on. Few of these young marriages survive).

'We wed in a church 2 years ago but it won't be legal until next year.'

'How many children do you have?'

'2 dogs.'

'Can you get me into the Church of Blood? It's been closed 20 years.'

'I don't think so. It was 4 years just drying out.'

The long palace of Petrodvorets rises behind trees on a steep bank of cascades and fountains which make it look bigger than it is. The waterworks are undergoing renovation so it's rather a shambles but the Gulf of Finland façade gavottes in lighthearted pomp through a medley of hipped roofs, curves, pediments, and orange-tawny stucco, governed by the power of 7. During the Second World War the Germans razed the palace almost to the ground and did their best to devastate the park. Only the brilliance of the reconstruction betrays the fact. These reconstructions of the destroyed Imperial palaces are among the greatest achievements of the post-war Communist era and probably would not have happened under a capitalist system.

We queue for nearly an hour in cold drizzle, because official parties of foreign tourists, including the Jehovah's Witnesses, are given priority. My gorge rises as yet another Intourist crowd with hideous faces and garish pullovers are let in ahead of us, and I marvel at the ordinary Russian's patience in dealing with such affronts. At the admission desk Maxim deftly disguises my nationality to avoid the surcharge and we don overshoes.

The rooms are enchanting, not daunting. Above one's head in the Throne Room, chandeliers hang with a massive pendant languor, their thickets of lilac glass as abundant as forest foliage; the lilac colour clashes with the scarlet of the upholstery, which the pale green and white of walls and ceiling cannot resolve, lending a strain of delinquency to this airy saloon.

Golden Neptunes, Apollos and Venuses are scattered in great number among the parterres and water gardens outside. Avenues terminate in pavilions (whose onion domes give them the air of futuristic transmitting stations), or lead towards the Stables (a Russian 'Tudor' Hampton Court almost as extensive as the palace itself), or turn into the circuitous pathways of the Alexandria Park laid out in the English romantic style of landscaping which weds intimacy to the sublime. Here woodland gives relief from the jerking gale until we break upon the shore where criss-cross waves are chopped by gusts.

Under a skidding sky I say 'Thank-you for engineering the cheap ticket for me. Russians are very alert to these things.'

'We have to be. Russians know many tricks,' he replies. 'But Russians have tricks not only to squeeze money out of foreigners. Even more, to squeeze money out of each other.'

'I'm sick of dollars. My visit to Russia has made me hate dollars. Just the word makes me want to puke.'

'Most people here can only dream about them.'

It's different for me. Dollars burn in my pocket like a reproach, like an invitation to criminals, a symbol of my apartness, of the abjection of the Russians. I don't carry them any more, or rarely.

'Were you in the military?' I ask, as we approach the Sea Canal with its parallel lines of fountains linking Palace to Gulf.

'I was supposed to go into the Building Corps. Unless it is a career, you cannot choose. They choose – Army, Navy, Air Force. Building Corps is worst – for idiots and criminals and troublemakers, lots of people from the South.'

'Why are they such a problem in Petersburg, the Southerners?'

'Because they are not at home. I was put in the Building Corps for being a rebel. But my father got me off it, saying my US passport was coming through. Conscription is for 2 years. The second years are called grandfathers [godfathers?] and the first years have to shine their shoes, wash their clothes, sometimes give up their food rations. Everybody steals. There are many bad stories. Once one of the first years did something wrong and a group of second years stuck a car tyre pump up his backside, blew him up and killed him.'

'Oh God, I want to go to the Circus.'

'Be sure to cover up. There are fleas. They will bite. Perhaps I shall come with you and bring my wife?'

Struck by icy blasts, we are waiting in an open kiosk by the jetty for the hydrofoil back to town.

'Is your father *really* mad?' I ask.

'No. He is a painter. But he needed this paper for a purpose.'

The play at the Maly, *Stars in the Morning Sky*, written in 1984 but unable to be performed until recently, also gave a sobering view of the – to put it mildly – tendentious nature of Soviet psychiatry. During the Moscow Olympic Games, the prostitutes were moved out of Moscow to lunatic asylums because the Communist Government had told the world that prostitution did not exist in Russia. . . . On stage they were busy shouting at each other, hitting each other, generally treating each other like shit, except when occasionally loving each other at which time they clung in a desperate convulsion of need. One learnt that 'hivno' is 'crap' in the Ukrainian pronunciation ('guvno' is the Russian, cf. Gamlet, Gitler and Victor Gugo). Lots of smoking in these plays and the smoke is always used creatively against the lights. The main character in this one was a whining red-eyed drunken derelict who frequently took from her bag a comb and pulled at greasy hair with it. Her lover was a 'mad' nuclear scientist – VV said that in the 1970s many scientists – and others – found freedom in the mental hospitals. Once they had the paper certifying their insanity, they could say what they liked.

In the kitchen Zoia talks of the Lady from Astrakhan who has visited Boris's café. Her husband runs a caviar factory and she's offering a kilo of good caviar for $10. I accept the offer. The Lady from Astrakhan is supposed to be telephoning in the next few days. At about midnight Boris returns home. Zoia has gone to bed. He and I are alone in the kitchen and I mention the caviar. He nods but is preoccupied.

'Racket want money from my café for protection,' he says, 'but I not pay. To-day a big man with gun come and fire rockets. Everyone under table. Don't tell mama.'

Though serious to the bottom of his soul he utters a laugh, which is a nervous reflex (Dima has it too. I remember once when we had a small row over something, Dima didn't confront me but tried to withdraw from it by laughing, but it came out all wrong – his hands moved agitatedly and the laugh was a weird bubbling noise – I felt as though I'd done something dreadful to him.) Boris says he rents the café not from the mafia but from the municipality.

'Will you pay the racket?'

'No. Not pay. Ah Petrodvorets. Did you see in study of Peter the Great the English musical clocks?'

His courage is imperishable. I hope *he* is too.

From Death's Door To Jetset. Briefly very cold, it is now very hot once more, via a violent storm at lunchtime. No city is subject to more extreme and rapid weather changes, and the great variety of spectacular cloud formations is a continuing wonder. The cause must lie in the proximity of cold arctic air to warm continental air. To-day the Pototskis have invited me to tea.

On the telephone the Countess Irina Pototska, who speaks beautiful English and doesn't use the title, said 'It will be difficult for you to find our flat, so we shall meet on the corner of the street. How shall I recognise you?'

'I shall be wearing a black denim jacket, black denim jeans, white shirt, and a red neckscarf with white spots.'

'And I am old and grey,' she replies, 'and therefore not very pleasant to look at, wearing turquoise ear-rings, quite large ones.'

They live a couple of streets north of the Lenin Park, over the Kirovsky Bridge. There is another cloudburst en route but luckily I have a collapsible umbrella, although everything below the waist is soon sodden. She is recognisable long before any ear-rings come into focus because Irina typifies the aristocrat circa 1930. A thin, bony, beautiful face; scarf tied as a choker and held with a large brooch at the throat; a dove-grey cloaklike coat; composed under a dripping umbrella. Coming closer reveals the lively, intelligent eyes, the gentle but self-possessed expression, and a skin of matt delicacy which seems to have been moisturised and softly buffed with papier poudré for 50 years. Her first words are 'Isn't the weather appalling?' We could be in Berkeley Square. She is about 70.

Quite right: their habitation would have been impossible to find without guidance. We wind through derelict buildings and pause at a black portal. It is absolutely pitch within; not a single glimmer dances there. 'You must navigate by counting the number of steps,' she says, as we grope our way up, holding fast to an icy iron banister which loops through several flights and landings. Finally she says 'Here.' Nothing whatsoever is visible but a key sounds in a lock and a blade of dull light cuts across the stone floor. She ushers me into a dilapidated communal flat and therefrom into their claustral apartment, 2 small rooms, damp and musty but made vivid by the books stacked at perilous angles, photographs, china, a wall-size oil painting of maidens picking fruit, several outsized pieces of carved furniture, and by the flourishing personalities of its occupants. The only floorspace is a narrow strip round a wooden table (with even less in the closetlike bedroom beyond). Nonetheless in addition to themselves, they find accommodation within it for 2 cats and their dog Sir Toby.

Her husband Alexander Pototski sits at one end of the table, dishevelled and pixy-ish, sharp blue eyes in a scowl, beautiful hands and nails contrasting with unkemptness. His mother was a celebrated maker of ceramics and since he was – and is – a Communist, he gave most of his collection to the Soviet Government. In retirement Count Alexander (who likewise scorns the title) is an art expert, though by profession a marine biologist.

'Specialising in crustacea,' he grunts.

'I like the House of Scientists,' I say.

'I hate it. It's vulgar,' he replies.

'That's one of the things I like about it.'

(The House of Scientists overlooks the Neva behind Zoia's building and was built by Rezanov for the brother of Alexander III, the Grand Duke Vladimir who gave the best parties in St Petersburg and was the patron of Diaghilev. To enter the palace you must push on the pert breasts of female gryphons, the chief device of the exterior. Inside, each room is different: rococo ballroom, Siberian gothic banqueting hall, baroque staircase, English Jacobean oak library, French saloon, Ottoman smoking room, etc: the San Simeon of St Petersburg, or like something a Scottish soap magnate might've put up around 1885.)

'And what's more, it was considered vulgar at the time it was built!' emphasises the Count.

'He can become quite indignant about it,' observes Irina, graceful as an egret. She has returned from the communal kitchen and is setting the table with tea, square biscuits, and a jar of preserved plums.

I: Before the war I thought – I wonder what it is like to live through a war? Then the war came and I thought – how interesting this will be. Such a fool I was.

D: Do you hate the Germans?

I: I didn't at first. Then the German Army became very cruel, especially here in Eastern Europe. We were accustomed to cruelty from Stalin – but Hitler became very cruel.

D: Worse than Stalin?

A: No. They were both the same, both terrible!

I: Before the Revolution our family had a flat of 8 rooms. Then workers were dumped on us to live in it and they hated educated people like us. The flat was in a large building on Ulitsa Nekrasova. All the flats were large and therefore many many people came to live on our staircase. But of the whole staircase, only 4 people survived the Siege.

D: How long did it last?

A: 900 days. 1941 to 1944. It is impossible to calculate but you could say over a million lives were lost from bombardment, hunger and disease. Altogether our country lost 20 million in the war – excuse us if we are sometimes suspicious of foreigners. [He smiles.]

I: Whole families died. I was on the verge of dying at one point and had to lie on my bed because I couldn't walk. We waited for food in queues down to minus 42 degrees centigrade sometimes, hoping a car might turn up with something, a piece of bread. That is why I now become very afraid when I feel cold. We had a small stove in our kitchen and everyone sat there to keep warm. A whole generation of my aunts died except one. She managed to survive – and was then arrested. That is a tragic story. I shall tell you later. There was no telephone, no transport, walking was difficult. So it was impossible to know who is alive, who is not. There is a cemetery where all the tourists are taken – Piskariovskoye – an awful place now with musicians and souvenir-sellers. We had to dig it with our hands to bury the masses of dead.

D: My landlady was evacuated. Why were you not?

I: Because Mother said we must stay – otherwise we shall never be allowed to return to our home, although . . . you know, in Russia we do not have this very strong addiction to *things*. Of course we like to have nice things and I love my gold ring but if I lose it I shall say 'Oh well, that's life.' During the Siege my mother gave a boy a precious stone because the boy said he could bring us potatoes and we hadn't seen potatoes for 2½ years. We did not see the boy again. But Mother was not angry because she said maybe the boy was killed or had a great problem.

D: Yes, I understand that.

I: There was a Jewish man called Ezrakh who built up a great art collection in this way during the Siege because when people are dying of hunger they will give a painting for a loaf of bread.

(The telephone rings. Before picking it up Alexander asks his wife in Russian 'Are you at home?'

'Niet,' and she serves up more tea.

'No, she's not at home.'

'Oh, is that X?' and she crosses to the phone for a cosy little chat with X.)

D: What happened to that collection?

A: Disappeared!

I: No, no. Some is in the Russian Museum. Some at Pavlovsk, I think. If you are starving you cannot think of anything else – I could not sleep for it and the rats came under my blankets because it was so cold for them too.

A: You see the bare spines of those leather-bound books? All eaten away by rats during the Siege. The city was gnawed away. Sometimes the rats ate children.

I: You cannot imagine how *ugly* the Siege was, so very very ugly. People were swollen up and afterwards went very thin. People walked like this. [She demonstrates a stiff backward-leaning shuffle.] People were dirty – there was no clean water. I worked as a washer in a chemist shop and would put snow in a bucket and when it melted I could wash the medicine bottles – which was very hard work because I had no strength. Do you know what kept me going? My mother had a picture which she had bought in England of a woman, an Edwardian beauty with firm plump arms and a big hat and a pretty dog. I looked at it every day to remind myself of how things could be, that things could be better.

D: I know all the cats and dogs were eaten. Was there cannibalism?

I: . . . I don't know what to say about that.

A: Yes, there was!

I: The chemist where I worked was opposite the morgue and we saw . . . things taken away, bodies for food. A friend of mine had a daughter of 3 years old who looked very healthy. She disappeared one day, taken, probably eaten . . . .

D: The Russian serial killer recently – he had 53 victims and ate parts of them.

I: Yes, terrible things happen now also.

D: How do you feel about the situation now?

I: Every day I feel like Alice in Wonderland.

D: Nabokov translated it.

I: Yes, but he called her Anya, not Alice. People do not go out and beg. They sit at home wondering what to do. All their money has vanished. Some have been through the war and are invalids – and here it is again for them.

A: I fear civil war.

I: No, no. It is not in the character of the Russian people.

A: Then I fear some great violence. I am afraid of this. People begin to be desperate.

I: We are accustomed to living with socialism. All more or less equal. And I liked it. Now it is different. I don't like capitalism because it is cruel and makes people greedy.

A: All economies are mixed. Pure capitalism doesn't exist anywhere – except in Russia now – we are experiencing a wild virgin capitalism. The absurdity of free market forces – as if we are not permitted to control what happens in any way. Anyway, free market is a highly controlled system – money control.

I: Our educated class are trying to leave Russia. But I feel very patriotic.

D: The new business class arouses great resentment.

A: Because they are mostly crooks.

D: Or are they forced to become crooked to achieve anything?

I: But one good thing! Nevsky Prospekt is alive again. Before it was cold and dead. Now it is alive!

It certainly is. The Headbanger sports a coronet of fresh scabs and out of a large untidy hole in the pavement comes the screaming sob of an electric blues band playing live down in Hades. Turning into Rubinstein Street, through a blast from the fish-shop on the corner, I soon spot VV outside the Maly Theatre, always there before me, very soothing in his good-natured reliability.

'Cor blimey, guv'ner, how's your mad landlady?'

'She's been cooking me beautiful salmon. Guv'ner sounds like Russian for shit.'

'Oh my giddy aunt! Whatever next?'

Gaudeamus is an avant-garde production with an athletically leaping cast, a black comedy about life in the Building Corps of which Maxim spoke so beguilingly. I now realise what that uniform is one sees so often about town, the least formal but in fact the most Russian (loose khaki trousers tucked into cossack boots, simple belted tunic, and round cap) – it's that of the Building Corps. One also learns, thanks to VV's conscientious elucidation in the glazed box, that cannabis is 'plan'; that 'kife' means pleasure in the sense of blissful comfort, an idle voluptuousness (an Arab word, also used in North Africa to denote cannabis, bhang); that it is a Russian trick to take a drag from a cigarette, swallow vodka, exhale the smoke. Throughout, something which is not part of the performance is dripping onto the stage from above.

Walking back along Nevsky Prospekt I say 'A boy told me he is in big trouble and needs money. The question is – is he ingenuous? . . . or do I mean disingenuous? I always forget.'

'You mean is he sincere or insincere?' asks VV.

'Yes.'

'Sincere is ingenuous.'

'Thank-you. What I mean is – his manner is very ingenuous. He seems to be the open type. But what he says sometimes doesn't gel. So I have to ask myself – *to what extent* is he genuous or ingenuous, no, I mean, genuine, that's to say, ingenuous or disingenous?'

'Let's have a look at him.'

'Er, no.'

'I could tell immediately.'

'Yes, but he's not something to be passed round for comments. I couldn't do that.'

(However, one can understand the growth of the secret police in

Russia. When in the foreground of life everyone is lying, inventing, dissimulating, it is the only way of establishing a sort of background actuality. But then, through the spread of anxiety, a secret police fosters the proliferation of the very thing it is trying to dispel: the murk in which events are buried.)

After learning a little more – but no names – VV bursts out laughing and says '$300 indeed! My Kung Fu master and I will recover the girl for only $50!'

He descends into the tube station and I walk home. It's about 10.45 pm, a fine clear evening, the Prospekt calming down – then the sound of gunfire. Not an explosion, not anything crashing to the ground, not a car backfiring – the banal flatness of the reports means 'shots'. I shrink into an entrance. A woman of about 60 years, well-dressed and square-shouldered, arms straight at her side, a bag of something in each hand, stands on the opposite side of the archway, stately, motionless, except for her face which is violated by twitching fears.

At home Zoia says 'Sonya telephone.' She is with the Mormon Boys in the Big Room.

Mormon Smile One, the bigger, says 'St Petersburg is so crime-free!'

'Er, are you sure?' I venture in amazement.

'Compared to American cities it is.'

'American cities are *completely* out of control,' says Mormon Smile Two, the smaller.

When they've gone Zoia and I watch Nevsorov and she asks 'Do you think he is beautiful?'

'No. But the eyes are good.'

'I think he is beautiful.'

Nevsorov is meanwhile inciting Russians to kill blacks (ie. Southerners) and the programme is cut off (but the next day he is back again as usual).

About midnight I call Sonya. Russians don't mind late phone-calls. It's part of their funkiness. A lady professor once said to me 'Phone after midnight. I should be back then.' Professors don't say things like that in England.

'Did you see Nevsorov?' I asked Sonya.

'No. What's he done now?'

'Incited Russians to kill blacks.'

'Doesn't he always?'

'They cut off the programme.'

'The day after to-morrow you can visit the gymnasts at the Dynamo Club. There are still problems with the ballerinas – and anyway they say you can only speak with them in the cabinet of the Director.'

'The Director is frightened they will seduce me?'

'Ha! What have you been up to?'

'Chasing wild geese.'

'Everyone knows the English are the most eccentric people in Europe.'

'Gladstone and his wife always took to bed with them a hot water bottle filled with beef tea which they drank in the course of the night. That's very Russian. Sonya, should I read Rozanov?'

'Good idea! Are you interested in the choir of the Capella? They have a special school. Their repertoire is very unusual.'

Boris hasn't come home. Zoia and I watch a bit of *Royal Wedding* on the box, starring Fred Astaire, Jane Powell, Peter Lawford and Sarah Churchill.

'See that one – he was President Kennedy's brother-in-law,' I explain.

'Fred Astaire was?'

'No, the other one – he married President Kennedy's sister. And that one, she was Winston Churchill's daughter.'

'Oh.' Zoia's very attentive.

'She was an alcoholic.'

'Oh?'

'And she was also a great friend of a great friend of mine called April Ashley who is a sex-change.'

'Oh!'

'And who married an English lord, April did.'

'Oh!'

Zoia is looking at me with an expression I've not seen on her before, a combination of terror and love.

At which point, to clinch my all-too-brief ascendancy, Kitty phones from Moscow.

'A lady kissed my feet when I gave her roubles and a soldier kissed my hand up to my elbow. And a Professor of Economics from England was mugged in a lift at knifepoint in a strange block of flats after being conned there by someone who overheard him in the hotel foyer trying to contact a

contact in the world of academia and the con-man then posed as that
contact. Isn't that awful? David was constipated for days and now has
diarrhoea and I have diarrhoea too but I wasn't constipated first. Mary of
course doesn't have diarrhoea. Tone is into icons. Jimmy keeps making
anti-Russian remarks in front of Russians and his suitcase was stolen or at
least he lost it on the station platform or something but probably he just
forgot it because after a car accident in his youth one of the things he
suffers from is short-term memory loss.'

The Dynamo Club. Boris rematerialised thank heaven, and it's his day off.
Please tell me you love me. Stop driving me mad – the Stones reverberate
through the flat (Boris's tape-copying was a great success). The lady
professor at the University, the one I had to phone after midnight, has
been channelling a number of useful and well-mannered students my way
as interpreters. Among the sweetest is a 19-year-old with hair in a
platinum ponytail called Natasha who spent last summer in England. It
was Natasha who accompanied me to the photographer Boris Smelov
when at last he was tracked down. We arrived at a tiny flat among the
Lines on Vasilievsky Ostrov, were admitted by Smelov's mother-earth
wife into a miniature interior that was pure Dickens – dark wood, fretted
screens, dusty cut glass, crammed with curiosities, fitting together in a
compact jigsaw. 'He's not at home, he'll be coming later,' she said – he
must have freaked out at the prospect of a Western visitor – and she
produced several thick piles of black and white prints, many of them
showing signs of stress. The spaniel nuzzled my leg and whimpered for
toffees while a peremptory hailstorm came and went; muddy old
photographs of Gogol and Bulgakov stared down from the wall; we sat
silently on top of each other in this Dickensian den while I sifted through
the photographs, waiting for Smelov.

He turned up roaring drunk, thin, battered, long straggly wet hair,
shouting 'Hooey! Hooey! Hooey! Hooey!' Natasha giggled. The wife
laughed until tears streamed down her plump cheeks. Catching sight of
his photographs, Smelov homed in and started to anatomise their
qualities through a gurgle of curses and obscenities, repeatedly distracted
by nothing. Natasha did her best to bridge the various gulfs but it didn't

matter – his amiable truculence overtook all. Here was a photograph of the woman, fat with bun, who translated Byron into Russian. She spent most of her life in prison but kept all Byron in her head. There was a photograph of Prince Lvov – he was mostly in prison too. Both dead now. Smelov rubbed a greasy finger over the Prince's vaudeville face, not caring, bursting out 'Hooey! Hooey!' His architectural photographs are magnificent and somewhere in them always a human being, usually very very small, but always there to be found, so that history, romance, story, humanity breathe in the work.

I chose 4 photographs: 1) the Fontanka in winter, 2 pairs of industrial chimneys venting black smoke across a low sun behind the classical façades, ice breaking up, a figure hurrying across a bridge; 2) a little boy on the steps of a brick laundry house, plants growing from the roof – he holds a gun crudely shaped from wood; 3) a station platform with posters, tragedy and happiness juxtaposed; 4) a disturbing view of St Petersburg from the wooden bridge near the Petrovski Bar – a lone figure, a bird in flight, and the very imperfections in the printing process have flecked the crespuscular sky with unusual cosmic activity.

D: I'd like to buy these 4. How much do you ask?

S: Give what you want.

D: If I give you 250 roubles each, that is 1,000 roubles, it leaves me 100 roubles for the taxi home.

S: No!

D: I've said something wrong.

S: This one! Only this *one* I sell it for 1,000 roubles!

D: Oh . . .

S: And the other 3! . . I give them you as a present!

Well . . . . that was what the Americans call a class act. And it is this Natasha who now accompanies me to the Dynamo Club. She arrives at Zoia's in slacks and jumper and we cross to the House of Sport opposite, where a car is waiting.

The Dynamo Club, 15 minutes away and reached via an explosive sequence of potholes, is a glassy 60s or 70s building, down-at-heel but with very extensive facilities. We are greeted by the head of the club who is accompanied by a little chap called Oleg. He looks 10 but they insist he's 14 and he has a nasty bruise on the side of his face 'from fighting'. Our driver turns out to be his father and fiercely ambitious for the boy who, it is predicted, will be the new star of Russian gymnastics. 'He was hanging from things by his fingers before he could walk,' says the father. The head of the club has had an offer from Greece to set up a gymnastic school in Athens which in the present economic circumstances is very tempting. It is conditional on taking Oleg along too who would compete in the name of Greece: dual citizenship is now possible for Russians. The head doesn't really want to go but Oleg's father is keen – the money would enable him to set up a taxi business in St Petersburg in a few years' time. We are joined by the chief coach, Alexander Dityatin, a redhead who is the greatest male gymnast of modern times – he won 8 medals at the 1980 Olympic Games.

AD: With gymnastics, you can't wait. The opportunity passes very quickly.

DF: Who chooses them?

AD: They choose themselves. But not everyone is chosen. Oleg is small for 14. This is good. Maximum height when grown is 1.7 metres.

DF: Do they eat special food? [They all laugh.]

AD: They eat what is here. We would like high protein, low cholesterol, but, well, it was easier for me because the organisation was better then, better food, better facilities. They go to sports boarding schools but these are being reduced. Everything is being reduced.

DF: The momentum from the strong tradition of the past is still there, as in other fields, but will it last beyond the next few years?

AD: It becomes more and more difficult. Fruit and vegetables are essential to a sportsman but they are very expensive now. Meat is important for warmth, especially in our climate.

DF: Are you tempted to work abroad?

AD: No – because although there is more money abroad, the important thing, the basic raw material – the boys – is much poorer, so it is not so interesting. In Russia the young boys in gymnastics are of a much higher quality. Oleg is just coming to a difficult physical period. He will grow fast now. This period 13 to 16 is difficult for the boys. He will mature into a man with changes in hormones, metabolism, physique, balance, etc.

Oleg's father returns. I present Oleg with a Boy T-shirt – *The strength of a nation lies in its youth* on the front – and the father tells him to take off his shirt and demonstrate the perfection of his body. They present me with an illustrated book about the club and a membership badge. Dityatin slaps his arm – his redhead's complexion is very susceptible to mosquito bites and this he says has now developed into a phobic reaction to their mere presence. I promise him the repellent which was among Kitty's largesse (while I retain the Jungle Jelly just in case – although the mosquitoes don't bother me any longer). But why is the Dynamo Club empty? One was hoping for displays. There has been a mistake in the information. They are all at summer camp in the countryside. Oleg is only in town to visit the dentist. We agree to visit the summer camp at a later date.

Natasha returns to the flat for a cup of tea and tries to help me make calls from the bedroom, but lifting the phone every so often, it seems Zoia is solidly on the line and we can't use it. After Natasha leaves, I sit in the kitchen as Zoia prepares dinner.

'She bad girl,' she says.

Can't believe my ears.

'I can read her physiognomy,' she continues.

What's up now? Why is Zoia in a rage?

'She ill-bred. She is the type who goes with men for money.'

'Zoia! This is madness. She is a wonderful girl from the University. She has been in England.'

'So now she thinks she is too clever to take off her shoes.'

'Who I have as interpreter is none of your business.'

'It is my flat. And she doesn't even say hullo!'

'That was my fault. I apologise. I should've introduced her. I thought you were occupied on the phone.'

'I think you are very well-bred man – and I am surprised by the friends you have.'

'Stop it. That's enough, Zoia. You are too rude to me!'

It's really getting out of hand – and she's been at the dictionary. 'Ill-bred' and 'well-bred' haven't made an appearance before. Why am I listening to such odious claptrap? Who the hell does she think she is?

'These girls are just after you! I saw it also at the Grand Europe Hotel – how the girls at the next table looked at you.'

'What's the matter with you? Why shouldn't they be interested in me? I'm not a horrible person!'

Then it dawns on me. This is no longer a question of defending her coffee-beans – Zoia is wildly jealous. Well, well, well . . . (And what happened at the Grand Europe Hotel? Nothing. I took her there for a drink after she'd taken me to the *Petersburg* ballet. Enjoyed it. Didn't feel stared at at all. Not that it would've mattered anyway.)

But yes, it's enough – I ring Leonid and ask 'Can you sort Zoia out? She's going crazy. If I invite a man here she says he's a murderer or a gayboy. If it's a woman she says she's a prostitute. It's just awful! She's had the Siege of Leningrad – I'm getting the Siege of Zoia.'

'Put her on.'

They talk for a while, then Zoia hands the phone over with a hoity-toity expression, nose tipped up.

In a voice of imperturbable lassitude, Leonid says 'She tells me that the girl was listening in on her telephone conversation. This is very bad.'

'Absolutely not true! The girl was trying to make a call for me – I was there the entire time. We aren't interested in Zoia's phonecalls, can't you see? Leonid, this is crackers. Do you think Lydia infects her with paranoia?'

'Zoia is trying to protect you.'

'Bollocks.'

'She said the girl did not remove her shoes.'

'Must I shoot her for not taking off her shoes?'

There is no resolution. He is concerned to the point of somnolence. After this call, the telephone rings immediately. For me.

'I can't come to the Circus with my wife. We must go to the cemetery. How can I return the tickets to you?'

'Oh Maxim – um – I'm having a fight with my landlady. She doesn't want Russians coming here.'

'I can understand her feeling.'

'Oh . . . .'

'Are you still there? Is there a postbox?'

'Er, yes – on the ground floor,' I tell him.

'I'll leave them inside it. By the way, what did you mean you can always tell Jehovah's Witnesses by their feet?'

'Did I say that?'

'Yes.'

'I must've been drunk.'

Give up and retreat to the bedroom. Yes, enough, had enough – of her, of him, of them, of IT – I wanna go home. No, not even that. I wanna *be* home without the hassle of travel, couldn't travel anywhere right now – let's lie on the bed and let all the crap sink in, sink through, drip out, and wish there were a sane person round here who liked me and would give me a long cuddle with no overtones, undertones, semitones . . . .

Listen to one of my homemade tapes (Turn Up The Bass, Dmitri!) through earphones:– Gloworm: *I Lift My Cup* (Shining Path Mix) . . . Fats Comet: *Stormy Weather* . . . Perfect Zebras: *Touching My Heart Again* . . . The Smiths: *How Soon Is Now?* . . . The Blow Monkeys: *Digging Your Scene* . . . Lennie Welch: *Since I Fell For You* . . . Gertrude Lawrence: *Experiment* . . . Les Negresses Vertes: *Zobi La Mouche* (club mix) . . . The Stooges: *Down On The Street* . . . Isley Brothers: *Inside You* . . . Toy Planet: *Rapido de Noir* . . . Kid Creole & the Coconuts: *The Lifeboat Party* . . . Eye to Eye: *Am I Normal?* . . . The Marvelettes: *I'll Keep Holding On* . . . Toots and the Maytals: *Funky Kingston* . . . Big Audio Dynamite: *In Full Effect* . . . Yello: *Vicious Games* . . . . .

Boris returns early and talks with his mother and puts his head round the door. 'Duncan, cognac? Da, da, da. Choot-choot!' He's a lovely bloke – must get it from his father. To-day there was no bread in the shops and he trudged everywhere looking for some – without success. It is so exhausting having these scenes with her. But she cannot be allowed to cut me off from everyone and everything the way she's cut *herself* off. And she is so *strong*. With people like that you either firm up or are swept entirely away . . . Can't get to sleep. *Make your move. It won't happen by itself.* To-morrow I shall ring Dima. What the hell. I want to see him. I want to. I need him. For once in his life someone needs him.

Get It From The Inside Out. Dima picks up the phone and gives his usual little nervous laugh: 'What do you want?'

'Can you meet me?'

'Yes.'

My mood rises in a rapid glissando.

'Now. This afternoon.'

'Yes. I am free now.'

'Let's meet at the Naval Museum. Is everything OK?'

'Yes, everything OK now. My situation good.'

'I have 3 tickets for the Circus this evening – you could bring Valentina.'

'Yes. What time we meet?'

White fluff floats slowly from the trees like summer snow. A man with a

Greenpeace T-shirt is sauntering in the Mikhailovsky Gardens with his 2 daughters, between the benches of individuals absorbed in books. The girls have matching red dresses and white bows in their hair and pick dandelions, linking them into garlands. From Rossi's pavilion comes the tinkle of a xylophone, quavering soap bubbles of Bach-ian sound drifting through the high branches. Having killed time beside a ring of forget-me-nots, I stand and walk to the Naval Museum.

Our appointments now are always outside, in public places, and always I am unsettled, convinced he won't come, but suddenly there he is, late, rushing towards me at an unexpected angle out of the matrix of the city, and every time he is not the person I have tried to maintain in my mind's eye but more lively, more rich in character, more than I've been expecting, and always I cannot believe it. There is something wild in his expression which is elemental, which arouses a kind of physical worrying in me, and when we meet there are 1 or 2 minutes of shyness as the faulty internal memory of him and the reality of him adjust and coalesce. I write scripts beforehand but in the event they are mostly useless because we are off in a fascinating new direction. Waiting, waiting . . . waiting is castrating . . . Russia is a labyrinth of waiting . . . . .

I'm waiting by the lime trees opposite the museum – he's running towards me, alone, almost ¾ of an hour late, and he runs straight past – what the fuck now? Nearby a man with a cylinder sells balloons. Dima buys one, returns inhaling the helium, and says in a squeaky parrot voice 'Hullo, Dooncan, how are you, hullo, Dooncan, how are you?' Helium does that – I didn't know.

'Stop it, stop it.'

'You understand?'

'Yes, but stop,' I say, rubbing the side of his head.

He insists on buying the museum tickets. I say nothing about his mafia problem and he doesn't refer to it but it's there – I can smell a nervous sweat on him – and will have to be dealt with. I feel a bit drunk actually.

The museum contains, for some reason, a model of Lenin's armoured car – carved from the tusk of a Siberian mammoth. The real armoured car used to be outside the Marble Palace but has been transferred to the Artillery Museum. Nazi exhibits – again, why in a naval museum? – include a piece of human skin and a bar of human soap from the concentration camp of Maydanek in Poland, and the tour ends with portions and models of nuclear submarines.

Dima says 'The brother of a friend of mine had to go to Chernobyl. The Government needed volunteers to clean up and do 10 minutes each person, so they went round saying you, you, you, you will go and do your 10 minutes and if you refuse you will go to prison for 3 years – and still have to do your 10 minutes. When my friend's brother came back from this task he heard that to drink mineral water helps to clear radiation out of the body and so he drink 5 litres of mineral water every day, drink, drink, drink. He lost all his hair and teeth. But he continued to drink, drink, hoping to clean his body. Then he died.'

Coming out and screwing up eyes in a superfluity of sunshine, I ask 'Is Valentina safe now?'

'Yes.'

'She's back?'

'Yes.'

'But she didn't want to come to the Circus?'

'She go to another place. We visit the Black Sea in 3 days.'

'How long is the train journey to the Black Sea?'

'One and a half days – but we fly.'

'You fly?'

'Yes.' So there's money for air tickets.

'And the grandmother?'

'OK. Good.'

Lack of words can make one's conversations very direct – can speed communication. And can hinder it – when everything is only good or bad, one's curiosity is largely unsatisfied. In fact Dima can converse much more fully when he's at ease – on this subject though he is blocked. I can't get more out of him at this stage.

A young man in a blue tracksuit is vomiting over the embankment into the Neva. You can see the streak of it down the granite face but it's a 'clean' stain – booze puke. His head is hung over the parapet, arms crossed beneath his chest, and as we pass him he is motionless, having passed out in this position. Dima takes my arm. We run across the road and sit in the Triangle for a while, making circumspect conversation.

'I hear you are taught Lenin was not so bad and Stalin was very bad.'

'Yes. But Stalin was a good economist,' he replies. 'If he wanted to kill 12 men he stood them one in front of the other and used 1 bullet. He was not Russian. He was Georgian.'

– Stalin, whose wife committed suicide – Stalin, who disowned his own

son when the Germans captured him during the War, who refused a
German offer of exchange, effectively condemning the son to death –
Peter the Great killed his own son – Ivan the Terrible killed his own son –
all 3 men slaughtered their subjects on a fantastic scale, especially Stalin.
These are not human acts. Only the gods of mythology act thus.

'Stalin had a young voice,' continues Dima, 'and spoke a little bit fast
without papers. But relaxed. Not Hitler style. Gorbachev's Russian was
full of mistakes. Yeltsin's Russian much better. Gorbachev couldn't say
'g' – he used the Ukrainian 'h'. Lenin liked to do the Russian 'r' like this –
rrrrrrrr. Brezhnev made a click noise with tongue when he talk and his
voice was deep, terrible, and he always read his speech. There is a joke.
Someone knocks at Brezhnev's door and Brezhnev pulls out a piece of
paper and reads 'Who's there?' There are many jokes about Brezhnev
because people were afraid of him.'

'You are a good actor. You do the voices well.'

'All Russians good actor.'

'The English too.'

But I can't let it rest and add 'So the mafia problem is finished?'

'Yes. No problem now.'

'You found the money?'

'Little here, little there, borrow from friends.'

'I think it was a mad story.'

He stares at me, biting his lower lip nervously. 'No mad, no mad' he
says.

One thing is sure – my refusal of his request for dollars has not caused
him to think less of me. It's as if he tried, failed, found the solution to his
problem elsewhere, end of matter. I attempt to explain my financial
situation to him, to exonerate myself in the event of there having been a
legitimate crisis. But he has disengaged, his anxiety evaporated. He
seemed to have been in a state for *some* reason. Shall I ever discover what it
was really all about? We are late for the Circus and take a taxi.

'Can I sit in front?' he asks.

'No. Sit beside me.'

'How much is Levi jacket in England? How much cigarettes?'

'Gawd.'

'Tell me. I am interested. Tell me about England.'

'Why don't you become a business man and help a poor writer?'

He laughs, innocent as albumen, saying 'I think you have very interesting life.' And quite abruptly he is away from me, not looking at anything, distracted, focusing if at all on a point in mid-air.

The Circus, still in its permanent tsarist building in Belinsky Square, is not outstanding , but fleas are not a problem either. Jugglers, dressed like the figure of Harlequin upstairs at the Yelagin Palace, drop things. A clown plays spoons and balalaika. The star of the trampoline troupe must be drunk – this is the last performance of the season and perhaps they've been slapping necks – because he keeps on happily missing catches, blithely crashing onto the padded border, reeling and falling and landing horribly askew. His colleagues are white with fear and the audience thrilled he'll break his neck but by a miracle of soppiness he doesn't.

During the interval we go for a pee and Dima drinks tap water matter-of-factly from the wash-basin, then pretends to croak his last, clutching frantically at the wall. 'Tsh, look, stupid me,' he frowns, showing with distaste a black smear he's caused across his freshly washed pale blue jeans. Very gently he touches my bare arm – 'You like ice-cream?' I look at him. I want to see him completely naked.

The ice-cream comes in a roll of greaseproof paper and I say 'Russian ice-cream very good. Your tooth is OK?'

'Yes. Tooth good now.'

'Everything is good now suddenly. You *look* good. But you always look good.' He beams and makes a skip as we walk round the curve of the gallery corridor. 'But are *you* good? That's the question.'

'Oh yes, best boy!' he laughs, digging me playfully in the ribs and shying away.

'Not always.' There are a million questions to ask about his life but I hold back and merely enquire 'What is kvass?'

'It was on sale on every street corner but this year you don't see it anywhere' (with the help of the pocket dictionary, the drink is decoded: a beverage made from fermented bread).

Second half. A fire-eater lies on a bed of nails and walks over broken glass, great bursts of flame issuing from his mouth. Plumed horses dance in the ring. A contortionist languidly ties and unties her limbs. The last act is a troupe of elephants – *Entry of the Gladiators* from the band and in they somnambulate. One of the elephants however is wide awake and angry and refuses to clamber onto its pedestal. From a primordial soul furious trumpetings shake the big top, reducing us to an agog silence – it's a different game now and we are chastened and absorbed by the power of its elephantine resentment. The trainer cracks his whip and the rebellious beast, offended by this impudence, rocks from side to side, cogitating upon the possibilities. Seeming to decide on anything-for-a-quiet-life, it tentatively raises a half-ton foot and places it with refinement on the small round perch, then does so with another foot, and shuffles forward its hind-quarters to complete the operation. But all at once this quaking heap is riven by an upsurge of behemoth energy and wilfulness, abandons all truck with gentility, emits fearsome trumpetings, retreats, pounds the floor of the ring, and finding no obvious exit, rotates in a dementia of indecision. Trunk and tail swing out symmetrically. The trainer recoils to avoid being slugged by the trunk and his professional smile drops off. Quickly he picks it up and slaps it back on again but carelessly, at a funny angle, so that one is no longer convinced by it. Though anxious, he does not lose his nerve, talks to the beast, cracks the whip, while the rest of the team, docile and hidebound, look on, faintly conscious of their own ridiculousness. The psychological battle rages for maybe 5 minutes, the trainer berating and cajoling, the elephant magnificently perverse. Except possibly for those sitting nearby, we all long for it to stampede the crowd and cause mayhem and at one point it looks as though it will oblige in an explosion of courage. The trainer wobbles but then hardens, stands firm and applies a superior determination to which, with an awesome series of trumpeting protests, the beast finally succumbs. The centre has held. This time.

Grand finale of all the acts – only the star trampolinist is absent, presumably suffering from concussion.

'I must go home,' says Dima. 'Telephone me to-morrow. I have free time to-morrow.' I give him a hug.

I do ring him to-morrow. Several times. But there's no one there. He's driving me crazy! Is he playing games or just absent-minded? Why don't I trade him in for a reliable model? There must be thousands of bright young people here who'd be very willing to help a wonderful person like me through the hoops of living in Russia. How did I get stuck with this one? . . . Because he has succeeded in arousing a great tenderness in me.

Boris turns up at lunchtime with a girl, the first person I've ever seen him bring to the flat. They drink champanskoye and coloured syrups in the Big Room to the thudding of early Stones – *Ahma kying beeya bayber buzzinarahnd yer hyerv*. I jump into a taxi and say 'Dostoievsky Street.'

These banya buildings are very large, 4 or 5 floors, each floor a warren of chambers large and small, wet and dry, used and unused – you may open a buckled, ill-fitting door into a room of nothing or into a corroded corridor or an oubliette with plastic chairs or a howl of heat or a cupboard full of twisted metal.

What's this slow bundle of rags coming up the stairs? Better let it pass. God knows what sex it is. It passes with a low hissing sound.

The General floor costs 12 roubles and the attendant, whose portable radio is playing music by Sting, hands over a large folded cotton sheet. Clothes are fed into a locker with no lock in a flaky blue-painted changing-room with benches where naked men read damp newspapers, drink beer, do nothing, chat, dress or undress – the vest (singlet) is a standard item in the Russian male wardrobe – and they take not the slightest interest in me. All this differs from the Lux floor in being larger, shabbier, more populous.

The shower room is immense, the true heart of the establishment. Lines of showers recede into the distance, divided by grey cement partitions, and dozens and dozens of males of assorted shapes, sizes, ages and racial types, are drawing down a diluvian gush and sending up an infernal steam from various places within it. They wash with great diligence and the washing alone can take up to an hour, each occupant carrying a small plastic bag in which he preserves the necessary accoutrements. A tattooed bodybuilder with busted lip moves like a diplodocus in the swamps and jets of splashing water. He has scars on the inside of his forearms and they have stretched as the muscles burgeoned beneath – an attempt at suicide from his earlier incarnation as a neurotically introspective weakling. A mafia-type has a number tattooed on his flank about 6 inches below the armpit – prison. Boys of 5 or 6 trot after their fathers. Men wash each other's backs. Teenagers compete in the heat, then dash yelling to the plunge. Old men, varicosed, scarred, arthritic, gnarled and twisted like ancient olive trees, mop their mottled limbs with sodden rags – a few of them (and nobody else) wear peaked caps (to avert overheating of the brain). But many of these old codgers are remarkably agile and well-formed for their age. Totalitarianism is a very male creation. It makes men physically strong and serviceable while a man's social and psychological independence is, ideally, reduced to zero. The cult of physical prowess therefore thrived here because it was one of the few areas in which a male could demonstrate his maleness.

Back at the flat Zoia says 'You had telephone calls. That girl.' She means Natasha. 'And Arkady.' He works with Rodion on *Hotel* magazine and would like to go to Oxford University.

Zoia continues 'I want to give you something.'

'What?'

'Sit in that chair.'

She goes out and comes back in with a towel which she wraps round me like a bib, tilting back the head. She goes out again and comes back a minute later carefully carrying a horizontal tablespoon.

'What are you doing?'

'Don't speak.'

There follows 15 minutes of kife. Bliss. She has warmed olive oil in the tablespoon and proceeds to massage it into my face. The blandishments of her powerful fingers, drawn up and outwards in firm sensual strokes, are irresistible.

'Zoia, this is amazing.'

She raps me on the head with a knuckle. 'Don't speak.'

'But it is.'

'Sh.'

'Now splash face with hot water and make dry like this.' She pats her face lightly.

Massage has become the sublime release here. I now have 3 full body massages a week – 2 with Pavel (fast & vigorous) and 1 with Kirill (slow & dreamy) but in case Pavel is offended by Kirill's intrusion onto his patch, Kirill does me at his family home in a towerblock to the north of the city. But neither of them has ever administered anything as sensational as this to my face. On television a pop girl is going through her gyrations.

'You like that one?' asks Zoia, still attempting to determine my sexuality.

'No,' I reply. Which somehow fails to resolve the issue for her.

She goes to a cupboard and hands me an object. 'This is Russian antique. For you.' It's a bar of chocolate. 'Russian chocolate was very good. Now even the chocolate factory has collapsed.' Something else drops from the cupboard which she quickly pushes under blankets – I think it was a gun. We share the chocolate. It tastes of powdery emptiness, a ghost from the past. I am about to give her a present too but the doorbell rings. Just when we are getting on so well – it's Lydia.

But I still bring forth my present, a large jar of Von's homemade Oxford marmalade which is probably the best marmalade anyone could have. Zoia takes a spoon and tries it: 'Mmm. Good.' Lydia does likewise – she savours at length, turning down the corners of her mouth, and finally says with a nasty curl in her tone 'I make marmalade too. Mine is better.'

The fucking cow!

I could kill her. She wouldn't pay a compliment to save her life. You cannot call this stringy belligerent carcass a sad character – she's too cold for that. But pitiful, yes. Zoia told me Lydia had a lover (how do you make love to a razor blade?) 12 years ago. The man was married but called regularly and always brought presents. One day he arrived without a gift and Lydia told him that, since he didn't respect her enough to bring a present, he should visit his wife instead. The man never contacted her again. One may've thought the recent economic ordeals, especially hard on the professional classes, had been the paramount cause of Lydia's implacable vileness, but this story suggests she was always a thorough-going bitch.

'Do you fear civil war, Lydia?'

'It will come. Let's get on with it. Let's get it over.'

'But you are fighting the last civil war. The next would be the world's first nuclear civil war.'

'I am sorry to disappoint you. It will not be so dramatic. But listen – Russia needs great strength at its heart or it is nothing. Out of the conflagration is born a new rigour, a restored destiny. Russia is a leviathan, the people its food – it can give much only when it demands much.'

The blood-red fascist light glows in her eyes.

'How much food does it need? I mean, will it want to eat me as well as you?'

'You make joke but – '

'No joke!'

'Listen! I cannot walk at night in my own city now for fear of attack! Is this the way to organise a society? Is this what freedom is?' Her mouth fastens furiously onto her cigarette and she sends up a pillar of smoke.

'You mean you prefer violence to be a state monopoly, as under Communism?'

'Of course! Doesn't everybody? Your precious human rights! Do you not realise that the criminals are intent on creating a system of ruthless control unequalled in our country since Stalin? I cannot believe how stupid you are! Your hostess will tell you – '

'It's not "hostess". It's "landlady".'

'Host. Hostess. You don't even know your own language!' She speaks to Zoia, switching into Russian with a metallic laugh, cutting me out with a sneer. The one who has the last sentence always wins, no matter what has been said before, and she knows it – her switch into Russian finishes me like a squashed fly.

'Oh fuck off,' I mutter and leave the room. Why am I so angry with her? It's her manners as much as anything else. But she's never sworn at me.

Next day I try Dima again. No reply. They must have left several days early for the Black Sea. Endlessly mercurial Funky Dmitri. It's all so impossible. Since Russian life is currently so fragmented, I have of my association with him only some pieces. I am trying to compose them into a picture but cannot. Therefore the association retains its mystery: an allure of luminous pieces. My eyes are as awake as 2 cut diamonds. *The Collected Poems* of T. S. Eliot are open on the bed but Eliot doesn't speak to me – I am not in the mood for wrought-iron vicarage gates.

Behind Dima's wide-apart eyes are spaces limitless and unfocused. Across these tracts moves his soul in its varying conditions: wholly apparent – wholly transparent – wholly invisible. I hear a voice calling to me from inside him but he does not hear it.

In his eyes, his attention dissolves and recrystallises and shifts away and dissolves and comes close and dissolves and recrystallises in uneven spasms of elation, despair, sweetness, devilry, fun, nervousness, love, generosity, greed, self-assertion, quandary and indifference. With every delight he delivers a headache, with every revelation a question, with every pain a ludicrous or touching compensation. Enough. It is time to . . . realise.

REALITY

CHAPTER SEVEN

At first, with Dima and Valentina on the Black Sea, all purpose is sucked out of the city, the air drained of light, the stones of significance. But then I begin to breathe more easily, as though a paralysing spell has been lifted. Torn free! (However, they will return sooner than I expect.)

On a hot day Natasha accompanies Alexander Dityatin and myself to the Dynamo Summer Camp. AD asks 'Have you remembered the mosquito stuff?' I have – and also mention the existence of mosquito nets. An English film-maker called Sian has one in her flat on the Moika, the only net I've seen in Petersburg. But despite his mosquito phobia, this new concept does not interest AD – indeed his lack of practicality on the matter is striking. He says 'Since the economic crisis, the basements of St Petersburg buildings have become wetter and wetter – many are permanently flooded – so there are more mosquitoes than before.'

We hit the forests and lakes – it's a 1½ hour drive into the countryside – and Natasha hands out chocolate biscuits. Were it for its forests alone, I should love this Russia. As Auden said 'A culture is no better than its woods.' How much wood and forest is left for an Englishman to enjoy in his homeland? Almost nothing – and what little remains they begrudge, they wish to flatten.

The camp is in a salubrious sylvan setting: brightly painted wooden cabins among an infinity of pine verticals. The air is cool, fresh and exquisitely scented. Even in the heat of this summer, the woods retain their moisture – the dryad's undryable eyes.

We walk to the gymnasium and soon Oleg and his classmates troop in with their coach who says 'Excuse them if they are a bit floppy. They have just come out of the sauna.'

It is difficult to believe that these young athletes are 14 to 17 years old. One of the 17-year-olds looks 9.

'They are chosen for being physically retarded,' explains the coach. 'Children of tall or heavily built parents are not selected.'

I address the semi-circle: 'What is bad about life in Russia?'

'Not enough food!' they chorus.

AD interjects 'They are using huge amounts of energy. They eat about 3 times the adult amount.'

'What is good about life in Russia?'

'Closeness of the people,' answers the 17-year-old who looks 9. He is cheeky and grown-up, his appearance deceptive, and he asks me 'Why do you like gymnastics?'

'Because it's so beautiful.'

They are pleased with this reply and start to throw themselves around the gymnasium as though gravity has no claim on them. In the austere perfection and command of his physique, the gymnast is the ultimate dandy. But he is more – he gives – he is the dandy in action. He is a magician of the body, a yogic youth, a sculptor of physical energy. He stretches and contracts time. He flies. And he is miraculous because incapable of deceit. But he is more – he competes – he participates – he is dramatic. He is explosive – yet concentrated. He is wild, elemental, and cannot be captured, his genius being in movement, but he is not capricious – he is a dictator not worshipper of himself. He takes nature but goes beyond nature, so that his achievement is finally in defiance of nature, in defiance of physics – in this his freedom lies. He knows the secret which fuses total abandon and total control into a higher functioning unity. Gymnastics is our physical violence in a state of grace. It is the body at the extreme of possibility. And in sport – as in art – only extremism counts.

Back in St Petersburg I apologise for being unable to invite Natasha up to the flat but she has no inclination to come anyway. Rising in the lift my nose begins to run which is unusual on a warm dry day. It drips. Then I see that the drips are of blood. Another nosebleed so soon – that's unusual too. Blood has splashed down the side of the lift cabin – everyone will imagine a dire deed has taken place. I pause on the landing until it stops which it quickly does.

The flat is filled with a loud vibrating noise and the first thing to be seen is Zoia's bottom. She is bending over in skimpy top and panties sorting washing in front of the noisy washing-machine and cannot hear the intruder approaching from behind. I drum on her back with my fingers. She snaps upright, chubby creamy dimpled thighs aquiver: speechless, scarlet, victim of a double shock: the surprise itself and the embarrassment of undress.

'I'll put the kettle on tra-la,' say I, leaving her to sort herself out. Minutes later Boris arrives home with a huge chunk of halva like tree bark and the 3 of us take tea in the Big Room. Zoia has concealed herself within pink dungarees and keeps on pushing at the hair at her temples, trying to appear normal, but her lingering consternation is delicious to me. I must dream up something else awful-but-not-really.

Boris browses among his collection of curios and passes across a trove of space memorabilia – medals, postage stamps, cards, ornate and colourful, manufactured to a high standard – and there is the astral smile of Yuri Gagarin, First Man in Space, April 12th 1961, star and sweet hero of my boyhood.

'This was the golden age . . .' says Zoia wistfully.

Yes, it was. And never to be recaptured. The wreckage of the egalitarian attempt is all around us. Communism was not of course based only on force. Russians traditionally love not so much the equality which gives rise to equality of opportunity as that equality which allows the merging of personalities. But they oscillate between loss of self in the group and a brooding sense of isolation and loneliness (Shostakovitch's symphonies alternate emphatically in this way). So the most painful aspect of Communism for ordinary Russians was that they could no longer say what they felt. Because of the necessity of silence, and because also the sudden separation of people who were emotionally attached became commonplace, Communism increased Russian telepathy. Not only in space but also in time: to wait for someone for 10 years was not unusual.

But when first thinking of Communism I do not think, I picture: Blyumkin is haphazardly drawing names from lists in front of him, filling in a stack of blank death warrants supplied already signed by Dzerzhinsky (founder of the KGB, after whom Dima's college is named – when will they change that?): given that the shortage of everything included a shortage of guilty people, random arrests were required to fulfil the arrest quotas issued by Lenin's administration. Russia, consumed by self-hate, could not stop arresting itself, wave after wave of arrests, tortures, executions, exiles. I laugh – in astonishment – having just 'got' VV's joke about the dog howling because it's standing on its own balls.

Russia has the most cruel history of any country in the world, and this city has suffered as no other in the 20th century – the Great War, the Revolution, the Civil War, the Red Terror, the Purges, the Siege, more

Purges, the Gulag, millions of souls lost, it's always in millions. This lends an awful grandeur, a terribilità to the atmosphere. Tragedy has deepened and elevated Russian literature but in the 20th century, in the course of which the tragedy and comedy of Russian life were increasingly transmuted into terror and absurdity, it became a crushing limitation for the Russian writer who, unless he capitulated to dishonesty or mere whimsy, found himself enfeoffed to 'the ghastliness of the situation'.

Let us take an example – nothing heavy from concentration camp memories but simply a banal quotidian fact: the Soviet Dental Service supplied false teeth of stainless steel. This is terrifying and absurd, surreal and true. Any literature deriving from a world of such facts can never escape nightmare.

After its hysteria of sado-masochism, Russia developed multiple sclerosis. Golden-age Yuri Gagarin rocketed out of the belly of a doomed giant who would soon be in a wheelchair. What is more, Communism minus Terror equals Tedium. Literature was left with tedium and absurdity, both by definition meaningless. The bosses tried to bring back terror. But they were stabbing in the dark. The system seized up altogether. Then it caved in . . . . The entire panoply of totalitarian shibboleths lie about like potsherds in the sand. A slogan which maybe has survived on a wall has lost all firepower, is as quaint as a rusted arquebus. And all this happened, as it were, overnight – in Russia things happen very quickly, or very slowly, or not at all. But 'menace' comes into the present from the future. So about Communism, shorn of its terrors, it is possible for the Russians to be nostalgic. But listen to Communism's greatest music – that of Shostakovitch. This will not make you nostalgic exactly. In this endures the authentic creak of terror and anguish.

Rachmaninov's Third Symphony (1935) would seem to be the last great work in the pure line of the Romantic Movement in the arts – and was written in Switzerland. Meanwhile back in Russia the emotional splendour of Tchaikovsky and Rachmaninov had transformed first into the violence of Stravinsky – who also fled abroad – then into the inventive distortions of Prokofiev, and lastly into Shostakovitch's mighty lament-into-mystery. Shostakovitch's most serious works are not without passages of brilliance and speed, but it is an animation which is danger, or tricksy mischief of life, or panic. The macabre elegance of the Ninth Symphony (suggestive of Tchaikovsky in a curved mirror on Mars) is no exception. Shostakovitch has much of Slav *force* and martial power too. But always the disquieting mysteries prevail, the slow revolutions of inhospitable galaxies, vast caverns of lusciously bleak introspection, neurotic and dismayed by turns. Peace of mind he never knows, until in the Fourteenth Symphony he begins to enter a kind of courtly abstraction. It is a song-cycle. Shostakovitch could not find what he needed in the permitted Russian poetry – which was too bound to society, too earthbound – so he used poems by Lorca, Rilke and Apollinaire: an icy death poetry. The work is of a bleakness so extreme that it attains to a kind of companionable warmth through its certainty of comfortlessness.

Shostakovitch wrote the great tragic oeuvre of 20th-century music – and the most frightening body of work in all music. Both victim and conqueror, he is unshrinking, as compassionate and full of wonder as the night. But finally in the Fifteenth Symphony, he goes beyond all this into the strangest dimension of play, dance and reflection. Surely here at last is an eccentric, aristocratic peace-of-mind. In such a scheme the mysterious cosmic joke is higher than tragedy. We are beyond death. But it can be reached only through tragedy. Any other route is an insult to what people have to undergo in this life.

After Shostakovitch, music in Russia – like literature, like indeed everything else there – had nowhere to go and could only request another world.

'And this is for you,' says Boris, handing me a tape of Russian songs. 'Michael Shufutinski – country songs. Villi Tokarev – prison songs. Viktor Zoi – very good singer – dead – car crash – 28 years old. Igor Talkov – also very good singer but – '

'Car crash?'

'Murder. A political murder.'

'No, no, no!' interjects Zoia passionately. 'It was a jealous woman, a lover.'

'Nonsense, Mama.'

'Yes, yes, yes, I know!'

They row in Russian, sometimes pausing to give me a quick reassuring smile before battling on again. Boris eventually throws up his arms and retreats to the kitchen to prepare his dinner.

When he's out of the room Zoia says in a low voice 'A Serbian girl is coming to stay here next week. Is that all right with you?'

'Yes.' But I worry that I'm to be thrown out of my room. 'Where will she sleep?'

'Here. In my bed.'

'But where will you sleep?'

'There. On the sofa.'

'And where will Boris sleep?'

'Poosh! Out!' She makes an expressive movement with her whole body as though slinging water out of a pail. 'He must stay with his father for 3 weeks.'

So the prison is opening its doors . . .

Rodion says 'I have to meet 2 prostitutes and make sexy photographs in a falling down building. Do you want to come?'

We take a tram and alight at Vladimirskaya Prospekt and walk towards the tube station, passing a black hole in the wall at pavement level from which blare the Beatles: *Take a goo-ood look around you!*

Outside the station Rodion's assistant, Arkady, raises an arm of recognition. He is standing beside a gypsy girl of about 20 years old. She has a slightly bruised appearance, long loose curly black hair, a very fine sulky face periodically emblazoned by a wholesome smile, and is wearing a black and red tube dress which is contracting, riding down the breasts, riding up the thighs. She keeps tugging the top up and the bottom down to prevent it shrinking to a narrow band round her waist. She greets us formally and is very well-mannered but tosses her hair rapidly from left to right to left to right to left, searching the street.

'Her friend has not come yet,' says Arkady, blushing and trying to flatten his spiky hair with his hand (but it always springs back up).

I hand round bananas which we munch before proceeding along the road minus Girl 2. Arkady has located a flosculous art nouveau block of flats previously squatted by painters then drug addicts, now empty and half-demolished inside but façades and several wings still intact. The courtyard is filled with dunes of brick and rubble, on one of which perches an orange bulldozer. We pick our way carefully along a trembling corridor, crunch over glass, dodge falling plaster, avoiding rooms to the right where precipices jut raggedly into mid-air, and arrive at several large light derelict rooms painted white, with expressionist black swathes, by its long-gone artist tenant. Warm sunlight falls across the rooms in shafts.

While Rodion examines these spaces from various angles, going 'ah' and 'um', I peel wallpaper, stripping it back in one particular corner, back through the harsh tangerine geometry of the 60s, back through the sombre geometry of the grey & blue 50s, back through the overlay of wartime newspapers in the Siege 40s, back through the thick red, green and brown paint of the savage dictatorial 30s and the manic revolutionary 20s, and back to the original purple & gold pre-revolutionary wallpaper – and, still peeling, to the primal insulating underlay of Tsarist newspapers. Apart from ourselves the whole site is silent, abandoned by workmen for the week-end – or maybe forever.

There is a distant cry of triumph from Arkady. He has chanced upon an interior wall exquisitely patterned with ravaged pink paint and vivid green mildew. Rodion speaks to the girl and against this backdrop she staggers onto a pile of split planks and broken bricks and starts to work, while Rodion, froglike, hops around clicking with his camera. The girl's battered high-heels make her position precarious and this tottering uncertainty is reflected in her face with appealing results – many different expressions of vulnerability move across it. At the same time she slowly peels down the clingy tube to expose her breasts. These large firm golden breasts sway or tremble or tighten as she does various things with her arms in order to maintain balance. There is a growing excitement in Rodion's hops; the camera clicks faster and faster. Now she begins to roll the dress up from the bottom and the 2 rolls meet in a lifebuoy round her middle. This is eased down over hips and legs, slowly, shot by shot, and kicked away into a cobwebby corner. She hovers there dressed only in a lick of white knicker and high heels, throwing back the hair, striped by sunlight, and looks at Rodion, wondering what to do next. He is still hopping and clicking, so she shrugs her shoulders and throws me a smile framed in red lipstick. Eventually Rodion gives her the cue and the panties start to come down, and his hopping and clicking grow frantic as he immortalises the stages of the final revelation. He halts the panties at mid-thigh. The film runs out. A Slavonic curse is uttered.

'You should send some of these pictures to *The Spectator*.'

'Do they publish photographs?' he asks.

'They do at Christmas.'

There are a couple of recent bruises and some small scars on the girl's

legs. Also a tattooed number on the hip at panty level. Prison. He winds
in a new film, the panties come off and there she is naked, reborn out of
her clothes like a baby, wobbling in heels on a pile of rubbish, tossing her
hair without embarrassment, without the coy nudge-nudge, nothing
lewd or artificial, entirely natural, innocent, and amused. Then Rodion
borrows my last banana. And so an hour passes.

At the end of it, Rodion packs up with a miserable expression.

'What's the matter?'

'She did not connect with the camera. In erotic photos you must be
exaggerated.'

He wanted the coy nudge-nudge. Arkady pats his own head.

The Palace Is Ablaze With Light. After breakfast Zoia summons me into
the Big Room and says 'We exercise.' I say 'Not on a stomach full of
porridge' and she says 'Very good to exercise with full stomach – work it
through – stop it sitting there.' So we stretch and twist and swim on the
floor until Leonid turns up with my double boat ticket to Vallam Island at
the top of Lake Ladago – it's dated after Dima returns from the Black Sea
so with any luck he'll be able to come too.

'How is Serafima?'

'She is going to the Black Sea for holiday,' he replies, mopping his
overheated brow.

'Does everyone go to the Black Sea in the summer?'

'If they can. Not so many as before. Russians dream of the South – but I
don't. The Crimea was visited by Ovid in exile – Pushkin and
Mandelstam were exiled there too.'

(Russians have a dream of the West, as Westerners dream of the East,
and all of us dream of the South, and in the South they dream of the
North . . .) (and Russia itself is where North becomes South and vice-
versa and East becomes West and vice-versa.)

Ring Katya who says 'You can come over if you come over *now*.' In the
streets a-shimmer with heat haze a sound is missing – the rumble of
the dented trams which gives Petersburg the soundtrack of a film from
the 1930s. There is a bus and tram strike to-day.

At Katya's her boyfriend shows me his tattoos, Divine on the left forearm and Sid Vicious on the right, and Katya says 'Sian invites you to the Magic Theatre to-night. Will you go to the Pop-Mechanika concert? It's going to be in that square opposite Sadko's.'

'Will it be any good?' asks a boy with black ringlets sitting in the window. He is Welsh, called Hugh, and gives English lessons, but his main objective here is to acquire an old photograph of Nicholas II – no luck so far.

'2 men said they could help me and we went to meet a third man in a park but he didn't turn up. Isn't that awful?'

'Awful. How are the English lessons?'

'OK. The one yesterday turned up for her lesson 2 hours late. But it was all right because I was 2 hours late getting up.'

'What's the Magic Theatre?'

'Dunno,' replies Katya. 'I asked Sian but she wouldn't tell me. I'm not going. I'm going somewhere else.'

On the way home I pop into the Hermitage – I quite often do – but remain downstairs, and stand still in the cool grey stone and marble halls of the Collection of Antiquities, shedding therms. Upstairs, where the picture galleries are, the palace is ablaze with heat, light and colour – on a day like this the last thing you want is to be in a furnace of genius oil paintings.

Not everyone knows that the Hermitage is a chain of linked buildings of which the Winter Palace, though by far the largest, is only one. The smaller buildings make a kind of sense but the Winter Palace itself, though uniformly rococo without (its fronts are painted aquamarine but before the Revolution the exterior was red), is spectacularly incoherent within. Indeed the whole linkage is a centreless constellation of corridors, landings, staircases, rooms great and small, in disparate styles of sumptuous, sometimes mind-boggling embellishment, with no aggregate effect except that of disorientation among copious treasure and untold marvels: it is for getting lost in.

One of the most breathtaking interiors I couldn't locate the entrance to, or identify on the floor plan, and only discovered it by crossing a gallery at one end – a powderblue and white plaster hall with clustered pillars and 4 white petalled domes like the 1,000-petalled lotuses of Brahma, Strawberry Hill meets the Arabian Nights, yet so light-hearted and unstrenuously itself. Absolutely enormous too, but – I couldn't find it again . . . The main staircase in the New Hermitage is another elusive masterpiece, neo-classical but very modern in feel, the steps rising between plain cliffs of polished stone to a pillared gallery. The effect is both grim and theatrical – one does expect votaries to perform blood sacrifice at the top (as indeed they *have* done) . . . The roof garden of lilac trees in the Small Hermitage is shocking in its modesty scale . . . and on the top floor during my first visit I was amazed to see one of Ker Xavier Roussel's finest pictures, done 1911-13 – terracotta dancers with cymbals and fruit on a fertile but sunbaked hillside rising against a sky of the bluest blues flecked with cloud. This picture possesses a particular kind of exoticism, one which displaces you outside *time* (Pasolini achieved something similar in *Medea*) . . .

Through this galaxy of worlds called the Hermitage shuffle parties with guides in diverse tongues, and curious tales may be overheard . . . In Tsarist days the doors of the Malachite Room were guarded by huge negroes, Coptic Ethiopians. Pushkin's great-grandfather was the Ethiopian favourite of Peter the Great, who had been presented to the Tsar by the Sultan via Count Tolstoy, Russian ambassador to the Sublime Porte. Peter loved his Ethiopian, granted him many privileges, and used his belly as a pillow . . .

Standing beside a blue and gold wall, a 60-year-old American male says to a 30-year-old Russian female guide 'I want to see what is most famous in the museum.'

'What?'

'Most famous. Just take me to the most *famous* things.'

'But so much is famous.'

'Yes, but I want to see the *most* famous.'

'What type of famous?'

'Er, any type, but the *most* famous, do you understand?'

'Matisse, Fabergé?'

'Perfume?'

'Not perfume. Famous. Leonardo da Vinci?'

'Yes, the Mona Lisa. I want to see the Mona Lisa.'

The Magic Theatre is off Moskovsky Prospekt in the Stalinist-styled south of the city. On the way we pass a steaming hill of blackish muck with people crawling over it – further out there is a steaming mountain apparently. It's a very sticky evening.

A dozen of us sit on benches in a dimly lit grotto capable of seating 20. Eerie electronic music writhes in the air. Shadowy automata come creepily alive. Goblins emerge from baroque towers. Acrobatic dolls dance in gothic castles. Lights flash, bells chime, snatches of folk melody drift in swirling sheets of sound. All that prostrate detritus which is for sale on street pavements – much of it has ended up here, organised into lunatic co-ordinations of post-industrial fairytale. It is not open to the public in the customary way. You ring up and order a performance.

The enterprise is the work of a Jewish family and since they are friends of Sian we are invited to dinner afterwards which takes place at a table filling the back room almost to the walls. There seems something special about it – the men wear those round caps, there is only candle-light, and the food is laid out in banquet profusion. They explain it is always so for them on Friday, Sabbath Eve: vodka, meat balls, red caviar, cucumber and tomato salad, vodka, rice, compote of plums, cakes, tea, and vodka. I am jammed between a husky-voiced woman addressing me with great emphasis but who speaks no English, and a bald man called Alexander who does.

'She say you must drink your vodka more quickly.'

I knock it back and say 'Did you know that the national head-dress of Albania is the white fez?'

'I think I knew it,' replies Alexander. 'Albania is even worse mess than Russia – total sovok.'

'But there's much less of it, so . . . Do you think I could have some more vodka?'

The woman huskifies approvingly.

'Have you heard about shadow economics?' asks Alexander.

It is suffocatingly hot – the vodka, meeting little resistance in such heat, drowns the brain – and someone has the idea of opening the windows. A succulent aroma floats in from the overgrown garden and almost at once a major thunderstorm strikes up, adding to the gaiety.

'Shadow economics is the popular name of what happens when the Communist world tries to become Capitalist. Shadow economics is people not paying taxes, taking money out of the country, getting bribes for contracts – this is the City of Bribes – and the shadow economy is much bigger than the black market.'

But enchanted by the steaming heat, the open windows, the dripping vegetation, the claps of thunder unfolding like hideous sonic flowers, I have returned in my mind to Vientiane 1975, at the moment when Laos fell very softly to the Communists, in a room at the Constellation Hotel, and later, at midnight, walking during a lull in the storm to the George & Dragon, an opium den, so named because it was run by George, a 22-year-old US army deserter, and his Laotian mistress who was in her 60s. To-night's smell of hot and soaking vegetation is identical. The light is identical – here electric summer night, there it was electric dawn. The sounds are identical – water smashing onto leaves, thunder overwhelming then draining out of conversation in waves. Alexander's voice rises into my attention as another roll of thunder fades but I've lost track of what he's saying and quietly interject 'I love the sound of the Russian language. Is it good for making jokes in?'

'That depends on who's talking,' he says. 'Russian is rich in synonyms which are useful for wordplay. There are not so many tenses however. There is no future perfect – this is a Western tense!'

'Also I am interviewing the Russians on love. But there's only one question: what for you is love?'

'Love for my children – and I love myself in them.'

The woman grasps my knee with her hand, huskifies, and pours me more vodka. I ask her the love question and she silently draws all her features into the centre of her face in a warm pouty expression and leaves it at that.

Leaning across to the man opposite – he's taciturn and poetic-looking – I say 'I'm interviewing the Russians on love.'

'I am not Russian.'

'Oh. What are you then?'

'I'm a Jew.'

'Oh.' It's a shock. 'Can't you be a Russian Jew? Like Al Jolson. And Irving Berlin. And the parents of George Gershwin.'

That screwy little thing directed at the floor, and prefaced by a nervous flash of the eyes, must be his smile.

'So – what for you is love?'

He inhales deeply, looks up at the ceiling, and says '. . . You do something for someone and it gives you pleasure. But you must receive something from the other too. Your question is better than the question they ask in the USA.'

'What's that?'

'Are you happy? For us it is a crazy question.'

'For me too.'

'Why for you?' he asks curtly, interested for the first time, as though to consider such a question crazy were a Russian prerogative – a Russian Jewish prerogative.

I stare out at the bouncing leaves onto which the rain continues to crash – and say 'Because I think it is crazy to make a fetish of happiness. Americans and mothers do this. But it's asking for trouble.'

'Why asking for trouble?' he pursues. His manner is at odds with the general conviviality.

Oh dear – the follow-through – all right, well, because happiness is only one element in life. Happiness comes and goes for all sorts of reasons – almost like a scent. You can't put it in a cage. To be happy all the time demands a kind of death. Endless happiness can come only at the end of a life.

'So what is life for you?' he harries, pouring a lot more vodka into my glass.

'Er, whoa, that's enough. Life is a . . . an . . .'

The Puppet Man, in reply to the question 'What for you is love?', says 'Sex! It's sex! I don't know what is love.'

And his wife Tania says 'I was very happy when I loved. But then you must pay for it. If you love all people, it is easier. To love one person is very painful.'

The question is put to a man called Kolya who is sardonic and emanates a quiet authority. He thinks before he answers. Nearly 2 minutes pass, everyone waiting in deferential silence, until he bursts out 'I never thought I would ever be asked this question and I haven't lived long enough or thoroughly enough to answer it.'

Madam Husky laughs like a drain.

(I got rather pissed and lost the piece of paper on which was written the remainder of the replies.)

I Am Ablaze With Light. On this night I fall asleep easily and deeply. Until 2.30 am when a ramshackle Boris appears in the bedroom doorway and murmurs 'Telephone'. Oh God, what's happening now? I take it from beside the bed. It's Natale in Palermo. I'm less upside-down than when Jill phoned that night. Nonetheless 2 worlds collide tensely in my breast as I struggle to come awake, to grapple out of St Petersburg and onto his wavelength – can't be done – I'm derailed –

'Natale, I can't explain how I feel. You sound so normal.'

'You are OK?'

'Yes. But you sound so far away. Everything is changing, boiling, and . . and I don't know what to say.'

'It's like you are inside a thermo-nuclear reaction.' He is a scientist but also a reader of souls.

'That's exactly it. You've got it immediately. It's so good to hear you.'

'I didn't hear anything from you. I was curious and worried.'

'It's very difficult phoning out. You can't just pick up the phone . . . I feel so strange talking to you but I want to talk.'

'Don't worry, it's OK. How is your finger?' He means the eczema.

'Oh, better now.'

'Really?'

'Yes, it went away.'

'Oh, good for you. Is the food all right?'

'Yes.'

After the call I drift with open eyes, listening to distant thunder while summer lightning flickers over my naked body.

Cannot return to sleep. I am burning and take a bit of tranquilliser but too late and awake at 11 in the morning, half slept, sweaty, all phlogiston gone. Whereupon my mother rings.

'You sound tired, dear.'

'This place is emotionally exhausting.'

'Will you stay the course?'

'Certainly.'

Arkady rings suggesting a rendezvous with him and his brother this afternoon – why not, they can wipe the dust from my eyes – and we arrange to meet outside the Moscow Station.

Zoia is leaving for the clinic and I apologise for last night's telephone disturbance. 'No, no, I understand, not problem,' she says, really not minding at all.

Men play chess under the trees of Ostroskova Square. Then a shock: is that Dima talking to someone over there? My body got there before the question in a horrible jolt of recognition – I walk towards the figure which melts into the crowd – surely it was a figment of that psychedelic heave of St Petersburg, of a 1,000 likelihoods popping and crawling in one's veins. Still, I'm shaken.

Arkady and his brother Timofey are standing outside the station, fresh as daisies, while I am wet with perspiration. They are twins; they have a psychomantic consanguinity; they both have hair which sticks up despite attempts to flatten it; they blush alternately like traffic lights; they both pronounce the 'th' as in 'thing' as 'f' which is quite common among Russians, but also the 'th' as in 'that' as 'v' which is less common; and sometimes they finish each other's sentences (watch out for unusual punctuation). But they are different too. Timofey is open and upright. Arkady has more inner turbulence – he always looks as though he's ashamed of something but-not-really – there's a twinkle in his eye about it.

'Sorry you couldn't come to the flat. My landlady doesn't like it.'

'Vat's not very Russian of her.'

'Some Russians agree with her.'

Arkady says 'Rodion said a very good walk, very Charles Dickens, is to follow ve railway track out of Moscow Station. But maybe it is – '

'Dangerous,' says Timofey.

'Let's go and see a Russian film,' I suggest.

'Vere are no Russian films now – all American films here.'

And the crappiest ones too. It's outrageous. How much more American junk does the world need? (Another thing – international companies like Benetton and Sony must use the Russian alphabet on the streets of Russia.) So we walk while thinking where we want to walk and the first stop of unusual interest is a Roman Catholic Church. There is a most dispiriting atmosphere inside, with ugly tight-faced priests in black clothes, and suddenly I recognise the prim chill of Poland. The place is largely run by and for Poles. It's not clear why Poland should be the most uptight country in Europe, perpetually trapped like a mammoth in ice. That it has been struggling against history for the past 300 years of course plays a large part but as significant surely is that Poland has the most priest-ridden society outside the Islamic world. Priests are fine – in their place. You can discuss mankind's metaphysical hunger with them. But a priesthood with power is bent on persecution, and perverts human zests and charms. Rise up, young Poles, and live! And God protect Russia from priests and other religious maniacs – it was Omar the Muslim who burned the library at Alexandria, and it was Justinian the Christian who closed the Academy at Athens.

(But unlike priests and their agents, it is not my business to take any man's religion away from him – unless of course he threatens me with it. In which case it is as reasonable as hoping to take a loaded gun away from a child.)

There is a further discomfort in this church – something irritating and untidy which I can't put my finger on – until the penny drops . . . It has pews. Pyoooooooooooooooze. How frightful pyooze are. Russian churches are pewless: everyone must stand or kneel: superior aesthetics.

When we step outside again it is as if Nature herself had acquired the priestly glower. Overhead is a mass of dark clouds tinged with greenish putrefaction. A wind hums. Individuals quicken their pace, trying to gain a destination before the waters break, but we are indecisive. Lightning flashes, the air cracks, large drops descend, hitting the pavement like transparent tomatoes. The populace scatters into doorways and under arches as the low hot sky sobs against the upturned face of the city and Petersburg goes entirely out of focus, becomes a rough sketch of itself. The broken surfaces of roads are lakes and streams all in splashing commotion, while the grain and speed of the rain make the buildings appear to ascend – but ascend not into the sky, rather to lift up into the depths of a waveless sea, into a possible future when the barrage has given way and palaces are submerged, when ornate rooms enclose giant blocks of silent water, when chandeliers are strung with green weed, and fishes with flicking tails cruise slowly up pillared staircases . . . . . I wonder what weather Dima's having on the Black Sea. I have heard that the Black Sea is the most unpolluted block of water in the whole of the Mediterranean system. No, no, that wasn't him I saw, was it?

10 minutes later it's over. The city refocuses its lineaments which have been given greater edge and clarity by the douche. We espy a porn cinema, its entrance on the far side of a muddy lagoon traversed by hastily improvised fruit boxes, and we retreat inside it to dry out.

The cinema is beautiful, with paired Doric pillars down either side, but the film is rubbish – a few muffs, no cocks, poorly simulated sex (all of which is still more than is permitted in London!), a French film with

Polish subtitles and Russian voice-over. We chuckle patronisingly and afterwards I invite them to the Baghdad Café if they know where it is. Arkady does. In Ulitsa Lavrova Petra. The café occupies a tiny basement with a jovial atmosphere. The ceiling is vaulted and painted all over with cochineal arabesques and in the corner a TV plays pop videos. You order at the counter and sit down.

'Plov and – '

'Plov finish,' says the Uzbeki woman, relaxed about the shoulders but her pencil is erect.

'Manti.'

'Manti finish.'

She indicates what remains – carrot salad, meat something, small loaves – and in addition we order beer and tea. The place is full but there is just space for us at a table taken by 2 American students.

'We come here a lot,' says one of the Americans. 'I like it coz it's colourful. Phew – it's like Communism painted the colours out of Russia coz traditionally Russia is very very colourful.'

'But there are amazing colours inside the people,' says the other American. This is a perceptive remark and I am immediately alert to him. He's called Greville Pinkerton VI. 'Call me Grev.'

'About colours inside – for example?'

'Well, listen, I'm involved here,' he murmurs conspiratorially.

'Oh, really?'

'She's 17,' he says.

What is it with this number? Keeps repeating. Reading the cassette notes to Rachmaninov's First Piano Concerto this morning – though first performed exactly 100 years ago, it was revised in 1917.

'And she's never had anyone before,' he adds.

The food arrives quickly, highly seasoned and excellent to taste. Arkady and Timofey engage the other student while I concentrate on Grev.

'Then she pissed off to the Crimea,' he observes ruefully.

'Really . . .' This is extraordinary.

'They still have a lot to learn about freedom of speech, freedom of action. It isn't easy with her. I have to push. She says no all the time.'

'Isn't that usual with virgins?'

'No, I mean even for just kisses and cuddles. But then she loves it.

Then she pisses off to the Crimea and only told me the day before, you know, like, by the way, I'm leaving to-morrow for 2 weeks. She's quite you know withdrawn.'

It seems Russians inure themselves early to disappointment – this helps them to minimise its pain. But it also means that they are often afraid of opportunities, or screw them up, or simply fail to see them.

'Is she more or less realistic than you?'

'Um . . . more realistic. Their idea of love is more linked to survival than ours. I mean, she's 17, I'm her first – we did it – I know why she went with me, I'm an American, I have money.'

'I think she sees more to you than that. Anyway money's OK so long as it isn't the be-all and end-all. It can be a catalyst. You need catalysts when people are from worlds so far apart.'

'Is that so? She teases me a lot. When I first came here I was amazed. We have this idea in the States of Russian women being heavy and ugly and the first day I walked down Nevsky Prospekt I couldn't believe it, loads and loads of beautiful girls in very short mini-skirts. I couldn't believe how sexy they were. But it's weird having a scene with one. They don't react in the normal way.'

'You're telling me . . .'

'You discovered that too?!' says Grev. 'Oh great – I thought it was just me.'

'Everyone thinks it's just them. Russians think it's just them.'

'But she should've given me more than 1 day's warning about the Crimea.'

'That depends.'

'On what?'

'Are you serious about her?'

'No.'

'Oh, you must be serious about it. Even if it only lasts for a few hours. It's so boring not to be serious about it.'

'But I'm not thinking of marriage yet!' he protests.

'Good God, I'm not talking about marriage. Marriage is the opposite of serious. Marriage is, you know, freeze-drying it. No – I mean, are you excited and moved by it? By the unlikeliness of it, even the impossibility of it. Look – you have just deflowered a 17-year-old Russian girl in St Petersburg – doesn't that strike you as something?'

'Um . . . well, I'd like to keep in touch . . .'

These TV-weaned kids from rich countries – is there no magic left in them? A pop video of surfers comes onto the screen in the corner and Grev says 'Wow, man, look! I'd love to be in California right now!'

'You have a wonderful name.'

'Yea, it alternates every generation between Greville Pinkerton and Simon – well, actually it's Simonides – Pinkerton.' He is a fine young man of 20 years, handsome, healthy, good-hearted, with no inner story. Grev, you should stay longer in Russia where the shocks eventually cease to come as a surprise, but where one continues nonetheless to be upset by them – thus making one pulpy and sensitive inside.

Arkady and Timofey walk me back to Zoia's.

'Somefing strange about vose Americans,' says Arkady, flattening his hair.

'In what way?'

'Vey were not reacting to where vey were,' says Timofey, flattening his.

'Mine was. But he hasn't realised it. He was on some kind of military scholarship.'

'Oh my God, I did 1½ years in Russian army,' says Arkady breathlessly. 'Horrible fings to eat. No – '

'No meat, no fruit, mostly very bad porridge, old and hard,' says Timofey, 'and tea – '

' – was mostly water wiv a little tea colour. In 19f century ve way to'

'avoid military service was to cut'

'off trigger finger, isn't it, which is'

've index finger of right hand but'

've auforities understood and'

've punishment was'

A dog barks at us from a balcony.

'prison'

'or worse.'

I bark back. 'Woof-woof-woof!'

'Woof-woof?'

'For the dog we say woof-woof. What do Russians say?'

'Gav-gav.'

'And for the cat – miaow.'

'Miaw miaw.'

'Cock a doodle doo.'

'Coo coo re coo.'

'Honk honk.'

'Hrew hrew.'

'Cheep cheep.'

'Pee pee.'

'We use that for when a child wants a pee. And for the owl – twit twoo!'

'Ukh ukh.'

'Ukh ukh? For the owl?'

'Yes. Ukh ukh.'

'What sort of owl's that then?'

'All sort of owl. Ukh ukh.'

'I don't get that one.'

They present me with a painted wooden bell which they have made themselves. And a cassette of Sergei Stadler playing the Paganini Caprices. Why, when later I listen to them, do these Caprices sound as though written for, in and about St Petersburg? Because this city claims everything and everyone which comes into its orbit. There is no escape from its sense of place, not even for a minute. Which is how all great cities used to be, but are no longer. They have all now joined at some level that international technoplastic club. All except this one. This is the last to go. The lack of modernisation is a joy. To save it, it must be restored, but a modernised St Petersburg would not be the town I fell in love with. Anyway, whatever happens, I shall never leave it now.

Giselle and Pop-Mechanika. Using Boris's double-cassette ghetto-blaster, I compile a tape for Pavel, *London Noise for Russian Boys*, and set out on foot. 'Do you have a record of Balakirev's piano music?' The girl on the stall beside the Philharmonia box office says yes, to-day they have one! In addition I buy Lyapunov's Second Symphony, new to me (it turns out to be spirited and melodic with a moving slow movement – why isn't it better known?) and read on the sleeve – composed in 1917!

I bump into Rodion who is shuffling about near the Armenian Church on Nevsky Prospekt.

'What are you doing?' I ask.

'I'm waiting for a girl. We take naked pictures – do you want to come?'

'Thanks – but I can't. There's going to be a picnic to Pushkin soon.

Will you come with us?'

'Yes, thank-you. I'd like to,' he replies, and adds 'You have a real St Petersburg face now. Tired, worn in – with alive eyes!'

A few steps further on another voice hails 'How're ya doin?' It's the Tampax Man.

'Fine. Was your client happy?'

'Oh yes! He appreciated the problems.'

'You look excited,' I say.

'Listen,' he says drawing closer, 'something incredible's happening to me. I was sent a poem to-day. Have you noticed that all Russians write beautifully? They're taught proper penmanship at school.' He smells of Lanvin eau de vetiver.

Late for Pavel, so take a taxi. The car radio is playing Neil Young's *Sweet Surrender* on Radio Novi when, not far short of the Needle by the station, the taxi crashes. He's gone into the back of someone. No one's hurt but there is much crumpling. The other driver, awesomely confident in his blamelessness, is ice cool. My driver, guilty as hell, complains vociferously with big arm-throwing gestures, his fake Rolex flashing in the sunlight. I push a bunch of roubles into his hand and trot the rest of the way to Pavel's – he's standing outside, his wiry frame swaying from one foot to the other, worried because I'm so late. Sliding in and out of sauna and shower, I hand my body over to him and he goes into action. Kirill is wandering round the place doing odd jobs and I'm careful not to appear over-familiar with him.

(Sometimes these little conspiracies are necessary to avoid hurting all that pulpy sensitivity. The next step is that conspiracy becomes reflexive. Russians are *the* experts at living multiple lives, surviving by decoy and mask. Besides, it is interesting to visit Kirill's home among the new blocks in the north of the city. The blocks are huge and abstract, archetypical of the modernistic workers' estates, but there are plenty of seagulls in that part of town, the air is better, and the simplicity of setting provides a refreshing contrast to the chancred opulence of the centre. In fact the standard of accommodation in the new blocks is far higher than in the historic part of town and therefore these modern flats are much in demand. Kirill is as dreamy as his massages. Although he speaks some English, he doesn't respond to *any* remark until about ¼ of a minute has elapsed, which makes for very lackadaisical conversation – he communes from a far-off but not unpleasant other-world.)

That evening VV takes me to *Giselle* at the Maryinsky Theatre – his girlfriend is in the corps de ballet – and afterwards a friend of VV's drives us to the much-vaunted Pop-Mechanika concert near Gostiny Dvor. The site is ringed by police boys but Pop-Mechanika have walked off in a huff without playing a note, for reasons no one can divine. I walk home at 11.30 pm in mellow gold sunlight under a rich blue sky.

Near the Moika, and the apsidal structure supported by Doric columns which terminates the Imperial Stables, a taxi draws up. A woman in furs (despite the heat) and long glittery ear-rings, jumps out and disappears behind one of the pillars. As I pass I see her with rucked up furs and skirts, leaning forward, legs wide apart on high heels and slightly bent at the knee, wearing stockings and suspender belt but no knickers. A stream of urine issues from a central point I only *just* cannot catch sight of. It hits the tarmac, runs round the base of the pillar, and across the pavement towards the open taxi door. On her face is an expression of kife with lowered eyelids, of longing gratified, of desperation released. She acknowledges me with a faint, mocking smile and an amused light in her eyes, finishes the task, throws down the skirts, jumps back into the cab, and is whizzed off into the night of another tortile St Petersburg day.

Grace, the Serbian girl, has arrived from Paris where she was born and where her family has now settled. She is tall and slim and walks with an easy upward-floating movement as though only half her apparent weight, an effect enhanced by the long sheenyflaxen hair which drifts slowly in the space about her head and shoulders. Her face is square with clear greenish brown eyes, a thin-lipped but wide expressive mouth, the snub Slav nose, and a small cleft in the chin. She has a robust, good-humoured nature, which brings freshness and carelessness to our ménage, but there is a piquancy too – the suggestion of some psychological complexity – in the way she occasionally narrows her eyes or gives a surly tightness to the mouth. In France Grace plays volleyball at a high level – and thank heavens she isn't 17. Actually she's 18 and has beautiful, almost horizontal eyebrows. We get on; we laugh. On television, military manoeuvres along Russia's southern borders are interspersed with Pepsi and Tampax advertisements.

Will Dima Never Stop Springing Surprises? Next days are hot, hot, hot. Grace goes in pursuit of volleyballers and Nikita proposes a trip out to Dyuny Beach from the Finland Station. In the train he says 'I was on television last night for the first time. When I saw it later, I was always nodding my head in a stupid way. Yes, I looked stupid! Why didn't the director tell me? That's his job. To-morrow is my birthday. Should I have a party?'

'Yes.'

'I don't know. I will decide when I wake up in the morning.'

The sand is pale and powdery, the water full of slimy green seaweed, and many people at this end of the beach sunbathe naked.

At lunchtime next day Nikita phones – yes, the party is on. Then Dima phones. My brain has a hernia. 'You're supposed to be on the Black Sea!'

'I was.'

'Then you are back early . . .'

'No.'

'Then I got the dates wrong – but I'm sure I – listen, yes! – come to a party to-night?'

'What time is? Oh. No, I must meet friends. We can meet after and walk in the white night. Is this a good idea?'

His voice has such a marvellous timbre and it sounds lively and relaxed. The holiday unwound him. We agree to meet by the Marble Palace on the Khalturina side at half past midnight.

'*Don't* be late, Dima. It's uncomfortable standing around late at night by myself.'

Whistling from room to room a catch from Alien Sex Fiend's *Ignore The Machine* – Zoia accosts me and says 'Don't whistle inside the house. You will lose money.' Oh boo! to nutty Russian put-down superstition. Her face is unusually drawn, her spirits low, and earlier this morning she dropped her guard completely by saying 'We were always told we lived better in Russia than in the West and we believed it. Now we know it is not true – and was never true.'

At 9 pm Grace and I move in balmy heat through the Summer Garden and along the Neva to Nikita's small, sweltering flat in Ulitsa Furmanova. Henrietta the English student is there looking gutted.

'My flat was burgled while I was in Tallin. Everything good taken.'

'Do you know who did it?'

'That's the really depressing part – it was probably someone who'd been there as a guest, as a friend.' But apparently Misha, her rave-organising boyfriend, has not been very sympathetic. 'I was going to travel in Central Russia with a girlfriend but I want to go home to London now. I want to get out of this mess.'

'How is it with your affair?'

'Russia certainly does something to the hormones!' She draws deeply on a cigarette. 'But I dunno . . . I never know what's happening. I'll know if it means anything to him', she says, knocking back the champanskoye, 'at the airport.'

Grace is surviving well on the other side of the room – she's found a Chilean under a flourish of black curls, Miguel, who lives in Berlin and is studying there to be an architect between sessions at the gym. DJ Groove sits on an adjacent chair and Henrietta fills in as interpreter.

D: I can't call you DJ Groove – what's your real name?

Z: Yevgeny. Which is Eugene. Zhenya for short. Don't you think this is a wonderful town?

D: Yes I do! What's the most wonderful thing which happened to you here?

Z: I fell in love.

D: With a machine or a person?

Z: A person. It's finished now.

D: So it was also the most unwonderful thing?

Z: No, no! It was one of the brightest moments of my life.

H: You're lucky to be out of it.

D: What sort of person are you?

Z: I am always looking for something new, always trying to do the impossible. I am attracted by kindness. And also by fun.

D: What makes you angry?

Z: Betrayal – from friends. Some people became envious because I have a little bit success as DJ and they did bad things to me. They hate anyone with talent or success – you are only allowed to have it when you are dead. But you know, if someone treads on your toe, you must tread on their toe *immediately* – otherwise there will be endless argument, otherwise they will tread on your other toes, your foot, the whole leg, not stopping until they have trodden on all of you.

D: Is this Russian philosophy?

Z: The philosophy of young Russians.

Nikita comes across sniffing a carnation and asks 'Did you see me on television?'

'Yes,' replies Zhenya, 'and you kept nodding your head.'

'There, I told you! Everyone saw it! I feel an idiot! Now you must stop talking and eat.'

A buffet of foie gras, Camembert, cold meats, apricots, plums, raspberries, backed by a bank of flowers in vases, has miraculously manifested along one wall.

'What happened with the Greenpeace man?' I ask Henrietta.

'Haven't I seen you since then? He said every Russian reactor is teetering on the edge of catastrophe. And they don't dispose of the waste properly. And he marched round town in a very aggressive way taking his readings.'

Nikita presses a plum into her mouth.

'So what was the result?'

'Normal,' she sloshes through the plum.

'Really?'

'God, I'm wilting in this wretched heat. Is there any more champagne? Yes, normal!'

'But it's not supposed to be normal.'

'Normal is abnormal. Something's going on. They bribed them.'

'Grace, do they have techno music in Serbia?'

'Hasn't Nikita got anything other than techno music?'

'No, it was the Greenpeace man and he said – normal.'

'I haven't been this year,' says Grace. 'I used to go every year to see my grandparents in a little village with cows and wild flowers and everyone singing at parties. But last time I went it was horrible – all the men singing the same songs but they changed the words to all about killing people.'

'Is your Russian as good as your English?'

'It's getting better now that I'm speaking with Zoia. She said you have a castle.'

'No – I told her it was only a joke.'

'She said you pretend it is a joke so you will not be kidnapped but really it is true, she can tell.'

'This is how things get out of hand in Russia. Fact and fantasy are too plastic. Believe me – no castle. Only 2 rooms in the grotty part of Notting Hill.'

'Grotty?'

'Most interesting part. I think Zoia is feeling jeopardised. Before in the flat it was 2 Russians to 1 foreigner. Now it is 2 foreigners to 1 Russian.'

'She warned me about you.'

'Why?'

'She says you know bad people.'

'What?'

'And you have too many phonecalls.'

'The cow.'

'And that you sleep too much.'

'The pig. I read in my room and I average 5 hours' sleep a night. I'm on an extended adrenalin burst.'

'Opposite for me – I sleep so much here but still feel tired.'

'That's a St Petersburg effect too.'

Grace has been here only a few days but already has the heavy eyes with the surface glitter stripped away to reveal emotions beneath. Her face is like that of all foreigners after a few days – a face not merely of fatigue but of one whose certainties have been undermined. This is the demonic power of Russia, its inescapable genius. Nor is it to be moaned about – for uncertainty is the mother of intelligence. Chaos is the mind's favourite food. One becomes mediocre to the degree that one is estranged from chaos.

'And Zoia said she showed you her photographs but you were not interested.'

'No, well, they were awful.' (It was after I'd shown her Smelov's beautiful photographs, which she dismissed with a glance, urging me instead to consider her box of snaps.) 'Zhenya, sit here. Do you pay protection for the raves?'

'Not my problem! I am only DJ! You want some raspberries?' Champagne is knocked down his bomber jacket sleeve. 'Once I saw how after the disco at 6 in the morning, which is when we usually finish, 6 or 7, some gangsters took girls into the cars. The girls didn't know them and were with other boys and didn't want to go but the gangsters carried them off. It happened right there, everybody watching. Nobody did anything.'

'Didn't their boyfriends protest?' So it does happen. What if Dima . . .

'They were too frightened. They would be attacked.'

'What happens if the girls refuse to go?'

'They cannot. Maybe they are beaten up and taken anyway.'

'Who was the person you were in love with?'

'She was studying with me at the Conservatoire. I found it difficult to approach her. I am a very shy person. Then it happened that she approached me – I was so shocked!'

'What time is it? I've got to go. Where's Grace? Henrietta, I've got to go. Best of luck at the airport.'

'Yes, I'll know then if it means anything to him – if he cries or something. I'll be a wreck of course.'

It's a relief to be out of doors in the after-midnight sultriness smoke-free. 'It's now or Neva!' I sing but my head is pounding. A purple light rises off the river whose surface is sliced by ripples into slivers of cobalt, black and violet. At the Neva door to our block I say to Grace 'You go on through.'

'Aren't you coming up?'

'I'm meeting someone.'

'What? Now?'

'I'll explain later.'

I backtrack, turn right into the short street leading to Khalturina, turn left. Dima is leaning against the railings of the Marble Palace, smoking. The cigarette end flips through an orange arc into the road and he walks slowly this way, screwing up his nose in a kind of bashfulness.

'Party good?' he asks.

'I drank a lot of champagne.' I kiss him.

'I drank a lot of yorsch.'

'What's that?'

'Vodka with beer.'

'So you are very drunk.'

'I drank a lot and went for a walk. No – I stayed where I was and the city went for a walk. Now we go for a walk.'

He is jaunty and suntanned, full of holiday, his curly hair bleached into uneven gold. Across the Field of Mars only a few frizzled lilac heads remain, crispy brown on sheltered boughs, and now the orange blossom is out, emanating a nirvana perfume. Dima takes out his cigarette, and a small parcel drops to the ground. 'Nylon stockings for my girl,' he says, sliding it into the back pocket of his jeans.

'Let me light that for you. I had a mysterious dream last night. A beautiful house reached by a flight of pale marble steps – and blood pouring down the steps like a river.'

'This is not very mysterious in Russia. I had a dream of going up – up –

up in a balloon – but it did not feel good. There was someone with a needle who could stab the balloon at any moment. You want to finish the cigarette?'

'No, no, sorry, take it. Come on, Phluphluns, this way.'

'Do you know the joke about the Polish abortion clinic?' he asks.

'No.'

'There is a year-long waiting list.'

I tickle him – he's very ticklish. He spits out the cigarette in surprise. We tussle against the wall of the Old British Embassy and his elbow knocks my nose.

'Yugh!'

It starts to bleed fast. I lean over, hands on knees, hang my head and let the blood fall which seems to trigger release of another sort because after a little while hot tears begin to ooze slowly from my eyes in sympathy and Dima, horrified by what he's done, or thinks he's done, puts an arm round my shoulders saying 'Sorry, sorry, excuse me please, Dooncan, excuse me, I idiot boy, please excuse me, sorry, oh God' during which I mumble 'It's OK, it's OK' and he continues with his apologetic refrain and I then stand upright, breathing deeply, throwing my head back whereupon the blood reverses and trickles down the back of my throat which I don't like so I move my head forward a bit whereupon it flows down over my lips and chin, mixing with a few hot tears, and down over my white shirt, soaking into it in larger and larger patches but it's all so stupid and I don't care, giving a little choking laugh instead, and Dima gives a little moan 'Ooooooo' and, taking a piece of tissue from his pocket, he starts to dab at my nose and face, trying to help, trying to clean up, trying to pre-empt the blood from drenching any more of the shirt, but in this way he dislodges any gathering clots and therefore the blood continues to fall and he's dabbing at the shirt making it bloodier and bloodier and I lean back easy against the wall, holding on to his shoulder, tears falling, blood falling, occasional bubbles up the throat or sniffing in the nose, letting Dima dab at me if he wants to, I don't care, and it goes on for quite a long time and the tears then cease and I become wide-eyed looking at the sky while the blood continues to drip, and the shirt continues to drink it, but less speedily now, and he tries to lean me forward again but I'm obstinate, I want the shirt to be soaked in as much blood as possible, I want to be covered in blood, I want to exhibit the blood, I *want to bleed*, but I groan 'Oh hell' anyway and my head falls against his and he says 'Dooncan, be careful of my clothe' and starts dabbing at my nose some more and I say 'Leave it, it's nearly stopped now' and the pressure from within has indeed largely expended itself and the drips falter and come successively to a halt nearer and nearer to the nostril until finally, at a definite moment as though a lock has turned, nothing more rolls down and he dabs the blood away from my mouth and gives me a soft, quick kiss on the lips. I have succeeded in covering my outside with my inside – the shirt is drunk on blood and my face, neck, breast and hands are sticky with blood. There are stars in the sky.

'Sorry . . .' he says.

'It's OK.'

'Very sorry.'

'It's OK.'

'I'm sorry.'

'It's fucking OK, Dima.'

'Me sorry.'

'Please, it's OK,' and I laugh quietly, holding the blood-wet shirt away from my body. It is drying quickly in the hot night but I take it off anyway and the air is sweet against my skin.

'Me stupid boy.'

'No, it's not you. I do have nosebleeds.'

'Without fighting?'

'Yes.'

'You must ask Rasputin to stop your bleed – he did this for the Tsarevich. You want cigarette?'

'No.'

'I want.'

He's run out of matches and intercepts a stranger for a light but the stranger takes one look at bloody me and legs it down the road as fast as he can.

At 2, 3 in the morning the light is eldritch and soft, a precipitation of lavender photons out of royal blue.

'You were on time.'

'I worry for you. I was thinking of that. My girl and I, we have gas guns. They are made in Germany.'

'It's safe for us, walking now, isn't it?'

'Oh yes. We are 2. And I have this.'

He pulls something out of his pocket slyly, and presses a cold closed knife against my bare ribs.

'Do you have a real gun too?'

'Yes – military gun. I made the oath to defend my country, then they give gun. Some of my friends went into the countryside with a metal detector and found guns from the war. They found skeletons next to the guns. I know someone who found 44 machine-guns in the forest and – '

He flicks through the dictionary. A bluesy mouth organ sings in a forgotten courtyard, its melody plaintive but not self-pitying. What is this bewilderment and pensiveness which creeps throughout the whole world now, this fretful nostalgia and scrying of the future? Maybe the species knows in its stomach that the old days are over and is sad about that, knows that old ways must die and tribes must fade if we are to continue, knows that everything must change now . . . . . A group of sailors serving in the Russian Pacific Fleet died from malnutrition. Their commanding officer was sacked but, well, this is what Dima's in.

'– and he ren . . . renovated these machine-guns from the forest and sold them to the South. You can find old rifles from the Revolution, from the Civil War. Returning to the city on the train, you must hide the guns to avoid problems with police. Sometimes on trains you see people with crazy shapes covered up with newspaper, guns they found. Where are we?'

I know where we are. Is it only Dima, or do all Russians have an appalling sense of orientation? He looks so lost and so sad for a moment. Sometimes he suddenly acquires this sad, lost look and it makes me want to reach to its source and reassure him and say 'It's all right. Don't worry. You're safe.' I put my arm round him and take him along a street, back up to the river so that he'll know where he is. A mild breeze skates off the water and I slip on the blood-red shirt, leaving it loose and unfastened.

He says 'Can you believe in winter all this water is thick ice? But not flat. With many big pieces of ice standing up very high. One cold night Catherine the Great asked 40 soldiers to her bedroom, only to stand there and breathe to make it warm. Some say she had sex with all of them!'

'Because she was the greatest woman Germany ever produced.'

'Can I ask you a question?'

'Yes – if I can ask you one.'

'Of course, so . . . is it true that people in England have 2 cars?'

'Some people, yes.'

'Phooooooooooo. Do you?'

'I have 1 car – I bought it from my sister and haven't finished paying for it yet.'

'What is your question?' he asks.

'My question? Oh, er – would you like to have 2 cars?'

'No. It is waste. You have one body and can only drive one car.'

'Do you like this new Russia?'

'I think so, yes, it's better than before when the KGB came in the night and take you and the neighbours and everyone would never know what happened, only guess because one day you weren't there any more. My great-grandfather was taken by the KGB in this way and never returned and – '

A drunken passer-by makes a remark and Dima answers in peremptory fashion.

'What did he say?'

'He say he wants to eat you. You look like red meat.'

'What did you say?'

'I say you are too tough for him. And there was never any information about him again and my great-grandmother went insane because of this. They had 8 children. She did not know what to say to her children. We never knew why they take him. Most people never knew. Often it was for no reason.'

'Keep it,' I say, referring to the pocket dictionary.

The weathered wooden lines of a beggar's face in apricot light make him look carved or petrified in his still doorway asleep at 3.30 in the morning.

'Do you have the dream of being chased and you can't run away?' Dima asks.

'Yes – as though your legs are held in slow motion by glue.'

'Yes, or mud. And just as the thing is about to jump on your neck you suddenly get free and fly up up in the air and it feels – oh, so good.'

'I know this dream well.'

'Stop.'

He takes out another piece of tissue, wets it with his saliva, and dabs the dried blood around my nose with a cautious but concentrated concern.

'Careful.'

'I shall tell you my big dream,' he says, rubbing flakes of blood off other parts of my face. 'I don't tell anyone this dream . . . It is to have a son. And to give to this son the love which I never had and the good things of life which I never had.'

'Will you have this son with Valentina?'

'Yes. She understands me.'

'Is that possible?'

'Can we go to your flat?'

'The woman is there.'

'Oh.' He looks away into blankness. 'Can we go somewhere to-morrow?'

'I'm going on a picnic to Pushkin. I thought you were away. It was arranged.'

'Oh.'

'But you can come with us.'

'I do not know them.'

'You'd like it.'

'We can meet the next day instead?'

'Certainly.'

Dima tries another stranger for a match but the man utters a whinny and capers off. There are few people around and those few give us a wide berth and it becomes apparent that *we* are the mavericks, *we* are the danger, *we* are the ones inspiring fear. It makes me laugh. So – to-night we have the power. We have claimed the city. It is ours.

Putting on a clownish face, I pull at my bloodied shirt, and burst out laughing and Dima laughs too. We laugh and laugh and laugh and start to run, first at a jog and then at a trot and then faster into a sprint along the empty avenues, façades sliding back on right and left and we are channelled between them and are sucked foward by an ineluctable force, propelled by an involuntary momentum, faster and faster down the street like a squall, feet thudding onto and springing off the pavement while the body shakes and leaps and flies over potholes and kerbstones, erasing all obstacles, and we run – well, it seems miles but it can't have been far – until we run ourselves out of breath and rein in, puffed out, lungs on fire, thighs trembling, tottering helplessly fowards towards the round and yellow moon which is large and low in the sky ahead.

'Where are you, Dima?' I shout.

'Here.'

'I cannot see you.'

'I am here.'

'Where? I cannot find you.'

'Here, I'm here.'

'Where are you?'

'Look at me.'

'Where? I cannot see you.'

'Dooncan, stop it – I am here.'

'Where?'

'You silly. I don't speak more.'

'Where?'

'Here . . . Look.'

He takes my arm. We shuffle to a halt.

'Where?' I place my hand flat against his belly. 'Here?'

'Yes. Here . . . Here I am.'

'Yes?'

'Yes. I'm here.'

'Yes.'

'Here I am.'

An absolute stop.

Still.

Quiet.

Warm.

The pavement is solid underfoot.

CHAPTER EIGHT

Picnic at Pushkin. 5½ hours sleep and wake up feeling good, though I shouldn't – champagne can give a nasty hangover. Zoia however is not her bumptious self. She looks nervous and hardly addresses me at all, reserving such spirit as she has for the new, favoured guest, Grace.

At 12.30 pm Grace and I proceed to the Baltic Station where we meet Yuri the Black Marketeer, Rodion the Eroticist, Arkady & Timofey each holding the handle of a big bag between them and, surprise, Timofey's wife.

'It seems odd that you aren't both married,' I say to the twins, 'and to the same girl.'

'Maybe we are,' says Arkady and 2 red clown's patches bloom on his cheeks.

'We have baby boy.'

'Is he in the bag?'

'He is wiv our muvver.'

The train is clean and hard-seated and although the journey is short it is not fast, with many stops at small stations. Pushkin has the leafy atmosphere of a middle-class suburb. They want to catch a bus up to the palace entrance but Grace and I prefer to walk and the party defers to our wishes.

'It used to be called Tsarskoye Selo – Tsar's Village – but after the Revolution they changed it. Pushkin was at school here.'

'He was killed in a duel.'

'As was Lermontov.'

It will be an educational day.

The park, where in tsarist days 600 gardeners toiled, is quiet. First we must do the palace, and approach its extremely-long-and-lively-rock-'n'-roll-but-unindented-blue-'n'-white-baroque-although-very-Russian-gardenside façade with joyous apprehension. What treasures lie within? Will the immense flat ceiling of the Great Hall 'work' in real life? Shall we be queue-jumped by Intourist groups of overseas religious cults? Alas, the palace is closed to-day. They deflect us to a Fabergé exhibition nearby – cigarette cases like chunks of Piccadilly Circus, ashtrays like Babylonian swimming-pools. And thereafter we stray beyond the terraces and into Stourhead sweeps, searching for the ideal picnic spot . . . . . the Palladian Bridge of grey Siberian Marble is modelled on that at Wilton (the first such bridge in the world and one of the most beautiful buildings in England) . . . . . until we enter upon a rustic region of hayfields and oak trees. The pelvis-high grass is green streaked with gold and smells sweet and we subside into it, spreading blankets and damasks. The propinquity of a palace is not something you want on a picnic. It should at most only be glimpsed in the distance, as in Beardsley or Watteau – and as it is here, betrayed by the merest blue and gold flourish between furbelows of foliage far away beyond meadows of heat haze. It is as hot as it could be, short of being problematic, and a faint breeze teases the long grass.

Everybody has brought something – Arkady & Timofey, a very generous pair, have brought most – and it is all put into the centre. Grace and I place cheese, chocolate, bananas; Yuri places vodka, mineral water, purple plastic cups; Rodion places salami, tomatoes, bread, butter; and Arkady and Mr & Mrs Timofey lettuce, sorrel, cucumber, tomatoes, hard-boiled eggs, cheese, salami, bread, and 2 large bottles of homemade raspberry juice, followed by knives, forks, plates and napkins.

'Davay!' proclaims Yuri, initiating the proceedings with a shot of vodka in which he is alone since everyone else prefers to eat before drinking. 'Tell me, what do you think of St Petersburg?'

'Rachmaninov with guns.'

'Ah, you were waiting for this question.'

'And it's one of the 4 mystic cities like London and Prague.'

'In Prague recently the Sicilian mafia and the Russian mafia signed a treaty to rule the world of crime.'

'And on July 1st our Government announced that foreign currency must not be used, only roubles. All people ignore this. So all people are criminal. But what can we do with an impossible law?'

'And I think Russia is very funky. I didn't think it would be. But it's the funkiest place in the world.'

'We don't know vis word funky.'

'Do you know this word, Grace?'

'Black American music?'

'Yes, of the 70s, but it has a more general meaning um . . . oh hell, how to explain funky um – your stripper in the block of flats, Rodion, she was very funky.'

'Sexy?'

'Yes but more.'

'Also on July 1st the price freeze on petrol was ended.'

'Have egg,' urges Timofey.

'You arrange to go somewhere – and find yourself taken somewhere else – this is funky. Russians share easily with friends, crash out on each other's sofas, this is funky.'

'Time doesn't exist in Russia I think,' says Grace. 'People sleep, arrive, depart when they feel – '

'Tell that to Zoia,' I protest.

'– without having to explain. There is fluidity between people.'

'Which means,' says Yuri, 'that there will also be the sudden break – enough – no closer – finish – end – also without explanation.'

'Russians can sleep anywhere,' says Rodion. 'Behind the wheel of a car, on riverbanks, walking along the street.'

Crickets make a hissy shuttle in the grass. Yuri with his coxcombical swagger strips off shirt and vest, causing a sensation which is however largely repressed – except in Grace who quickly leans across and touches the spider's web tattoo with her fingertip, avoiding the nipple with its few yellow hairs. Rodion goes 'Haw!', slightly peeved, and Yuri blushes deeply which suits him. Blushing suits everyone. The blusher feels a fool but others are very attracted by the evidence of emotional arousal and vulnerability. Russians blush readily – this is funky. So do Italians. I've only ever seen one French person blush.

Arkady says 'I like banana. But many people do not. Vey fink it', 'like soap,' says Timofey.

Rodion, inspired, asks 'Is funky like soul?'

'Very much! But not the same. Funky means alive, rhythmic, worn in, playful, sexy, yes, we've said that, emotional, bit sleazy and can be unpredictable, direct, flexible and relaxed but not *too* relaxed – cool isn't funky – funky is more endearing, and it's physically warm, warm-hearted too, aware but not enclosed, wise *and* innocent, loose but – '

Arkady, lobbing a tomato to Grace, asks 'One word means all vese fings?'

'No. Strands of these things.'

The tomato hits Grace on the shoulder and rolls, unsplit, into her lap. She is absent-mindedly gazing at Yuri who is lying on his back with eyes closed. His breasts are larger than hers. 'It must be the best word in the world,' he mumbles.

'Not always. Sometimes funky don't drive you on de floor – it drive you up de wall! It can phase into untogether, and then pain-in-the-neck, and stops being funky.'

'What is the 4th', 'mystic city?' enquire Arkady & Timofey.

'He didn't tell me.'

Rodion stands up and waves to a couple at the edge of the field. It's Masha the Sculptress and Misha the Poet, minus daughter-and-Airedale. Everyone looks in their direction, all eyes narrowing against the migraine of sunlight through which they swish towards us. 'I invited them,' says Rodion. We all stand up and shake hands and they say 'Don't stand up' and we all sit down, spreading back into the lush walls of grass.

'Scintillae!' declares the Poet.

'We saw tops of heads only,' says Masha with a bountiful smile, dropping a large transparent polythene bag of biscuits into the centre. She is in a good mood to-day. Must've sold a statue.

Rodion whispers in my ear 'Do you think Grace would pose naked for my magazine?' He grins mudlarkily but is serious.

I bare my teeth and gnash them at him and put 3 questions 'of English interest – forgive me' to the gathering:–

1. Does anyone know what happened to the family of Elphinstone who used to figure hereabouts?

2. Are there willows here? The willows of Catherine the Great are descended from Alexander Pope's willow at Twickenham. After Pope's death the villa and garden were taken over by Sir William Stanhope who sent cuttings of Pope's beloved willow all over Europe – but especially to Catherine the Great.

3. Does anyone know the whereabouts of the 50 place dinner service commissioned from Wedgwood for the Chesme Palace, painted with British scenes (every one different)? (The Chesme Palace, on the southern outskirts of St Petersburg, is where the Romanovs would halt for a breakfast en route to more definite places, just as the Devonshires used to halt for breakfast at Chiswick Villa on their way out of London. The Chesme Palace and Chiswick Villa, 2 breakfast lodges: I can't think of any others, can you?)

Arkady and Misha the Poet are in magnetic tête à tête and the word 'funky' pops up between them several times.

'You want china?' asks Yuri. 'I can get beautiful Lomonosov china.'

Arkady asks 'How do you spell it? T-h-u-n-k . . .'

The Poet rolls 'funky' round his mouth and asks 'Is it related to fun?'

'Yes.'

'And to fuck?'

'Indirectly.'

'Is SPID [AIDS] bad in England?'

'Yes.'

'Not so in Russia.'

'Soon.'

'All virus very bad,' says Masha.

'Not all,' says her husband, kneeling in the grass, hands trapped between thin thighs. 'Often the most beautiful flowers, striped tulips or striped camellias, are created by virus infections.'

Gently Yuri is scolding Grace for refusing vodka – with his hurt voice and smiling eyes – so of course she has some, swallows, coughs, flushes, has some more, and Masha says 'Excuse me' and picks up one of the plastic bags and takes off through the grass with a swaying motion of her wide bottom to a distant tree where she is soon to be seen hopping upwards, grabbing blossoms, and detaching them with the weight of her descent to earth, and popping them into the bag. Arkady says the tree is a lipa and its blossoms can be used for making tea. At a later date the dictionary reveals 'lipa' to be the linden or lime tree. Lime tree tea. Never had it.

'I think your wife is a passionate woman,' says Yuri.

'She is!' says the Poet in an unexpectedly shrill voice, throwing out a random arm.

I have a vision of Yuri going down on the Sculptress, his face completely buried, labia majora flapping about his ears.

'Do you know what a Novgorod woman did,' he continues, 'when she discovered her husband was being unfaithful? She carefully opened a condom she found in his jacket pocket, put ground chilli inside, and resealed it. He had to go to hospital afterwards for treatment.'

'She should have put in powdered glass,' suggests Timofey in a surprising tone of priggishness.

Rolling over to Grace, I ask 'What's wrong with Zoia? She is so subdued – and very distant with me. We've had rows but were never distant before.'

'She says you eat too much. She says because of inflation she is not making money out of you. She says she'll never have another Englishman to stay.'

'So she's damning the entire English male sex because of me? Her problem is she's overdone it, taking in 2 guests.'

'She told Leonid he's not giving her enough money for you.'

'What did Leonid say?'

'Feed him less.'

Timofey's wife, who has no English, has been attending to this conversation. She speaks to her husband and Timofey says 'My wife says she understand nuffing but love to listen to your voice speak your tongue.'

I redden with pleasure. A compliment always touches us, this is understandable because it is a delight to be praised on a planet of ravening envy where little that is human comes free. But curiously, even if we don't believe the compliment, even indeed if we know it to be the basest and most self-seeking form of flattery and that the flatterer is lying through his teeth, is *still* touches us, it always works. Flattery is irresistible. No one is impervious to it. There are people who pretend to be but they are deceitful or deluded – wantonly flatter them and they collapse into strings of syrup before your very eyes. And when the compliment is felt to be genuine, ie. is an expression of the other's authentic pleasure, it becomes more than an enhancement of self. It is a true gift, a quantum of joy which is transmitted and shared. All gifts are acts of sharing, a form of congress, the opening of an emotional conduit. This is the great thing about presents: they embarrass, especially when unexpected. To be embarrassed is to be liberated.

Seeing me blush, Timofey's wife blushes too, and then Timofey does likewise, disconcerted yet charmed by his wife's directness, and when Timofey blushes Arkady blushes, and seeing all this blushing, Grace needs no persuading to participate since she already has a proto-blush from the vodka, which brings a blush of happiness to Yuri while Rodion, the one who doesn't blush, becomes embarrassed by being the odd one out and starts to blush too, so that we all flower in and out of each other via blushings, all that is except the Poet who kneels before us, separated, head on one side, eyes shining, soft smile of a saint, while over his shoulder in the distance his wife is hopping upwards, grabbing blossoms, and detaching them with the weight of her descent.

The Poet questions us: 'Have you ever tried to commit suicide?'

'No.'

'Sort of.'

'No. A friend of mine just had a crack at it.'

'Suicide can be very beautiful.'

'Not when it fails.'

'Have you?'

'No.'

'Are you thinking about it, Misha?'

'No.'

'Well, you *are* thinking about it . . . but you're not thinking about doing it.'

'No.'

'In England 4 times as many men as women commit suicide because men are not allowed to express their feelings.'

'Like in Russia. What is the suicide rate here?' wonders Rodion.

'Lack of information. But froo roof boom boom!'

'Maybe not.'

'Like in war you mean suicide go down?'

'I once wrote a song, *Life is Naff and so is Suicide*. About being trapped.'

'What naff is?'

'Opposite of funky.'

'I tried when I was 18 with razorblade,' announces Rodion, brightly proffering his wrists.

'Why?'

'I felt bad.'

'Will you try again?'

'No, because now I am a father.'

Yuri passes round the vodka to toast the new-born nameless poppet. The Poet sighs and with a heavy countenance says 'Perhaps I shall become a businessman. From asphodel to infidel.'

'Yuri told me business is the new art form.'

The Poet's face opens. 'Why not? Voltaire sold Swiss watches to the mandarins of Peking, after writing to Catherine the Great for help. She had them transported on one of her camel caravans . . .' He says no more, lost in the silence of unattainable altitudes.

We gather up our things and migrate across the park to the Chinese Village, collecting Masha from her tree, Rodion leading the way with bouncy step and going up on his toes. The Chinese Village, built to designs by Cameron, Catherine the Great's Scottish 'poet-architect', is under restoration, but still dangerously derelict, and picketed off for safety. We duck through the lozenges of wire and make for the great rotunda. Externally its roof is a dome-shaped lawn of weeds. The interior is a wreckage of pink stucco, virulent green mildew and exposed red brickwork. The inside of the dome bears the remains of trompe l'oeil coffering (an echo of the Pantheon) and across it the green contagion bursts out in magnificent swatches, while beneath, ghosts swirl in organdie to a polka. Here, in a tall blancmange of cooler air, the conversation turns to loneliness.

'Everyone experiences loneliness,' explains the Poet, 'but there are many forms of it. The father seeing the bond between mother and child and feeling excluded – this is the man's loneliness. The mother seeing the father free to go off while she is imprisoned in the home with the child – this is the woman's loneliness.'

'I prefer the loneliness of not having any children at all,' says Yuri.

'Are children funky?' asks Rodion.

'Very.'

'Everything is being born in them.'

The Poet says 'I want to go and live in Montevideo, birthplace of Lautréamont and Laforgue and Augustini.'

'That's no solution. They all died young.'

'So have I missed my chance? I do not think so.'

'Going away from problems is traditional in Russia.'

'The country is so vast, and even at the height of totalitarianism was so filled with anomalies and ineptitudes, that the idea of just running away, burning all your boats you say, making an absolute break, has always been one solution to a Russian's problems.'

'But Russia is *so vast* that it becomes inescapable – however far you run it's still Russia . . .'

'Under Communism you could not leave your place.'

'Under the Tsars too. And yet throughout Russian history people have just disappeared out of lives.'

'Oh Sea-Poet, blow a blast on your conch!'

'Augustini was murdered by her husband.'

'Such things immortalise one's verse. With Masha's help . . .'

'Are you a sea-poet in fact?'

'I am a poet who longs to cross the sea, knowing it will bring him no happiness at all.'

'You must cry your sea.'

'I do. But it is not enough. Laforgue was wrong when he spoke of the superiority of tears. The better the artist, then the greater the division in him between the man who suffers and the mind which creates.'

'But you must create wiv your heart also.'

'This is inspiration – *this* we assume.'

'Is Chinese Village funky?' asks the Sculptress, opening her arms to include it.

'Very.'

'Was Caferine', 've Great', 'funky?' ask Arkady & Timofey.

'Oh one of the funkiest – the Empress of Funk! All that sex and buying Voltaire's and Diderot's libraries and murdering her husband and building palaces for her boyfriends. Really funky people are not self-conscious. If you think "I'm funky" you aren't funky. Why ever did I mention the sodding word?'

And hoping to get off it, I relate Dima's anecdote of Catherine the Great and 40 soldiers and possibly having sex with all of them.

Arkady & Timofey's top-tufts slowly erect while Grace's brownish green eyes revolve then stop revolving.

'Impossible!' she insists. 'She couldn't even have 20 or she would die.'

'Pshaw.'

'Not pshaw. You know those sects?'

'Seventh Day Adventist and things? They're everywhere, aren't they?'

'There was one in which they sacrifice a virgin to men. And she couldn't even have 20 men before she was dead.'

'Well, if the object was so sacrifice her, I'm not surprised. And I'm not suggesting that Catherine went the whole cycle with each man. She was probably already in a hyperorgasmic state after the first 2 or 3.'

'No, no, no, even with 4 or 5 men it is impossible.'

'Why are you so adamant?'

'They did an experiment. They put 4 women mouse in a cage with 1 man mouse and that was OK. But when they tried 4 men mouse with 1 woman mouse, she died.'

'Indeed this is a powerful piece of research. Have you told the feminists?'

'But Catherine the Great was not a mouse – for the Mother of Russia anything is possible!'

'Rodion, I have an idea of a column for your magazine,' says the Poet. 'Instead of horoscope like they all have, you can have – vaginomancy! Divining the future by reading cunts. I offer my services.'

'Oh, give us a poem, sir!'

The Poet breathes heavily in and out for several moments, and says no, but when pressed says yes, and announces the declamation of a poem he composed only last week, *The Longing for Cause and Effect*. It will be included in his next collection to be called *Suction*. It translates roughly as follows:

> *Lifting your chin above a furious catfight in the yard,*
> *You enquire after my serotonin levels.*
> *'What is charisma?' I ask.*
> *'The absorption of one's surrounding space.'*
> *You are as warm and remote as casuarinas.*
> *The eggshell ceiling cracks*
> *And sky drips down your tanned face –*
> *All this the dream-boosting effect of night-long light.*
> *Trying to escape, I corkscrew in the wrong direction*
> *And pop above the waves.*
> *Does the quantitative always turn into the qualitative*
> *If applied with sufficient gusto?*
> *Shsh – it is ready.*
> *Please pour.*

Motes of dust spangle the air. With melancholy eyes the Poet looks aloft and gives his saintly smile. 'The roof could fall down on us this very minute,' he warns, 'so let us go into the sun.'

We straggle out of the rotunda and across the grass introspectively and it is Yuri who eventually breaks the silence.

'Was Stalin funky?'

'No.'

'Therefore Stalin was naff?'

'No. Stalin was a butcher.'

'So Ivan the Terrible was not funky also?'

'I think Ivan had his funky aspects. For example, he took both male and female lovers.'

'Is funky happy?'

'Sometimes – which includes happy to be sad.'

'Is funky good?'

'Not necessarily. But it's interesting, and on the side of life.'

'Then I think Stalin can be funky too!' says the Sculptress pugnaciously. 'He moulded Russia like clay, not like butcher, and was the creator of our post-war greatness. You do not like him because he was Communist.'

'I do not like him because he is surrounded by skulls. And he's too close for comfort. In 1,000 years' time people will consider him a character like Nero or Caligula. Monstrosity becomes ridiculous if you go far enough back in time – isn't that awful?'

Here is a bridge over a stream, with an open pagoda at either end, and there, down on the riverbank, stripped to the waist, brown slip-on shoes covered in chalk dust, lying in the foetal position on stones and weeds, a boy is fast asleep. Do you recall Rodion's earlier remark about sleeping on riverbanks? I have noted previously that Russians are bad at synchronisation. Which is true. But they are brilliant at synchronicity.

'There,' I say, '*that* is funky.'

'Ah! Now I understand!' exclaims the Sculptress. 'Funky. It means – beautiful!'

Not far from the park gates is a monument to the memory of all Russian Jews exterminated by the Nazis. Yuri stares at it with a frown and asks 'Duncan, when do we discuss business?'

Saturday. To-day is even hotter than yesterday. Ring Dima. I'll call at his flat and we can go on somewhere from there – he agrees but sounds sullen. Ring Leonid and ask 'What's this money problem with Zoia?' He mumbles in his funereal fashion. I know he is not to blame – we all came to an agreement about money. But economic circumstances have overtaken it. It's vexing that he didn't broach the matter before, because I have to live here. Besides, for whatever reason, it isn't nice that Zoia is down. She must shine as an exemplar of invincible fortitude – which she is.

After the phonecall I say to her 'Zoia, I am ignorant and vain and blind and arrogant and thoughtless and stupid and greedy and I'm sorry. Excuse me, I didn't understand!'

'No, no, no!' She's horrified that her complaint has reached me.

'Yes, yes, yes, I am, I know it!'

'No, no, no!' She denies there is the slightest problem, absolutely refuses the extra money, so I dump it on top of the piano in the Big Room. Zoia becomes warm, round, fluffy and smiling (and later in the plenitude of her recovery bakes 2 enormous cakes, one with apricots, the other with strawberries).

Grace says 'I have learnt something in Russia. If you want something, you must do it yourself. You cannot depend on others. You must make the situation yourself.'

The lift is occupied so I walk down the stairs. There is dog shit at the bottom making an awful pong. In the Gorky Gardens the Fountain Boys try to sell me souvenirs. The young tourist hustlers, selling books, postcards, T-shirts, military gear, flags, work in groups of 2 or 3 and pool their takings. The ones around the Winter Palace are the slickest and least charming but the Fountain Boys are fine, though none of them is to be trusted at any level. These souvenir hustlers, with their wares in carrier bags, are among the most frantic representatives of the new commerce and are not necessarily mafia-controlled, but must all pay the police a fee to work their areas. The souvenir stallholders are less frantic and *are* mafia-controlled.

There is 'an atmosphere' at Dima's flat. The grandmother is not there. Valentina is tight-lipped. Dima, fresh and glossily damp from the shower, is restless. He flashes me a smile to mask his feelings, and puts bread, butter, cheese on the table. Valentina withdraws to another room. Have they had a row? Maybe the hot weather is getting to them.

'I brought you some tea and coffee.'

He picks up the packet of tea and looks at me haughtily. 'Indian, good. Georgian tea was good when it was collected by hand in different qualities. Now it is done by machines and all mixed.'

'Do you read much?' I ask, picking up a book on the table.

'I like science fiction. Eat something.'

'Is everything OK?'

'Yes, very OK.'

'But Valentina – '

'We had little conflict.'

'Serious?'

'I do not have words to explain.'

'Sorry – I always ask too many questions. If I could speak Russian – '

'No, no, no, it's OK, it's OK. But – more easy to say feelings with vodka.'

'You want vodka?'

'You want?'

'No, no.'

'To-morrow I must begin college. I go away.'

I am scythed by a blade. I'd no idea it was so soon.

On our way out of the door he stands with feet well apart, legs straight, looking down at Valentina. They speak. We leave.

Outside Dima is more at ease, with a feral glitter in his eye. He goes ahead with lilting step and we walk towards the big wild park south of the Obvodny Canal. The back of his neck – from this angle it looks as wide as his head – and the hair is cropped short upon it, curls tousled on top. We cross the road into the park. The unhindered-by-ozone sunlight floods the scene, revealing every detail. Grass and woodland ring with clarity. No sky was ever bluer.

Walking ahead along the path, he half turns round and says 'Ooo, hot!' and pulls off his top with a twisting movement of the torso. His back is very tanned, a rich gold, almost orange, and more muscular than I remember it.

'I want to find a quiet place to lie in the sun.'

'Yes, we can find this place I think,' he replies.

A few people sunbathe in the long grass but as we continue into a wilderness of overgrown coppices it becomes quiet, peaceful, the air fragrant and scored by the occasional sound of bees. We pee together in a bush and flop into grass and I take off my top too. The hot sun against the body is like a sublime drug. Dima is lying on his belly, head on crossed arms, looking at me with one eye.

'Time stops. Some heaven,' he says.

I say 'I want to sleep with you.'

'I don't sleep with men,' he replies without moving.

'I don't want you to sleep with men. I'd hate it if you were sleeping with men. I just want you to sleep with me.'

He lifts his head and laughs. 'Oh. You are jealous type. Me too. I must find light.'

On springy legs Dima moves across the glade, searching out a smoking sun-worshipper which isn't easy but eventually he finds one. I pick up our things and follow and we go deeper into the undergrowth and find ourselves in a circle stamped out in the thick grass and waist-high plants by a previous visitor, a perfect suntrap, soft underfoot. We sit and share a bottle of water while he finishes the cigarette with eyes closed against the sun.

'Dima?'

'Yes?'

'Take off all your clothes.'

'Why?'

'Because I think you are beautiful and I want to look at you.'

'Here?'

'Yes.'

'All?'

'Yes.'

He pauses only a half second, then slips off his shoes and socks, stands up, unbuckles his belt and undoes the fly and pulls off his jeans and underpants with the minimum of fuss, and lies down on his back in the grass with a low 'mmm' sound.

I stare at him, heart beating loudly, staring but hardly seeing.

'Can I touch you?' I ask.

'. . . Please.'

With that one word 'please', all the questions, contradictions and upset, all the false starts and false ends, all the frustrations and misunderstandings of the past weeks, contract to a point and explode. So – finally it happens. Nature takes its exhilarating course. The great resolving chord is struck. The luminous pieces come together and fuse. My life here achieves focus, meaning, direction . . . This isn't easy to write. I can't convey it – and I don't want to. Can you be satisfied with that, please?

He smells and tastes of heat and soap and smoke. Afterwards we are both so natural, unselfconscious, eye to eye: the wave has passed through, sweeping away barriers. So now I look at him with ease. He is lovely. Miraculous. Various golds tipped with red here and there and blue eyes.

And though not thin, of an extreme muscular leanness – they are worked hard in the services. Scars on the knees.

'Always falling,' he explains.

And on the hands.

'Fighting.'

There is golden hair on his legs and a blade of golden hair grows up to his navel but above that the body looks hairless. And I've always meant to ask – the chipped tooth?

'Oh – too much vodka one day. Same time I did this.' He indicates the scar above the right eye where a damp caramel quiff has glued itself to his brow. The face, sensual but not soft, with full red lips, is very expressive – he looks different in every photograph – and out of it comes the rich-toned voice with swoops in it, full of humour and deception. Now there are no spaces or sadness behind the wide-apart eyes – his warmth of personality has filled up behind them. While I look at him there is a low booming inside which makes my ears warm – until a stray thought . . . not a thought really – more a filament brushing the consciousness. It is the sense of surprise. I can't believe it. I am living the unbelievable. Everything is gradually pervaded by the glowing silence of amazement.

The trees continue to stand overhead.

The sun shines on and on.

He smiles and says 'This is a crazy situation for me.'

'Yes. But life's no good without crazy situations.'

We snooze against each other.

Time passes.

And the spell is slowly dispersed by an increasing awareness of the sharp cry of seagulls and a tipping of the light . . . . . Other facts intrude . . . . . He tears at some wild flowers.

Walking back towards the road, talk is of the necessity of exchanging letters. 'You must write like this.' With a stick he draws my name in capitals in the dust of the path. 'And send to home. Not college. They destroy foreign letters.' Suddenly he looks startled, for a few seconds and for no apparent reason – this is another of the things he sometimes does.

To-morrow he goes, first thing in the morning. A period of training in the north, and when he returns to his college studies, I shall have long gone.

'I must give you some things.'

'You already give me things,' he replies.

We taxi to the flat. I dash upstairs, fill a carrier bag, dash down and give it to him.

'It's too much,' he says, screwing up his nose – the way he does when he feels he should show reluctance but is open to persuasion.

'Yes, it's too much. Come on, let's go for a drink.'

Palace Bridge is covered with fresh horse dung from the nags returning from their daily tourist stint in the Square. He is walking along, eyes on the ground, swings them up, takes my arm – 'I know good bar.'

The Petrovski Bar, on a large moored riverboat, is new to me but recognisable as the dark hulk peeping in from the right in Smelov's panorama of St Petersburg. It is cosy and windowless inside. Orange and red lights glow from behind bunches of plastic flowers. A TV is on. No Russian beer, so we order 2 Belgian ones and 2 Fantas and take a corner seat. 'What's this?' He picks up my lip salve *Chap Stick* and reads the writing on the side, with slow deliberate enunciation so that it becomes a found poem.

> Lip
> Balm with sun screen
> Aids
> The prevention
> And treatment of
> Dry, cracked
> Sun and wind
> Burned
> Lips

'You must come and stay with me in London.'

'Oh – it is my dream . . . . .' Then his eyes get the glaucous look, misting before moistening almost to tears.

'What's the matter?'

'In Navy I cannot.'

'Maybe it will change.'

He brightens. 'In Russia that is always possible. Yes, I am sure there is a way!' And drinks quickly, nervously. 'Tell me about London.'

'Oh well, it is not as beautiful as St Petersburg – architecturally London is the most capricious town in the world – but it has everything, astonishing combinations of elements, no uniformity at all – it's the same with the people who live in it – London is the only great city which doesn't impose a style on you – you can be whatever you want there. I have been thinking about this. Compared to New York, Paris, Rome, these places, London is a mysterious labyrinth.'

He gazes at me and says 'It is expensive.'

'Don't worry about that.'

'But maybe I am a . . .' He speaks in Russian.

'Not so expensive.'

'No, no, you don't understand. I must speak better English.' He punches the side of his head in irritation. He forgot to bring the dictionary I gave him.

Scrambling through the possibilities I suggest 'You mean it will be expensive for me because you don't have money?'

'Yes, yes! I do not want to be a . . .' He writes down the word which a dictionary later reveals to be 'burden'. As on other occasions, his pride and thoughtfulness come together.

'OK – let's say that if I have the money, you can come. Davay!'

'Davay – it is what cosmonauts say before they go up in the air. Davay! Listen. We can meet – but only for quick time. In 2 weeks from Monday. I must be back at the college in St Petersburg for 1, 2 days then.'

'Meet where?'

'Near my college. By the Alexander Column. Mid-day.'

'Is it allowed?'

'No, but for a short time is OK.'

'How will you get out?'

'That's my problem.'

'I think you are beautiful outside – and beautiful inside.'

His eyes fix me steadily, without an obvious emotion. What thoughts slide past behind them like ticker tape? It flashes into my mind – does he think me a fool?

'Does it sound stupid when I call you beautiful?'

'No. Why stupid? I am glad.'

The low sun shines horizontally across the Neva onto the Winter Palace, making the long lines of windows appear to be glazed with solid gold. We embrace. He turns, before going out of sight, to give his big semicircular wave.

Sunday. To-day is overcast and sultry. The flat is empty. From time to time I dump the spoon into the bowl of porridge, raise it to my lips, but there is a heavy feeling in the stomach, no appetite, feel swollen about the eyes, hardly slept, borne up on a great surge of exultation, and yet I feel at rest for the first time since coming to this city, so that swollen eyes, heavy stomach, none of it matters. So much nervousness has fallen away. There is a confidence now. I feel earthed, connected, thoroughly entitled to be here. But my goodness, when dreams become reality, you can be thrown – somewhere between myth and delirium. Lying lengthwise on the bed, I think of his generosity.

'Come, eat with me. We have money,' he said one day, tapping his pocket.

And his forgetfulness – which is living in the present. When he is with me, he is really *with* me. But when he is not . . .

There is a glorious wild streak, entirely opportunistic, without thought for consequence. There are times when it appears to border on mania or half-wittedness. It is an aspect of his passion – as is the way he can consume a bottle of vodka or packet of cigarettes straight off.

He is the rascal, the dandy, the naif, all in one. A laughing boy visited by sudden timidities and terrors. He has levity without insipidity, insouciance to the point of negligence, a natural grace and courtesy which enable him to apologise.

He is unreliable, full of astute or callow surprises. A warm carefree personality, but one which finds itself imprisoned in a very constricted life situation. Proud, hungry, self-seeking, naughty and quick, he can transform into pure giving and caring and surrender, pure openness and intimacy – he can do this. And threading through him is a sense of honour, a wish to be fine, to do the right thing . . . . . . A sudden flash of him older – 30, 35 – teeth yellowed by tobacco, body bloated with alcohol, gambling debts, petty crime, grinning like an idiot, dreams all crushed, lost in a bleak and loveless underworld of thieves, addicts, fools, a vision of utmost degradation. No, he is too clever for that one . . .

Zoia and Grace have gone out somewhere and I go into the Big Room and play the dance tapes which will bring me a few hours closer to the final meeting by the Column which probably won't happen – I'm resigned to that. No, I'm not resigned to that.

> Blancmange: *Living On The Ceiling*
> Can: *Father Cannot Yell*
> Van Morrison: *Sweet Thing*
> UK Subs: *C.I.D.*
> 2 Unlimited: *Workaholic*

As I dance and think of yesterday afternoon, death crosses my mind like a faun. A man in his prime suggests eternity but a young man evokes the transience of life . . . Getting into this. Moving well, Ooo – that was a good hip movement. Let's try it again. Oo, yeah. Getting into it now. Rhythm has taken over – boomberlada – boomberlada – boomberlada – boom!

> She Rockers: *Jam It Jam*
> Smokey Robinson: *You Really Got a Hold On Me*
> Fern Kinney: *Groove Me*
> Wings: *Good Night Tonight*
> Checkmates: *Proud Mary*
> Alien Sex Fiend: *Ignore The Machine*
> George Clinton: *Loopzilla*
> Dream Warriors: *My Definition*

Dima is reflecting in the window looking onto the Church of Blood. He is playing cards . . . I like the way Dima sends himself up sometimes. Von once said that she found so-and-so sexy and I asked why and she said 'He's sexy because he can send himself up.' And sometimes there is a foolishness in Dima's face which adds to his timeless quality. . . . . If you physically touch someone, you automatically know them better. It's automatic.

The tape runs out. Put on Rachmaninov's First P.C. Ooops – that was a mistake. A sob breaks inside me – hot knife through butter – too much – take it off immediately.

At the kitchen table, above our dinner, I am looking into Grace's greenish eyes and telling her that I have been involved with someone here but he's gone away and maybe I'll never see him again.

'How do you feel?' she asks.

'Fantastic! I can't help it. I do. I feel like a king.'

'Can I read one of your novels?'

'I'll give you the weirder one.'

Zoia enters and says with great solemnity 'On television there is a very beautiful programme about prostitutes.'

I try not to look at Grace and she tries not to look at me but it's no good, we collapse into laughter and Zoia leaves the kitchen with a sickly expression on her face. We are cruel but do not mean to be.

At midnight I slug vodka in the bedroom and try to read and can't and it doesn't matter because I'm humming so beautifully, warm and peaceful inside and out and easy firework displays going off in my head every so often and you know, everyone is a dropout here, it really is terrifying and marvellous, the whole society has dropped out, crashed out on sofas, letting go, making do, not making do, leaping, fainting, slobbing around, you can do anything, whatever you want, whatever you can, whenever you want – I light a cigarette, stub it out, and at half past midnight or so a voice sounding from another galaxy, but a friendly, neighbourly galaxy, telephones. Mira Apraxin.

'Come to a boat party.'

'Whose?'

'Mine.'

'OK. When?'

'Now.'

'Now?'

'Now! now! now!'

'No.'

'The boat leaves from the pier near you in 15 minutes. A big boat. We sail out to the Gulf of Finland with champagne, buffet, dancing. Very international. Belgian, Russian, Finnish, Icelandic, French people.'

'Why didn't you ask me before?'

'I only decide to do it to-day. We sail back under the open bridges at 5.'

It sounds great. I'd love to. But it's the wrong day. Already I am soaring in this warm haze and don't need anything else at all.

I am so happy.

CHAPTER NINE

The Ship to Anywhere. Is in fact the 3-day trip across Lake Ladago to Vallam Island. Who will occupy the Dima-less bunk? Grace can't – she's volleyballing like billio every day. Vallam is a religious spot, once known as the Mount Athos of the North (and recently returned to the monks by the Russian Government in joint ownership), so the offer is put to Maxim, priest-in-embryo, and he accepts.

The tram to the wharf jolts past a small riverside edifice and he says 'That used to be a church. Now it's a condom factory.'

'I like the way St Petersburg recycles its old buildings. In London they usually demolish unused churches.'

'They are not very good condoms.'

'That church on Nevsky for example which is now a swimming-pool – brilliant.'

'They're too thick.'

Our boat is called the Alexander Ulyanov (the name of Lenin's brother who was hanged in 1887 for his part in a plot to assassinate Alexander III) but was built in Germany in 1979 for ploughing up and down the Rhine, not for crossing large lakes. It is very low in the water and at a glance there look to be insufficient lifeboats. The cabin is narrow, clean and comfortable, and leaving our bags there, we join the mix of ordinary Russians – teenagers, family groups, no solitaries – who line the rails as the white boat sidles into mid-stream. Soon we are advancing with glycerine rapidity between green fields, green woods, green grassy banks at sundown, the endless northern sundown of melting peaches, crushed strawberries, pale welkin blue, duck's egg blue, eau-de-nil, aquamarine, ultramarine, turquoise, electric blue, royal blue, cobalt blue, woad blue, navy blue, a whole Thesaurus of blues except Prussian blue, all the clairvoyant and poignant blues of Russia.

We have brought a few provisions but the ticket includes food – though not on the first night when recourse must be to the pay-menu in the restaurant. Caviar, tomato & cucumber salad, chicken or beef or shashlyk

– go for chicken and salad . . . Most of the passengers must have come otherwise prepared, because only 3 tables are occupied . . . Over the tannoy a man's reassuring voice keeps the passengers abreast of things – there will be dancing in the disco later – and the voice is followed by anodyne music reminiscent of the kind which accompanies porno-graphic films from the 70s. The chicken arrives, theoretically. It has no taste but resembles a knot of bleached car tyre rubber threaded with sinews, into which bones have been inserted like broken knitting-needles. I bounce it a few times but there's no way in. Maxim tears at his with strong incisors, a spark of amusement behind his specs, and says 'In Russia people are turning into animals.'

'So you said.'

'A neighbour of ours was in hospital having a baby and an unmarried woman was having a baby too and screaming with pain and the doctor delivering it said "Stop screaming, whore – you weren't screaming like that when you were fucking".'

'Are you turning into an animal?'

'Sometimes – in a shop trying to get food perhaps.'

We buy mineral water and pass a booth staffed by a pretty girl with dark terrier eyes who, among the souvenir key rings, iconic postcards and bicycle pennons, runs a crucial lifeline in homemade shortbread and cupcakes – we take most of them and a bag of nutty bon-bons too.

'What do you think of Nevsorov?' I whisper in the television room. Everyone looks round so we leave and crunch our bon-bons elsewhere.

'He's a sensationalist. But he's a patriot. And I'm a patriot!'

'Sounds like trouble.'

'It's not the same thing as fascist. Are you not a patriot?'

'No.'

'Don't you love England?'

'Yes. Very much. I hate it too.'

'What do you hate about it?'

'Many things. Its *shame* for a start. In the 19th century there was a priest called Hopkins who was the Rimbaud of England but he was *ashamed* of it and hid himself, only to be published 29 years after his death. Therefore – and unlike Rimbaud's – his poetry is a bore. Not part of the life of literature but of the archeology of literature. The English are ashamed of almost everything. They can hardly breathe any more they are so choked with shame.'

'What else?'

'So much isn't allowed, it's a joke. And if there isn't a law against it, the English go round pinning up rules, and talk about what's done, what's not done, what they like, what they don't like. Prohibition becomes internalised, instinctive after a while. English women are more free than English men.'

'I think women generally are more free than men,' he says.

The disco is packed and the bar serves drinks of uncertain character in dayglo colours – ½ an hour in the queue – I buy 2 orange ones – it's a colour that's recognisable, drinkwise. There is a vacant sofa out on the landing.

'I met some Jews the other day and when I referred to them as Russians, one was very offended.'

'Of course,' he says, sipping casually. 'How can a Jew be a Russian? They have different blood.'

'Oh, blood, yes. That stuff.'

'The Jews stabbed Russia in the back.'

'What do you mean?'

'The Jewish Revolution. 1917. Russia drank the poisoned cup – and like Christ it suffered for the whole world.'

'Like Christ?'

'Russia was crucified like Christ and by the same people.'

'Christ wasn't crucified by a people but by a bunch of priests.'

'But they said let his blood be on our hands and on our children.'

'Priests do talk like that. Blithely damning the unborn. But wasn't it Roman soldiers who actually did the job?'

'It's no use talking to you.'

'Please, go on.'

He delineates the Nazi Theory of Jewish World Conspiracy without seeing it as such and ends by declaring 'That's fact.'

'But history is the product of numberless conspiracies,' I reply.

'Russia was bewitched by Judaism seeking world domination. Its objective was the destruction of the Russian Orthodox Church by atheism. Marx was Jewish.'

'Engels wasn't.'

'Everyone knows the 1917 Revolution was Jewish.'

'But it was dedicated to the overthrow of capitalism and Jews have traditionally been the avatars of capitalism in Europe.'

'You don't understand. I knew you wouldn't understand. I'm giving you history, not my opinions, but you don't understand.' There is a quivering 17-year-old intensity to his belief. 'Do you have Jewish blood?' he asks.

'Not that I know of. I'm not a Jewish apologist, if that's what you mean. I know very little about this subject. I am aware that the Jewish settlement in Eastern Europe was very extensive compared to the West and developed a distinct Yiddish culture. Do you know a problem created by Hitler? We are not really allowed to look into this Yiddish world any more. We can only gawp at it and think "holocaust". We can't look at it critically. But what you are saying is that the Russian Revolution had nothing to do with the Russians.'

'That is true.'

'Was Lenin Jewish?'

'¼ Jewish.'

'Trotsky?'

'Ukrainian Jew. Stalin killed him.'

'Stalin?'

'He had this other name which means Jew's son. You must understand that "Soviet" and "Russian" are totally separate things.'

'No, they're not totally separate.'

'Just as Nazi and German are totally separate things.'

'No, they're not either, I'm afraid.'

'The pure Russian spirit was contaminated by Jewish ideas like a virus.'

'Why was huge magnificent Russia so feeble that a handful of Jews could destroy it?'

He crosses his legs and stares at the upper knee. Then blurts out 'You don't believe in God, you don't believe in prayer, you don't believe in the Bible, you don't believe in anything! You think Russia is a bunch of fleas! Satanists are proposing a monument to Satan in Moscow – perhaps you believe in that!' He takes off his spectacles and nervously polishes the lenses. He's getting upset.

'Actually I do believe in prayer. It orientates psychological forces. We pray all the time. To pray is to meditate, to wish, to place one's wishes in a larger context. If we didn't pray I'm sure we'd go crazy.'

'Good!'

'But it's no substitute for action.'

'Do you believe in life after death?' he asks.

'Yes.'

'You do?'

'Yes. Because I don't know – therefore I must gamble. If I gamble on death, after death I shall certainly lose, but if I gamble on life I might win.'

'You are too smart alec.'

'Yes. I'm sorry.'

We have to share a cabin later. Don't want relations to become too strained. I'll buy some ice-cream. Vanilla with chocolate flakes: 2 of them cost 64 roubles 80 kopeks. Maxim says that last year 2 cost 86 kopeks. Music has begun. The girls are flagrantly cruising the boys who are dragged, protesting with leaden feet, onto the dance-floor and have their male hands forcibly applied to female buttocks and bosoms. The girls' determination to get their rocks off despite the odds against them is very heartening – they are like English girls in this respect. The dancers fidget awhile to unfamiliar rap and techno rhythms but when the DJ plays Bill Haley's *Rock Around The Clock* the place erupts. Each seems to have rehearsed a rock dance routine which they now go into, all reserve abandoned, blatant groping underway, abetted by the ungainly pitching of the boat – a storm is revving up.

Maxim says 'The music hurts my chest' and outside on the landing adds 'You are lucky. You live in a cellophane bag in Russia.'

'Listen – it's very difficult for Westerners to cope here. Very testing. We have the economic advantage – but you have the psychological advantage.'

'No, it is psychologically bad for us too. Because of the collapse of our world, many people don't know how to live any more.'

'Why do Russians think that all Westerners are mollycoddled, that only Russians can have problems worthy of the word?'

'By the way, I'm not anti-Jewish, I'm anti-Zionist. They stab us in the back but we do not return the stab.'

'Jolly decent of you.'

'There is no anti-Semitism in Russia. Do you know about the Jewish Freemasonry Conspiracy?'

'Look, the achievements of the Nazis do not suggest that these Jewish conspiracies of yours are very effective, so why not stop worrying about it so much?'

'How could the Nazis kill 6 million Jews when there were only 600,000?'

'Even less excuse for all the fuss then.'

'I think we must stop this conversation,' he says.

'Yes. But one thing more – I'm beginning to see something. Tell me what you think. You nationalists have a problem that the German nationalists in the 1930s did not have: nobody has defeated you. Nobody has conquered the Russians – and nobody wants to conquer the Russians. Whatever one finds here is a Russian accomplishment. But you don't like that and so you ask "Who did this to our country? Who ruined it?" Russian nationalists accuse the Jews of making the Revolution because the nationalists cannot confront the idea that Russia could do such a thing to itself. Have you read *The Gulag Archipelago*? Is this the story of a Jewish conspiracy in which Russians played no essential part?'

'I knew you wouldn't understand. . .' he says in a philosophical tone which is not patronising. He has that holy, novice, deadly confidence.

For me – as a naïve, gullible, simple-minded Englishman – it *is* perplexing, the extent to which Russians appear to have collaborated in their own terrorisation. But they usually don't see it like that – Marxism taught them that men are merely the slaves of History. How far have Russians taken on the real question? Which is not how could Stalin kill millions of people, but how could we do such things to ourselves?

(But surely no Russian could read *The Gulag Archipelago 1918–1956*, every page of which freezes the blood, without experiencing his own form of psychosis, as no German can read the history of Nazism without a similar convulsion. These convulsions take various forms, not all of them apparent. And by no means all of them are forms of self-questioning – one for example is the rejection psychosis: imagining that it did not happen; another is the justification psychosis: imagining that there was a good reason for torturing millions of innocent people to death; most often a third: that it was somebody *else's* fault. But *any one of us* reading such books finds himself among material very difficult to deal with, especially on the nature of God's supreme creation, Man.)

The universal rituals of preparing for bed restore a degree of homely proportion. Maxim climbs fully clothed into the upper bunk, folds his spectacles into a hard flip-lid case, and undresses problematically beneath the blanket, arranging his clothes neatly on the rail behind his head.

'Don't worry,' I say. 'I shan't rape you.'

'I hope not. I have sex only with my wife.'

No sleep. People sing and make parties all night and doors bang in a round-robin of copulations. Also – the boat is pitching to excess and may conceivably capsize. Ladago is the largest lake in Europe – the water is very rough – so much for the lacustrine diversion. This is 'the ship to anywhere' because it doesn't much matter where we go – it's become part of my strategy for shrinking the next 2 weeks. To anywhere, yes – but please, Lord, not to the bottom. Maxim, secure in his Lordship's arms, sleeps like a babe.

But anywhere is of course somewhere. The next intrusion into one's quest for oblivion is Maxim pushing on the blankets and saying 'Hurry or we shall miss the boat!' It's several moments before meaning comes abreast of sentience. This is the small boat to shore. The crispness and clarity of the early morning air singing down from the Arctic is a tonic indeed, while the vividness of the colours on a cloudless day is hardly credible – blue, green, yellow: in the course of a troubled night we were transported to an Isle of the Blest. The lighter, bumping up a tangy spray, chugs past chapels which resemble oriental kiosks on wooded promontories, and into the shelter of a birch-clad harbour.

Apart from a few monks and farmers the island is uninhabited. There is only one building near the quay, a small café selling cigarettes, sweets, coffee, expensive foreign tinned drinks and nothing else – the Cure come loudly out of a double-breasted radio. Breakfastless, I yearn to divert to this establishment but Maxim says no or we'll miss the abbey church, so we climb the stony path with the others to the monastery complex which is silent and empty except for the occasional black-cloaked monk rippling along rotten walls. Piece by piece the fabric is emerging from dereliction but it has yet a forlorn, shattered air as though a major world war passed through some years ago.

The interior of the great 5-domed church is clogged with scaffolding but there are intimations of bygone magnificence – and of magnificence to come. We boat-people look wan or imbecilic, drained by the vodka night, blinking and swaying while the guide – a tall man with white hair, red face and a stick – gives gurgling vent to a stream of information which has no end and I tell Maxim to leave off translating it. When finally the guide's mind runs out and he prepares to shuffle his flock down to the crypt, a woman asks a question and this renews him – his inner resource plays for another 10 minutes. Far be it from me to suggest that the Mount Athos of the North is other than a site of the utmost fascination – it's simply that no sleep for one who was already underslept has rendered me all but deceased. So I tug Maxim's elbow and suggest we wander the isle aimlessly.

The landscape, warming to the ascendant sun, is both secretive and cheerful. The forest, flowered meadows, purling rivulets and rocky coves loosen one's various levels of urban tension which unfold like patterned tablecloths and float freely in the soft breeze. We come upon a pasture beside a stream, with so beautiful a view of receding deciduous trees and such a delectable chemistry of aromas that we decide to lie here and finish the remainder of the provisions. The stream is dappled with the circular leaves of water plants. Chamber groups of flying insects perform tiny quartets and trios from their outposts in the long grass.

'Madame Blavatsky has been appearing to people,' he says.

'What fun.'

'This religious market-place in Russia now – I would ban it!'

'I think the appeal of Western religious bodies is not the creed but the support system. People only take to religion for one reason – to feel safe. Maybe they feel safer connected to a support system beyond Russia.'

'Russia needs to be reborn,' he says.

'That's what we're in right now, isn't it?'

'We're in a swamp. You know these swamps with mirages? You see someone calling for help for example or you see a meadow and so you move towards it, but when you approach, the meadow vanishes or there is no one calling for help and you are in fact in the most dangerous part of the swamp and you just sink. Russia is this swamp.'

The sun shines onto his gold-rimmed spectacles and red hair. His whole head is aflame.

Feminist Film Party. For breakfast this morning we have semolina with smetana and fresh strawberries, and to accompany the dark invigorating tea, Zoia has wrested from the clutches of impossibility a great trophy of sophistication: fresh milk in a carton.

She says 'I think your book is very good' (she must've borrowed Grace's copy).

The strawberries explode serenely in my mouth: are they intrinsically superior to Western strawberries or is it the improvement of the taste buds due to an absence of processed food?

After the boat trip, among my phone messages was one from Valentina. I rang her and with dictionary help discovered she was proposing an outing to Pavlosk. With Dima away, my instinct said no and I made my excuses.

Katya rings with a same-day invitation to a party being thrown by Sian, the chubby English redhead who organised that evening at the Magic Theatre. It isn't in Sian's Moika flat which is too small but in the one where she *used* to live a couple of buildings along from Zoia's, a ground-floor flat with tall round-headed windows looking over the Neva to the Peter and Paul Fortress.

It's a close humid evening and when we arrive about 2 dozen people are shuffling about, including several semi-drunk actors and a number of independent-looking women, Sian's colleagues in the feminist film-making group. The windows are open to admit a restorative air off the river. The room is furnished with chairs and sofas from the early 19th century, and down one side a long table is so burdened with red caviar, trout, chicken, salads, tomatoes, apricots, cherries, apples, strawberries, bananas, tangerines, that you couldn't squeeze another plate onto it.

'It's because after this I have to starve for 18 days – and I mean *starve*,' laughs Sian with rotund equanimity. 'Only hot water – for 18 days! It's to reduce my fibroids. But *you* don't have to eat all this – I'm not Georgian. Georgian hospitality is the most aggressive in the world – they won't leave you alone – you've *got* to eat and eat – you've *got* to get drunk. It's all about status and power, not about being friends. The guest is not considered in the slightest. The guest is *forced* to conform.'

'Well, it's also an assault on the guest's reserve, isn't it? To take him out of himself and bring him in to the new place. How does hot water reduce fibroids?'

'When you starve you start to use up the most useless parts of the body – which in my case are the fibroids.' She puts a cassette into a red plastic radio and says 'Dance, everybody!' but no one moves – it's too early at 11 pm.

Though nervous of all these strangers, I feel very lit up inside. Near me is a woman of medium height and short dark hair, not pretty but with a sturdy body and sexual in the way it shifts beneath a close-fitting floral print frock. Her name is Tamara. She speaks fluent English and works with Sian and is also a feminist – I use the term to indicate a woman who makes her own decisions about her life, one who doesn't defer to the role designed for her by males.

As I bite into a tomato, a stream of red flesh shoots out in the direction of this woman. Fortunately she's seen it coming and dodges the offensive pulp which descends harmlessly onto the parquet beyond her.

'Terribly sorry,' I say as soon as able, wiping a slurry of seeds from my chin. 'Not normally so clumsy. I must be over-excited.'

'Why?'

'Dunno. Yes I do – because I'm involved.'

'With whom?'

'A teenage couple. No – the boy really.'

'This is interesting. Is he beautiful?'

'Yes,' I say, cleaning up the mess on the parquet with a paper napkin.

'Does he know he's beautiful?'

D: Not in the sense you mean, no – which is one of the reasons he is.

T: Why is he not with you to-night? He is with the girl.

D: No. He's gone away, training in the Navy.

T: Not very convenient.

D: No.

T: Are you seeing the girl?

D: No.

T: He'd be jealous?

D: It would give the wrong idea. And she doesn't speak any English. It's very difficult. But she wants to see me.

T: Is she beautiful?

D: Yes.

T: All this beauty. It could get complicated.

D: Yes. Because neither of them is *merely* beautiful. They both have their wised-up side.

T: Are you jealous of the girl?

D: No. To be jealous of someone I have to be able to identify with them.

T: Is she jealous of you?

D: I shouldn't think so.

T: Is she jealous of him? Most Russian girls want a Western man.

D: I don't er –

T: Or is he jealous of you?

D: Oh, maybe we are all 3 jealous of each other!

T: More champagne?

D: He invited me to go with them to the Crimea. I said no. Anyway – she was kidnapped by the mafia.

T: My God, it *is* a story.

D: He asked me for the ransom.

T: How much?

D: 300 dollars.

T: My God. A Russian can live for a year on that.

D: I refused.

T: So he thinks you are a mean Englishman.

D: I'd rather he thought me mean than stupid. If he thought me stupid, we could never be close.

T: How did you refuse?

D: I said I didn't have it.

T: Was that true?

D: I could've borrowed it somehow. And I said to him 'I don't know you.'

T: Oh, this is bad.

D: I felt bad saying it.

T: You are very cruel.

D: Please don't say that. You are too quick.

T: But the girl – what happened?

D: He solved the problem by himself.

T: But you took the risk. She might have been hurt.

D: Maybe it looks like that. But my guts said pull back. This was not from selfishness. You see how it was – I had no way of knowing what was true, what to do for the best, so I had to follow my instinct.

T: You are trying to convince yourself.

D: Of course. I have a great fear of being unjust to him.

T: What is truth for you?

D: In this case it would be someone trying to tell the truth. Truth being a motive.

T: So if you knock a person down in your car by accident, it has not actually happened?

D: I felt I should not finance a situation I knew nothing about. And thereafter the situation vanished.

T: And if you discovered that this had been an attempt to trick you?

D: Oh God, I'd be relieved! It would mean he was in much less trouble.

T: What would you say to him?

D: Don't make a habit of it! The little devil . . .

T: More champagne! Weren't you a little devil at his age?

D: Yes. A boy who hasn't got a bit of the devil in him isn't worth anything. The buccaneering temperament. Before taking the girl, they'd taken the grandmother.

T: What?!

D: Is it the sort of thing one would invent?

T: She came back, the grandmother?

D: I think so. Then went away again.

T: This is too complicated!

D: I'd give money for good things but not for bad things.

T: Good, bad, truth, trick – in our country it can be neither or both.

D: Oh yes, I think he was in a tight corner over something but perhaps it wasn't as he presented it. I don't *know*! Anything is possible . . . However, one thing I do know – he is innocent of any crime.

T: Russian men cannot easily be open. Can Englishmen?

D: Sometimes. So can Russian men sometimes.

T: Will you ever know the truth?

D: Maybe. In years to come.

T: And what if he told the truth?

D: I . . . I'd ask him to forgive me. I was suddenly so out of my depth – and still am. I . . .

T: I'm sorry. Don't worry. Is he a violent type?

D: No, no. He can defend himself but he's not a thug. He has this young gentleman aspect.

T: He was angry with you?

D: I don't know what it was. By the way I'm not mean with him.

T: You are generous.

D: He gives me things too.

T: What sort of things?

D: All sorts of things. He gave me a cassette of Russian rap. He gave me a beautiful book about St Petersburg. And a Russian phrase-book and –

T: Are you learning Russian?

D: Yeah, I will. He has a generous heart.

T: You mean he asks for 300 dollars not 30!

D: It's true – easy come, easy go, not petty in his thinking.

T: Ah, before you came along they were simple young lovers!

D: Now you are being sentimental.

She chinks her glass against mine and says 'Touché!' Why am I being so open with her? I've not gone into it with anyone else. The feminists are dancing with each other now, touching each other, laughing, while the men – including *their* men – huddle in sluggish corners making no waves. Tamara and I sit in one of the open windows dangling legs over the pavement. A group of boys stop and look in, joke with us, move on, except one who detaches himself and tries to make conversation with the party inside. He is from the Caucasus, tall, thin, black-eyed, floppy-haired, with a large bony nose.

Katya exclaims 'I love his nose!'

'You know what they say about noses.'

'No, no! What, what?!!' chorus the feminists.

'Big nose, big cock.'

They squeal.

'The myth of the small cock,' says one.

'There's another myth,' I say, 'that no woman is interested in the size of a man's penis. Size is not a problem for women – but they can be interested. Several women who appreciate size tell me it's not length they enjoy but thickness, girth.'

'Oh yeah! Girth, girth, girth!' they chorus, shimmying together, laughing. The Caucasian boy laughs too, without understanding this English exchange.

'Can I come in?' he asks.

'No,' says Tamara.

'Oooooooooh,' he moans and moves on.

T: Do you believe in monogamy?

D: Sometimes.

T: But it's so tiring looking for new people.

D: A man is programmed for adventure, isn't he?

T: And a woman isn't?

D: A woman is circular, a man is linear.

T: I want to be linear!

D: You can be.

T: You say I'm circular.

D: Do not follow it.

T: You know women's voices are deeper than they were.

D: How do you know?

T: They've done research with old recordings. What do you want to do with your boy?

D: Travel round the world with him.

T: My God.

D: But to do this, his present life would have to be broken – which might be a disaster.

T: Why disaster?

D: If it is to change, it must come from him, not me.

T: My God, at 16, 17, nothing is solid anyway. You are trying to be responsible!

D: Don't you see? He has to be his own man, or he'd end up hating me.

T: All life can drain away while you are being responsible.

D: You mean decency shrivels the passions?

T: It's a danger, isn't it?

D: But one can be passionate for example about justice.

T: The abstractions are different.

D: In truth I feel reckless.

T: You have the power to change lives. But things will change without your permission. These teenagers can change you.

D: Is it possible he will feel trapped?

T: With the girl?

D: No. In the military. I long for him to be free. I would always help that.

T: Maybe he wants you to help but doesn't know how to tell you. What does he want?

D: Who knows? She is his home.

T: Rock to-day can be water to-morrow.

D: Is that a Russian proverb?

T: Maybe he is using you.

D: Of course he is. I want to be used. And I am using him. But it's more than that. Mutual use, it's not a bad place to start, is it?

T: No, no, it's the best.

D: This idea that the affections are cheapened by any connection with reality, it's not –

T: No, no, I agree. It can't just be 2 fantasies staring at each other.

(Seeing lamplit gyrations within, and party-goers in the open windows, cars intermittently stop outside and their occupants ask 'What are you selling?')

D: Most murders in this town are not crimes of passion as in London but hard currency murders.

T: It is good you do not forget this.

D: I met a couple of ancient aristocrats recently who were pining for the good old days of social equality.

T: Oh that never was it! It was the Russian hating the idea that anyone should have something more than him.

D: No, these 2 old people – I think they were genuine in their noble dream of a just society.

T: Do you know what was so terrible in Russia? To be betrayed by people you trusted. It happened very often under Communism with so many informants. Malicious envy is a very Russian characteristic.

D: Something happened to you.

T: And betrayal still happens in this present time of mania.

D: What was it that happened?

T: Not now – I shall tell you another day. When will you see him again?

D: Next week. For the last time. I don't know. Perhaps. For a few minutes. It's so . . .

T: Little?

D: No. Yes . . . Concentrated.

T: You must learn detachment.

D: Oh, bugger detachment!

T: Do you want to dance?

D: Anyway – for this teenage couple probably I'm not real. Just something from a film. They'll both forget me. I was just some bloke one summer.

T: You have only to wear this beautiful white shirt and they will remember you for ever.

D: I'm a bit nervous when they're both together with me.

T: Because they are 2, you are 1; they are at home, you are alone in this strange foreign place; and when they talk about you *in your very presence* you do not know what they are saying.

D: That was another reason for not going to the Crimea. I wasn't prepared to sit in a corner like a lemon.

T: You haven't given me the first reason yet.

D: Oh – you know . . .

T: Remember how young they are.

D: I usually don't. They've been living together for a year. Doesn't youth give them power? Of time ahead, of ignorance.

T: Greater than your power? You may become his eternal dissatisfaction.

D: Why?

T: Because you remind him of what he will never have, never be . . .

D: If he wants to be a miserable sod –

T: Why are you laughing?

D: He's a wonderful person! Very bright and talented and up. He could have whatever he wants, be very successful in life, if he put his mind to it.

T: But in Russia it is always –

D: Oh screw all that in-Russia-it's-always stuff. Russia's future will be fantastic! Can't you *feel* it? Yes, let's dance.

The Caucasian boy returns on the pavement outside, washed, changed, holding up a bottle of vodka. 'Please let me come in,' he asks.

The feminists form a phalanx in the windows, laughing, teasing: 'No, no, you can't come in!'

Katya says 'Maybe he has tattoos. I'm mad about tattoos.'

'I've never seen so many as here. Except in Britain.'

'They have them in Denmark.'

'And in Japan.'

'My boyfriend's best tattoo is across his back. It was my Christmas present. It says "I Love Princess Katya Galitzina." It's the nicest thing that's ever happened to me.'

A couple more cars stop outside. 'What are you selling? Are you selling something?' And the Caucasian boy, with his head on one side, continues 'Go on, don't be mean, let me come in, please, can I come in?'

The consignment of caviar arrives in round golden kilo tins. Then Grace and Zoia make a trip out of town to the beach.

In the afternoon, looking at the Winter Canal – what is different about it? From the bridge on Ul. Khalturina the canal is a strip of denim-blue water into which the overlooking yellow buildings reflect ripples of hot gold. And at the far end where it enters the river and a Quarenghi masterpiece, the foyer of the Imperial Theatre, makes an unusual but very satisfying overarch to the 3 curved lines of the small granite bridge – hang on – yes, that's what's different – the low apertures in the termination of the vista are blocked by something massive on the other side, something 20th-century and elaborately metallic. Walking down the side of the canal, hemmed by the New Hermitage, and passing under the arch, a panorama opens up to reveal a flotilla of warships strung with flags sitting on the expansive peaceful breast of the river.

In the evening Zoia says 'The beach was very good. We had red champagne and black caviar and Grace had a beautiful swim.'

But when we are alone Grace says 'Zoia said "I don't think you have a beach so beautiful as this in France. You must swim. It is healthy." So I went in the water and suddenly realised I was surrounded by dead rotting fish and came running out. What kind of doctor is Zoia?'

'What we call a GP. General practitioner.'

'She has some very strange ideas on health. She was reading your book with a dictionary on the beach and came to a strange bit and said "I think he has sexual problems." '

'Bloody cheek. I wish she had some. She seems to have given up that side of life. Does she have any lovers?'

'Not for 6 years.'

'Did you ask her?'

'She told me.'

'She will again.'

'How do you know?'

'She's dormant, not extinct, don't you feel?'

In the Big Room the 3 of us compose a comfortable family group. Most evenings Grace and Zoia play card games or chess or chequers in here – how Zoia loves those battles! Despite everything, I have developed an enormous fondness for her. Zoia's former existence – financial security, reasonable expectations, good pension in the offing – has been completely wiped out. Occasionally the fatigue and disappointment show. She is quiet for perhaps a whole day, humming to herself, avoiding eye contact. But a whole day is rare. She soon bounces back. On this evening Grace does not play with her but places a cushion against me on the sofa and lies against me to watch television. Between sips of vodka I stroke Grace's hair and woodland-creature eyebrows and kiss her clear brow, while Zoia

pretends to be going through the classified ads in the newspaper (she and
Boris often do the buy-and-sell columns together in a white heat of
absorption). But her attention is on us.

'Zoia, what are those warships doing on the Neva?'

'For Navy Day,' she replies, not removing her head from the paper.

'When's that?'

'Sunday.'

Later that night at 1 am, when Grace and Zoia are in bed, the telephone
rings. It's picked up in the Big Room. Whoever it is talks for half an hour
or more and then Grace comes to my room with the giggles, saying
'Arkady is on the phone. He's drunk. I can't get him off. He wants us to
go on a crayfish hunt to-morrow. Will you speak to him?'

'Arkady? Hullo.'

'Hullo.'

'You're drunk?'

'Yes.'

'In that case I'll have a vodka.' And pop to the kitchen and take a large
shot from the fridge. 'Are you still there?'

'No. I want to propose – ' He dissolves in giggles too.

'Yes, the crayfish hunt – what time?'

'6 o'clock.'

'Yes, good.'

'In ve morning.'

'No!'

'Yes.'

'Too early.'

'Grace said same.'

'Where are you?'

'Wiv friends. We are drinking.'

'I know.'

'We are drunk – but it is the blindness of Milton!'

'You are very clever, Arkady.'

'6 o'clock is only a few hours soon.'

'I'll be asleep.'

'Come here now. We can play cards to fill time. King. Or Preference
wiv an "a".'

'Do you still play vint or pique-dame here?'

'You know vis opera by Tchaikovsky?'

'From a story by Pushkin?'

'And set in St Petersburg.'

'What *is* a crayfish hunt?'

'Do you know what happened yesterday? Vey changed Pushkin back to Tsarskoye Selo. You fink it a good idea? Come drink wiv us now.'

'How about the day after to-morrow?'

'Ah, vat is a new life! Don't know if possible. Perhaps a mushroom hunt.'

'Arkady?'

'Yes?'

'I'm collecting bad Russian words.'

'Why?'

'For an article. The Art of Invective in the Post-Soviet Era.'

'I know many.'

'That's right. Give me the worst you can think of.'

He gabbles in Russian.

'What does that mean?'

He gabbles some more.

'Come on – what does it mean?'

'Go. Fuck. Your. Muvver.'

'Ooooooooo. In England there is worse.'

'What?'

'Go fuck your father.'

'Ooooooooooooooooo. Bad.'

'And worst of all – go fuck your Airedale.'

The Party At The End Of The World. Nikita rings in a sentimental humour, having returned from a loving interlude at the Riga Festival, and invites me to a party followed by a rave at a swimming-pool. Henrietta's boyfriend Misha Vorontsov is staging the rave (called Aquadelik) and she has already invited Grace and me along.

Hugh, the Welsh boy, rings.

'Have you found your photo of Nicholas II?'

'No. But guess what. My gums have swollen up. Isn't that awful? The hospital put compressors on them. But it didn't make any difference.

They say it's not eating properly – and the water.'

Nikita's pre-Aquadelik party is for a troupe of English fashion people led by Andrew Logan – they've all come on from this Riga Festival – and is held in an enormous artist's squat near the Cathedral of Blood: empty high-ceilinged apartments opening one into the other, with missing floorboards, missing pieces of ceiling and wall, and rudimentary amenities. The beauty of dereliction arises from a variety of structural and decorative layers, both inside and out, being visible simultaneously in complex effects of shape, colour, texture, pattern. Let it rot! The supreme moment is at the point of maximum rot short of collapse – which in addition to its visual interest has a terrific emotional tension, i.e. will it cave in while we are here? Let it rot? No. Patch it up. Thereby adding further layers of richness.

A small high-tech Japanese television set is on a box in the middle of the floor of the largest room. The English fashion people turn out to be ferocious ravers, and to music from a hidden source, they dance like banshees, screaming and stripping off their clothes. Nikita asks 'Are all English like this?'

'There's a big mad streak which can emerge. It's the result of the ruthless oppression of the erotic in English life ever since Byron.'

'At my birthday party, after you left, there was a live sex show. Galina and a boy made love on the carpet. We threw flowers over them. The week before she had sex on some tramlines.'

Here is a painter called Africa.

'What for you is love?'

He replies 'This is a word I do not use.'

Here is another painter, called Andrei. He is wearing heavy cream cotton trousers with fine black stripes woven into them, like the peasant wears in the Ethnography Museum.

'How old are you?'

'17.'

'Are half the people in this town 17?'

'No.'

'Do you live with a girl?'

'No. I live here. Sometimes with my parents. I can live in St Petersburg with very little money – which would not be possible in the West.'

These places, it transpires, are not absolute squats but unoccupied buildings in which space can be rented for a nominal sum.

'I tried to commit suicide 2 times,' he says. 'First time pills, second time cutting my arm.'

'You were unhappy.'

'Not unhappy. Not crazy. It was a period when I understand more than I could bear to understand.'

'Was your childhood happy?'

'Very much. I was a child film star from 6 to 9 years and very happy because I did not go to school.'

'What do you like to eat?'

'I like to eat mushrooms. Up to 80 for a trip. They grow in the woods not far from the city. Some people eat 150.'

That seems excessive. But who am I to talk? During my 20s I was taking plenty of drugs – not from any addiction – I could never get it together to get addicted – an addiction requires major organisation. Nor was it to blunt or escape from life. It was the opposite – to throw oneself into it, to increase it, out of curiosity, a compulsive drive to see how far one could go overthenexthill/roundthenextbend, and to make oneself more seduceable. As a young man I had a very very strong head. I could drink gallons and not become drunk. I had to break down a lot of walls inside.

For example, the decision to take up cannabis was quite deliberate. As a non-smoker newly arrived at the University, it was clear that in order to smoke cannabis comfortably, effectively, I'd have to become a smoker per se. So I bought 20 Piccadilly at the Cadena Café – was sick once – never looked back – a 20, 40, 60-a-day man. The following summer (1968) it was opium and Dexedrine in Istanbul, aged 19 years. There is a swagger in the mere recording of the facts but compared to many I was a late developer. The era was supportive. Drugs were fashionable. Then LSD, Mandrax, the snortables – a headlong rush at my inhibitions, limitations, repressions. LSD was especially thrilling. The human brain is the most complex object in the visible universe (apart from the universe itself) – I wanted to explore it. And to explore the heart too – which was more difficult, the heart being the most complex object in the invisible universe. I became very wild in this passionate pursuit of a larger existence.

Indeed one day I thought I'd do the unmentionable. Be totally, unforgivably outrageous. Instead of the daily razzamatazz of pills, puffs, sniffs, booze, or whatever else might be circulating among the crashers in the bleary pick-me-up dawn of 1 pm, Lancaster Gate, I took – God so help me – nothing. Nothing whatsoever, except a cup of tea . . . yuk . . . foolhardy . . . crazy . . . sordid . . . but I took it anyway. Nothing . . . At first nothing happened. Then . . . still nothing. Then something quite unexpected which took my breath away. The walls stopped moving. Normally they palpitated like the bellies of aroused toads, making a singing or wheezing sound according to one's temper. But now – no – yes – they were motionless . . . It was quite a moment. I shouted through to Jill 'Hey, come and look at this' and she came through but couldn't see it. To her they were just ordinary, moving walls, and she went back into the kitchen to count her Mandy bottles. Then by degrees I noticed that somehow the colours of the room had altered. They had become simpler. For example – green was more or less green. You know, normally green was at least gangrene. And the large terracotta cushion which had so often, along with the floor, risen rapidly into the air to support my sleepy form – usually that cushion looked like the face of W. H. Auden in a state of advanced and complaining metempsychosis. But that morning – no. A simple terracotta floor cushion. It was a major revelation. A mind-blowing Zen thing. 'Is *is*,' I said aloud and I could feel the tears welling as, in a transport, and in the kitchen, I groggily pieced together the components of a fried egg sandwich from among the detritus of last night's fun. 'Do me one of those, will ya,' asked Jill. Had I seen God? Was I God? Then the headaches started . . . . . I know people say one hit an yer hooked, but taking nothing wasn't the beginning of a habit. 'Nothing' didn't begin to get a hold until after my 30th birthday, when I became *afraid*.

On the high-tech Japanese television set is the opening ceremony of the Olympic Games but no one pays attention.

Nikita and I leave, arranging to meet everyone later at Aquadelik, walk to my place to collect Grace, walk to Henrietta's 'sort of you know chunk of palace', and in the silky-hot night walk over the Kirovsky Bridge with a view of the dim hulks of warships dressed in brilliant strings of lights. The bridge and embankments are also dressed up, in bunting and Russian national flags, for Navy Day to-morrow. That is, to-day – since it's after midnight by the time we reach the Olympic-sized swimming complex in rectilinear brick, tile and plate glass (opposite the Gorky tube station, near the Mosque). Armed guards patrol the entrance of transparent walls where a throng of wildly dressed, thwarted liggers outside merges visually with the throng of entrées within: only a sheet of barely perceptible glass divides triumph from defeat. Henrietta has the passes, talks knowingly to one of the soldiers, and without anyone quite realising it the transposition has taken place and we are on the inside. Success seems to be only 'a knack' – for those who have it.

The noise breaks over us like surf.

'Where shall we go first?' shouts Henrietta. People run up and down open tread staircases in a froth of decibels. And all at once our homogenous party has dissolved into the larger, liquid, looning context. Do allow for that in the following description.

Various bars, massage rooms, solaria – but the pool pulls magnetically, a giant modernistic echo chamber, water floodit beneath and a neon blue light thinning upwards in the air and as it ascends to a clammy darkness, splays of blue and green lasers suddenly shoot the whole length of the space, intercut by strobes. There is a bar at this end, a tiled esplanade at the other serving as dancefloor, and people are swimming, splashing, dancing allegro vivace among aggressive light projections. The area is patrolled by soldiers festive in berets, combat gear, guns, but minus shoes and socks. We are not allowed into the main area until also barefoot. Most of us change into swimwear in the changing-rooms where attendants guard clothes. But you can strip off poolside if you like. All drinks are served in plastic cups –

swim
drink
swim
drink
swim

meanwhile Nikita is in another bar with painters who don't want to dance, don't want to swim, don't want to take off their clothes, who want to smoke dope and get drunk. Yuri says 'Let's talk about business – see you in the pool!' Bacchantes swarm into the bar. We leave. 'Rodge!'

'Any spare girls around?' asks Rodge. 'I hear there's screwing in the changing-rooms.'

'Yeah?'

'Yeah. And boys are touching each other up in the showers.'

'Yeah?'

'Yeah. A couple were fucking in the pool. Those people are swimming naked.'

'Where?'

A girl with black triangles on her cheeks comes up to us and says 'The universe is not rigid but dances and wobbles. It behaves approximately. To call this "chaos" is incorrect. To call Russia, ie. the universe, "chaos" is incorrect. To survive, to grow, the universe must be approximate. Rigidity is death. Anarchy is death. The universe shimmers between the 2 without ever touching either. All natural laws are extrapolated from approximate conditions. Russia is approximate. Even its nuclear reactors are approximate.'

'I see.'

swim

dance

Yuri swims up and hauls himself out of the electric blue water in a pair of swimming shorts printed with yellow and purple palm trees. 'Do you know anyone who wants to buy an incubator?' he asks, looking up at the lasers. 'My friend has incubators.'

'I'm drunk. But I don't feel drunk. Or do I mean the other way round? I'm not drunk. But I feel drunk.'

'I must have a woman to-night!' he exclaims and gives me a smacking kiss on the ear and dives back into the pool with a bellyflop whose terrific report cracks the building end to end –

dance

boom-boom-diaghilev

boom-boom-diaghilev

I dance to Zhenya's technogroove

for more than 2 hours without break among various recognisable and unrecognisable people – everyone is dancing with everyone – and during this period I go to Goa, to the Barbosas, a fishing family on Calangute Beach, to their house where I lived for 3 months, 17 years ago from this dancefloor, a house placed with a few others among palm and jack fruit trees, typically Goan, single storey, half hospitable and half secret, with a large verandah supported by fluted pillars and sheltered by a steep overhanging roof of mottled tiles. One could sit in the shade there, biscuit brown, genitals barely contained by a twist of blue seableached cotton, enjoying the occasional breeze, sipping coconut fenny or Indian gin, losing one's thoughts and collecting them again in spasmic clusters.

At the front of the house was a large glade where neighbours used to pass and a small white stucco chapel stood. To one side was a simple loo enclosed in palm leaves and when you visited it, there would be a squealing rumpus below as the black-and-pink pigs gathered to gobble one's waste. Several times a day I went to the well to fetch water, first in a yellow plastic bucket, but I couldn't make it sink and changed to a copper one. Mr Barbosa was a bit creaky and coming to the end of his fishing days. He enjoyed a drink. Mrs Barbosa had delicate health but was very solicitous and (though this wasn't part of the arrangement) would bring me fish or heart curries if she thought I were becoming too thin. Their son Benjamin and I would talk for hours and hours, then he'd go and play football or do his homework and I might visit Gabby and Ringo, a warm-hearted German couple who lived 10 minutes away up a quiet track.

Ringo had a finger and several teeth missing and always a lump of opium the size of a cricket ball on the go. Eaten raw, opium can sometimes produce a rebellion by the stomach but Ringo seemed to have passed this stage and indeed I never vomited from it either. But the taste is very bitter. Being maddeningly sticky too, opium is difficult to use, hence the phenomenon of opium dens wherein it is organised by professionals. Opium dens were rare in India and surprisingly also in Thailand. The most civilised were in Vientiane, and in pre-airport Penang's exquisite capital, George Town.

A 'pipe' of opium is traditionally 3 pipes – each being of one pellet ideally absorbed in a single slow inhalation. Others may differ but for me a night's resort would consist of 3 'pipes' (i.e. 9) between about 11 pm and dawn, interspersed with meditative slumbers on a soft couch or bunk and many cups of weak tea brewed by the young apprentice of the owner. There were usually 3 or 4 other customers in addition to any companion I might have – one hardly ever went alone. All was ease and dreamy cordiality on dark velvet nights, candlelit within and stars in the open window.

Left to my own devices, in Goa, I smeared a little of the brown gluelike matter down the side of an ordinary cigarette. Very unsatisfactory, because the opium does not burn properly in this way. I suppose one could have done what the Romantic poets did and dissolve it in alcohol to produce laudanum (where, in a decanter on the sideboard, it would have been indistinguishable from sherry or tawny port). But this takes planning and time. Ringo it was who devised the method of taking opium by vigorously stirring the pellet into hot coffee.

At some stage we would transfer to a small wood-and-palm-thatch café on the beach and eat pomfret or kingfish and banana pancakes with honey in the afterflush of a sunset into the Arabian Sea. And eventually I'd return to the Barbosas and read and write far into the night, sustained by French blues. Manufactured by Smith Kline & French, blues came in pretty rubber-capped phials from the chemist in Mapusa.

Every Wednesday there was the travellers' market up at Anjuna Beach, the main hippy settlement at the time. It was reached by walking through a palm grove at the northern point of Baga Beach to where a ferryman would punt you slowly across the river, after which there was a short walk over the rise of the projecting headland and down through rocks and light jungle. Every few weeks there were more ambitious parties on Anjuna, invariably coinciding with an astronomical event. A mobile generator would feed an electric band wailing under stars from a platform on the sand. There was free food of a murky, mystifying sort, and naked swimming which sparked phosphorus over the body. A creature with rough skin and sharp fin once grazed my flank in the midnight waves. It was large, probably hungry, and that one little tap carried the sense of an enormous weight and power behind it. Terrified but stoned, I paddled coolly to the shore. Next day we saw what it was – not a shark – a school of dolphins was running down the coast. One Anjuna party was for an eclipse of the moon. The moon duly turned green, then red, then bromide brown, and the dancers cartwheeling in the light of a huge bonfire resembled blood-sodden Aztec priests with virgin hearts between their teeth. Fab. Benjamin disliked going on the beach after dark and when I asked why, he said it was from fear of sea spirits. One of them had taken a relation of his and deposited him further up the coast the following day, dead, entirely blocked with sand from mouth to rectum . . . Happy days? Searching days . . .

And yes, pre-airport Penang is likewise wound snakily into this Aquadelik dance – the hotel in Chulia Street turned out to be a brothel with latticed rattan walls between rooms. The night was loud with the sound of Russian merchant sailors getting their rocks off, and once the rocks were off, which seemed to happen very quickly, the long interval until breakfast was occupied by the singing of sad Slav songs in resonant bass voices. In George Town heroin was widely smoked by people such as taxi-drivers as a casual, irregular high. That's how I took it too, rolled into cigarettes. I bought a gram in a glass tube with scoop-cap from a charming half-caste girl with fire scars all up the side of her body. It was 'brown sugar' with rocks in, very good quality – not to try it would be rather like finding yourself in Strasbourg and refusing foie gras. You used the tube like a mini-rolling-pin to crush out the rocks, then sprinkled the powdered narcotic into tobacco. I'd never dream of using a needle for anything – I'm far too vain. But I smoked it daily for 19 days, mainly in the back of rickshaws with the hood right down, staring beadily at pedestrians. Very dull – I prefer a freer, breezier effect. (Morphine, in the form of an off-white powder with a brown shadow in it, had no discernible effect at all.) As I've written elsewhere there were no withdrawal symptoms. But when several months later I flew from Bombay to London, after a year of travelling in the East, I did experience entry symptoms, and left much of myself smeared across the intervening space . . . . dance on . . . . .

Yuri is dancing with Grace – here is a triple rhythm – petipa petipa petipa – and Anna Benn, an English redhead, is talking to a group of masked harlequins, their costumes dripping red blood in a red light . . . dance on . . . and during the dance I too discover the secret of the universe, that everything in the universe, including thought and emotion as well as physical phenomena, is manifested in waves. People are collections of waves too, not enclosed entities. The fundamental law of existence is the wave. Matter struggling into form, form struggling into consciousness, it can be done only via waves. Something can exist therefore only in movement. Therefore everything is alive. The greatest possible wave is the breathing of God which cosmologists refer to as 'the oscillating universe'. The universe is not a machine, it's an animal!

Beside the pool, Galina (the Tramline Screwer) says to Miguel (the Chilean Berliner) 'Pleasure and death converge in the nirvana principle,' and she dives expertly into the water.

Then I dance for another hour, with Grace. In a panic surge of abrasive pulsations comes *Song of Life* by Leftfield – or something very like it –

'Spaceships are the children of mathematics.'

'Mathematics is a mystery *because* it works.'

I see Rodge moving away. He waves and mouths a silent 'Ciao.'

Then I'm tired and retrieve my clothes from the male changing-room where several boys and a girl are lying naked, drunk, asleep, on the long wooden benches.

Nikita, Grace and I go into the main sit-down bar and drink Concorde – tins of strawberry champagne (low alcohol, 7.5%) manufactured in

Britain. Never heard of it. Where do the Russians find these things? Serve chilled, it says. The tins are warm, almost hot. Foul sweet perfumed taste like melted-down boiled sweets. Nikita has a brandy with his but knocks it over. 'No, I will *not* lick the table,' he mutters, trying to focus, sit upright and square his shoulders – but his head keeps nodding like a model dog's in a car rear window.

'What for you is love?'

'Ooooo . . .' He smiles and rolls brown eyes under the crewcut. 'I was in love but what was love is no longer love so I must revise my opinion and think that maybe it never was love and therefore I don't know what love is because I was never in love. For me to be in love, the other person must love me first. This is very Russian – not making the first move.'

Yuri, who has joined us with a bouquet of vodkas in plastic cups between his large hands, declares that 'Love is when you begin to live for another person.'

'Have you found a woman?'

'Yes. She is waiting. I am enjoying myself first.'

'This also is very Russian,' says Nikita and his head falls onto the table.

'But,' continues Yuri, 'if you live for another person, that person soon ceases to be interested in you. As soon as the other person is completely sure of your love, you lose your magnetism for them. That happened to me – I lost her because I lived for her!'

'But that's the opposite of what Nikita feels.'

'No, if you want to be loved, you must not surrender your will to the other person,' says Yuri. 'You have to keep your own personality. Then the other person will love you.'

Grace rallies. 'Every relationship . . . is different.' And her head falls forward onto her breast.

'Sometimes,' says Yuri, leaning across and touching her knee, 'you love separate things more in other people. But taken all together, it's best with the one you love.'

But Grace is somniferous in a chair and Yuri, with no depletion whatsoever of vitality, says 'Adios!' and gallivants off. It's 6 am. Time for us to go too.

The air is misty fresh in the bugling sunrise. There has been brief, light rainfall – or else a heavy dew, because the sky is cloudless – and as we cross the narrow park between the swimming-pool and the main road, the clean-cool smell of wet vegetation invigorates the lungs. A rickety tram clanks its few carriages round a bend in the tramlines laid through cobblestones, but apart from the driver there is only one occupant. Otherwise there is no traffic at all and the streets are empty. In the course of the night most of the Navy Day flags have been stolen from the Kirovsky Bridge and here, at about mid-stream, we are arrested – by the sky, vast and pale blue, turning white at the eastern horizon to the left, and by the sun, strawberry-coloured, looking too big and pushing up through narrow bands of mist. Only ⅔ of the disc is presently visible above the horizon. But its slow upward slide is detectable with the naked eye.

A fine pearly mist pervades the city, not obscuring any of it but casting all in a pastel soft focus sparkling here and there with jewels. From the western side of the bridge dozens of small boats and yachts can be seen anchored on the river, bobbing but still asleep. The warships are dressed with flags, but it's too early even for them to be awake. It is very quiet. The only sound is the call of landbirds and seabirds. Hugely grand, St Petersburg is nonetheless dwarfed by the greatness of sky and river. No other city is so penetrated to its very heart by the grandeur of nature. This renders it both epic and intimate. The cosiest moments are susceptible to epic intrusion. And vice versa.

In the east the too-big strawberry bulb of the sun continues edging upwards minute by minute, until the whole disc wobbles free of the horizon, and rising on up through the low tiers of mist, it rises free of the mistline also, and attains to a round incandescent orange of godlike assertiveness, although the eye may still look upon it unharmed and the light which pours from it is soft, steady, clear.

On this riverine or indeed maritime summer Sunday at 6 am, the city is the most beautiful I have seen it, blessèd, shining like new toys in the early morning sun. For the very first time it is not haunted in the slightest degree, but entirely clean and undefiled, entirely healthy, in every way at peace. It is breathing light. Young. Perfect.

. . . The moment of rapturous pause on the bridge has expanded to more than 30 timeless minutes.

Grace says dreamily 'The expression on your face is so strange . . . How the sun changes – it's very grotty.'

'What do you mean?'

'Interesting. You said grotty means interesting.'

'No, it doesn't mean that.'

'Very funky?'

'No. Funky doesn't mean beautiful,' I reply, putting my arm round her.

'You teach very bad English.'

'Yes.'

'Zoia noticed us in front of the television,' she continues. 'Do you know what she said? "You must not have something with Duncan. He is too old for you." '

Navy Day. Get up at 1 pm, hot, sweaty, head *very* thick. Zoia recommends exercises, so the 3 of us squirm on the carpet and take turns on the swivel disc, without much effect, so I go for a walk round Palace Square where a Navy brass band – with 5 trumpeters in a line (one wearing mirrored sunglasses!) is playing *that* song. It was used in *Brothers and Sisters*, I think, or was it in *Stars in the Morning Sky*? The title continues to elude me – it is a flowing march of infectious and cavalier jauntiness, with a touch of bitter-sweet, and of all the Russian popular tunes has proved the most adhesive, the most evocative.

Back at the flat we eat meat, and Osip Kokoshin telephones: 'When are you leaving? I want to give you a small parcel for Layla.'

'August 6th.'

'Hiroshima Day!' he exclaims.

'You remember everything.'

'It is nothing in particular to remember this. Winston Churchill compared the Bomb to the Coming of Christ. Many people date the New Age from this day, August 6th 1945, the coming of the cosmic fire to Earth.'

Zoia's pretty niece arrives and the 4 of us cross the double courtyard, past fecund piebald cats lying drunk on heat while pigeons feed on scraps all round them, and out onto the Palace Embankment to witness the naval pageant. Normally so spacious and thinly populated, the embankment is now plumed up with blue flags and packed with motor traffic and sauntering crowds. Lines of cadets trundle along behind officers, making a tattoo of taps with their steel-tipped boots. Uniformed ratings with shore-leave stride about spick-and-span – a number are walking alone, interesting in their solitude. For what reason do they prefer to be, or find themselves, alone in this male-bonded profession on its special celebration day? Ex-sailors wearing bits and pieces of their old uniforms embrace in reunion groups – they make much noise and have impromptu vodka parties under trees or in public gardens. There's a fair volume of vomiting done by this element as the afternoon proceeds, whereas the sailors in service are orderly and well-behaved. A number of ex-sailors form a bolus and parade a flag with a red star in its centre, stamping their feet and roaring in rhythm. On the battleships and submarines, young conscripts lean forward along the rails, longing to be ashore, waving to the crowd.

Zoia says 'The Communists organised many days of this sort to replace religion.'

At 4 pm the warships fire the gun salute. Barrels dart tongues of flame and massive detonations bounce among the palaces.

Nina (Serafima's friend) and her husband wave and run across the road.

'You look marvellous, Nina. You've put on weight.' She is divided for a moment between looking marvellous and putting on weight. 'Is Serafima with you?'

'She is on holiday in the Crimea.'

'Nina, what for you is love?'

She ponders awhile, and replies 'Suffering.'

'Zoia, what for you is love?'

'I can love a man not for his beauty or his money but only if he is interesting. He must shine with interest. Sex is one of the things which can make a man interesting.'

At 5 pm a blue propellor plane performs spins and drops and loops to 200,000 open mouths and periodically shaves the tops of our heads, making the ears ring.

Lydia joins us. A wonder has happened. No pine-green tracksuit but a white blouse and wheat-coloured slacks, a touch of lipstick – and she's smiling, not the smile of obsidian but yes – this must be it – the curative smile. A smile from so unexpected a source does indeed have therapeutic powers.

'You are in love, Lydia.'

'Don't be stupid!' She is still hitting volleys – but almost waggishly. 'Have you got a cigarette, Lydia?' I seem to have taken up smoking again.

Because we awoke so late, the afternoon has passed quickly. Already the sun is descending. There are fireworks. Mortars make booms of a satisfying depth and bunches of hot gems trailing orange sparks are thrust up into the blue. They explode into sprays of coloured stars which hang and fade. This effect is repeated over and over again. Enormous amounts of smoke are accumulating in clouds which slide furtively along the river with clandestine intent. All yachts and boats and ships sound their horns in a din.

After a flurry of indecision because she cannot be duenna to both girls, Zoia departs with her niece (and Lydia), leaving Grace to walk arm in arm with me round 'the ring' – my standard walk in St Petersburg: along Palace Embankment, over the Kirovsky Bridge, through the Fortress, back over Palace Bridge.

'You haven't asked me the question about love,' observes Grace.

'I know. That's because I'm only asking Russians. What for you is love?'

'I don't know. I was thinking – if he asks me, I don't know how I will answer. But love – it makes life dramatic, doesn't it? What for you is love?'

'I knew you'd ask me! I was hoping you wouldn't. My thoughts on this subject are, well, it doesn't seem to be about having thoughts but about feeling *new*.'

'I wish I had a sailor,' she muses reflectively.

It is evening. We pause on Palace Bridge, snuggling into one of the granite loops, as we paused on the Kirovsky Bridge this morning, but the spectacle is very different. Despite the magnitude of the river here, smoke invades the banks of buildings as well as encompassing the flotilla between. It is very unevenly distributed, in dark thick swirls, or stretching in horizontal sheets which drift brown above the water, or creep over its surface in a grey film and trap the light of the falling sun in such a way as to turn the far side of the stream into a lava flow of orange fire. The city is half visible, half invisible. But the distinction becomes increasingly blurred, the light modulations increasingly erratic and original, as the smoke continues to diffuse and enwrap. It licks round bridges, devours whole blocks, coils over the superstructure of battle-ships, sniffs along streets. The tops of towers and domes and pediments emerge out of a ghostly acrid fog – the smell of gunpowder is sharp in the nose but does not make us cough. The flank of the Winter Palace rears up an unusually vivid green, its crest progressively vanishing behind dim palpitations. There, a line of statues in a pool of clarity floats against a blue sky, while beneath, a wall of black smoke is fingering upwards towards their ankles. The sunset glimmers hellishly at the back of the Museum of Anthropology in level tiger stripes.

Out of the smoke and into the smoke the crowd dwindles away. A couple of ex-sailors pass by with linked arms, stripped to their blue and white vests, quietly singing a song. And suddenly – Valentina appears out of a cloud. She is very suntanned in an indigo mini-dress, long black wavy hair all loose, walking towards us, laughing among a group of friends. I am taken aback. She greets me shyly but shows no surprise, as though she had expected us to collide.

She says 'Dima is away 3 months.' (One of her friends interprets.)
'Does he like it?'
'No.'
'I may see him this week.'
'It is not possible.'
'He said he might be back for a day or so.'
'His college is chaos. But when can we go to Pavlovsk?'
'Will you go to college too?'
'I will study History at the University there,' she says, pointing behind her into a heaving swell of black smoke.

Grace and Valentina look at each other curiously. For the first time I glimpse steel behind Valentina's coquettish ways. Afterwards Grace asks 'Who is Dima?'

Jill (the suicidiste) and our mutual friend Barbara arrive in St Petersburg from London.
'You've got your legs back then.'
'Not entirely. We have a message from your mother. She said "Smother him with kisses." '
I wait for it to happen, or something like it, but they just stand there, so I say 'Thanks for the message. What did you bring me?'
'Nothing,' says Jill.
'Not a chocolate, not a peanut? I've been here for months.'
'We didn't know what you'd want,' says Barbara.

Clearly they think I've been at the Grand Hotel Brighton all this time.

'Excuse me a moment, I must make a phonecall.' And I withdraw to my bedroom. 'Oh Mrs Podnak – is that you?'

'Certainly is.'

'I've been trying to reach you for ages. I've got a question.'

'Fire away.'

'What for you is love?'

'This is a feeling I would wish everybody to experience but it is not given to everybody – unfortunately. Was there anything else?'

'No. That's it.'

'Right you are. Good-bye.'

Then I take Jill and Barbara to the Baghdad Café where VV will join us later. Hope he finds it – there's a little confusion because the street only days ago changed its name back to Ulitsa Furshtadskaya. The girls like it. We pounce on champanskoye.

'Kitty said you were having a nervous breakdown,' says Barbara.

'Bollocks. What gave her that idea?'

'Don't know.'

'Oh God, these yankees . . Tears are part of the human equipment, you know. That wasn't a nervous breakdown – it was intensity of being.'

'Let's have another bottle,' says Jill.

'But finish this one first.'

'The stew is delicious. I was determined you wouldn't stop me coming to Russia,' she says.

'But I'm the only reason you're here!' I'm furious with her. 'Hope you apologised to the person who had to clear up the mess. Why did you do it?'

'I went on a downer.' She cries and says 'I don't know why you are taking it so personally.'

Maybe I'm a shit but – one of my oldest friends tries to kill herself – and one mustn't get personal about it. One mustn't dig. One must pretend it didn't happen. So of course I dig. While we have our row, Barbara drinks and chainsmokes in silence, offering nothing on the subject. She says 'I miss the children.'

VV shows up – a convict cut has replaced the mop of hair – and says 'Did you hear about Aquadelik? They found a dead boy floating in the pool afterwards. But it wasn't drowning. It was a drug overdose. There wasn't water in his lungs.'

'I'll order another bottle. Everyone seems to be cropping their hair.'

'They say that in England a bottle of champagne costs 10 quids,' he replies.

'Quid.'

'Yes, quid. 10.'

When the girls leave for Moscow, they give VV and myself a delicious bag of goodies each.

I do not know how to write the next section. So forgive me now please.

This is the day of my brief farewell meeting with Dima. It is hot and sunny. But he doesn't show up. And I don't know what to do . . . I have walked at the appointed time (midday) along Ulitsa Khalturina in a state of nervous apprehension – on the pavement outside the New Hermitage, sparrows flutter in dust-filled hollows, giving themselves sand baths. Palace Square is almost empty – the Hermitage is closed on Mondays. Nonetheless the poor moth-eaten dancing bear is padding from one foot to the other for any tourist who happens to pass. No one is standing by the Column. I sit on the steps beneath it and as the moments slip away so do my hopes. A painful dialogue takes place – he is often late, be patient – no, he couldn't make it, don't expect anything – Valentina said it would not be possible, accept it – but one always hopes – pace up and down – round and round the Column – do I want to buy postcards? No thanks. So . . . that's that. That's life. Someone you once met. Will he bother to reply to a letter? Probably not. Out of sight, out of mind. I'm history. No, no, he must have been delayed – or prevented – he will write explaining what went wrong – you must trust him – obviously he will not come now. An awful dejection thickens inside me. Was Dima real? Will the photographs, when developed back home, reveal a blank where he should have been?

I ask a nearby tourist the time. After 2 o'clock. Better unhook from this situation, better escape from the Square – a sick weight in the stomach – walking towards Ulitsa Khalturina I look over my shoulder, the moment of possibility relives, but it's a self-inflicted torture, nobody, that's it, finito.

Before disappearing into the street, I stop and stand facing the Square, bidding my private adieu, pathetically glued to the spot. A tiny white-topped figure comes skidding into sight on the far side. A shout, a wave, we run, stop short of each other confused and out of breath, there's anguish in his eyes, they are intensely blue, he mouths 'I'm sorry' but no sound comes out. My heart having shot from boots right up and out the top of my head, I don't know, I can't –

'I was on duty. I must –'

'Doesn't matter.'

'I have only a few minutes,' he says.

He looks anxious and radiant. His voice has a curious stammer.

'Will you get into trouble if they see you?'

'It's OK for a minute – I must do this – I – '

'I thought you weren't coming.'

'Of course I come.'

'But I thought – he's not coming.'

'No, no, if I no come, I send someone with message.'

He looks up at the sky while saying this, his lower lids flickering slightly, then looks down and takes from his pocket something wrapped in a piece of cloth and hands it to me. I slowly unwrap it and in the palm of my hand an ultramarine shard, broken off from his Siberian crystal, flashes in the sunlight. I stare, not speaking. He looks round about, quickly undoes his belt, slips it out of the loops, and presses it into my hands.

'It's too much.'

'No too much,' he replies.

'But what will you tell them?'

'I will tell – I will tell them . . . I don't know what I will tell them.'

He presses his lips together in an uncertain smile, emphasising their redness, and looks away.

'Write me letter. To-night I leave for more training. Always something else to do, never free, ha.'

'I'll meet you again. In St Petersburg. London. Somewhere.'

'I hope. And we will drink a little sea of vodka together.'

'Definitely.'

'You know it?'

'Yes.'

'Dooncan . . . I have very good time with you.'

We don't speak more, not tongue-tied, but silent. We look at each other, not searching each other's soul, not any kind of examination, but beyond all ulterior motives, our stares flowing together in a gaze of steadfast candour. Everything is accepted and understood in this, the possessionless gaze, a look you may trust for ever – because you will always be able to reach the centre of one who has gazed thus. There will not be many in a lifetime. It seems to go on for ever, but how many seconds pass?

He is so full of promise and beauty. Then an aching sadness seems to enter his eyes, and drawing Dima's head forward, I kiss his face. We hold each other – he gives me a sudden intense hug and leaves, walking rapidly away across the Square, holding up his trousers with one hand. Halfway across he stops and waves. Stopping at the main road he waves again, growing smaller each time, receding, shrinking. At the last, before vanishing into the trees of Gorky Gardens, he turns a third time and gives one of his huge waves, 5 semi-circles, left right left right left. And is gone . . . . There is a terrifying silence, the strangest silence I have ever known . . . . Then a click as we both snap back into our separate worlds.

Didn't move an inch until he was completely out of sight and for some time after that. The whole encounter happened so fast and yet all in slow motion and so forth . . . Afterwards I was unable to orientate. Not because of any panic. I had no interest in orientation. Everything was centred on an inner heat. What one may call the recrudescence of contingency took place without my interference – the sun exploded in my iris. Feet began to move of their own accord. Step . . by . . step. And when I came to, it was in front of the newspaper desk at the Astoria Hotel. Where I purchased *The Times*. The headline read: *World Financial Markets Tumble*. I looked at the girl and laughed and so did she.

This was the first foreign paper I had bought since arriving in Russia and perhaps a subconscious reflex was throwing me into the future – after all it wasn't into the present but into the future that my friend had vanished. The following days passed quickly, smeared together in various introspections and mealtimes and sultry sunshines, in a deep seething enchantment of the soul. This wasn't pleasant, or unpleasant, but more – it was riveting, wholly absorbing.

Grace said 'Ah, he has gone – so your story in St Petersburg is ended.'
'Yes. Or just beginning.'

Then she went too, flew back to Paris. Actually she failed to fly at her first attempt, prevented from boarding the aircraft by petty bureaucracy. But she got away the day after. I was sad. But the days were not empty from these losses. I felt full. And the frisson of stepping out from the flat onto the street beside the Winter Palace or the Neva always worked its magic. Boris returned to live with us. And in August, the month of the Caesars, the blue and yellow of summer deepened to purple and orange and the streetlamps were finally lit, giving an extra charm to cobalt nights on neo-classical avenues. The light tension still held however, violet twilights of stars never achieving darkness. At 1, 2, 3 am the sky reflected in the waters of the Neva a zillion infinitesimal nuances of blue . . indigo . . silver . . Gamlet came on at the Pushkin Theatre. Darkness gathered in the wings.

Osip in the Ice-Cream Parlour: Apocalypse Part 2. He wanted to meet me at the left hand sphinx outside the Academy of Arts, because he said that on certain days it spews up pure gold (the pair of sphinxes were discovered at Thebes and brought to St Petersburg in 1832), but I was too tired to walk there and suggested we meet outside Gino Ginelli's Ice-Cream Bar.

Ginelli's is down steps, a typical Petersburg half-basement, but very Western inside, with lots of lit-up plastic, and it's expensive (veluta only), and empty except for a group of black marketeers in a corner. One of them, giving Kafkaesque side-glances without moving his head, looks familiar – it's the tracheotomy man from the Dostoievsky Street Baths. He nods in return, dropping the tip of his nose abruptly – I have an irrational fear of his head falling off and rolling forward to our feet.

At the counter I purchase 2 ice-creams but have insufficient money for 2 beers as well (why on earth did I choose this absurd place?), so I get Osip a beer and for myself an orange juice, and carry them on a plastic tray to where he is happily humming in a plastic inglenook beneath the pavement-level window.

Immediately he starts to buzz.

'The natural destiny of Russia is different from the West. The task of Russia is to prepare the Earth for the coming of new human beings. The interest here has moved on from nuclear weapons to psychotronic weapons – the Iron Curtain will become the Diamond Curtain! I am not sure if St Petersburg can survive the year 2012. Many psychic people have seen it inundated by a great wave. Whether this is real wave or metaphysical wave is not certain. So much pollution has accumulated here. Russians want the good life – but who will enjoy this? People with cancer. So the good life is not so good. Anyway, ha! I hope to be in China! There are in China good places and bad places. The best places are the tea mountains, 3,000 feet, best climate in the world, 10 degrees in winter, 25 in summer, full of flowers, very clean air and water, and excellent food. This is east of Tibet and north of Vietnam: Yunan. I think I shall love it!'

'Osip, what is love for you?'

'I understand it as cosmic archetype. Love is the act of pouring out awareness. This benefits not only ourselves but also the Great Meditator. It is necessary not only for our self-realisation and self-awareness but for His too.'

'So on the human plane,' I ask, 'you would say that love is the discovery of cosmic archetype in another person.'

'Exactly! In fact our whole life is the translation of archetypes into human life. So to find this in the intimate world is very exciting. But Jung said every archetype contains the lowest and the highest, evil and good. You must keep in mind the higher archetype or be swept away and lose your foundation – remember that your foundation is up, not below! In all our affairs it is necessary to work always on the highest possible level.'

'For me,' I say, 'the main problem in advanced consumer societies is vapidity, which one could interpret as the crushing of the archetypes.'

'Consumer capitalism needs to limit people to banal functions,' he says. 'The Bolsheviks made this mistake too – with different methods. It was Lenin's greatest error to work on the lowest level. He was not stupid. In fact I believe he was a sort of reincarnation of an Egyptian pharaoh. His social system was that of the Ancient Egyptians. He was even mummified and buried in that funny little pyramid in Moscow!'

'But the Ancient Egyptians were very successful.'

'Yes, you're right. Lenin's problem was that he had no initiation into the ancient mysteries – and so he failed. He made the mistake of trying to operate on the very lowest level. Russia was literally *forced* downwards. And now you see the result.'

'And yet no other political system in Russia was able to achieve what Communism achieved – to lift Russia to the pre-eminence of a superpower.'

'And the effort broke the country's back! Do you know, in 1990 70% of all industrial production here was *still* devoted to military sector, 70%! And it was higher before. Such an imbalance has destroyed our economy. You see, such superpower things are possible for a while by force of will. But mere force of will leads inevitably to collapse. Another legacy of Communism is a lot of repressed energy – and much of that energy is *anger*. Besides, our superpower status under Communism lasted at most 30 years. This is nothing. Communism was only a phase in Russian history. Russia is a young country.'

'About this new religion which you say will be born here – who is doing it?'

'I am doing it.'

'You?'

'Yes.'

'Do you have any followers?'

'No! And I don't want. It is a difficult hidden mystic thing I am doing. Look – if I am making my way along a dark lane in the middle of the night, do I want followers? No, no, no! I will spread my religion not with followers but with computer programs. You know, the psychological infrastructure of this nation has something in common with a computer – a closed system. Turn this switch and they become free, can say what they like. Turn the switch back and again they are slaves. This is the danger for Russia. In the Communist period, *real* dissidents, actively important dissidents, were not more than 100 people at any one time. This is not very many for the authorities to deal with.'

'It's always only 100 people in such circumstances, isn't it? But the reigns of terror killed millions.'

'Yes. They went like lambs. Because they were innocent, they couldn't understand anything else.'

'And now?'

'Russians in authority can still treat those beneath them with a horrifying contempt. And it is with this same contempt that the global industrial complex has treated the planet. The Secretary General of the United Nations said that we have perhaps 10 years before we kill the world ecologically. Russia's mission is to stop that happening. Russia will do it through the development of psychotronic devices. They will intercept the electronic technology and jam the destructive system. Electronics are very vulnerable to psychotronic interference. You remember how successful the USA's electronic weapons were against Saddam Hussein? If he had had psychotronic development, they could have done nothing with those machines. USA and Russia will be friends. Russia will offer to patrol Muslim world which is a great threat, and in return Russia will overrun Japan which is a great threat economically. Or perhaps China will absorb Japan. It is not quite decided yet. But all this is an objective necessity. It is no longer about making money or the personal aggrandisement of states but about saving the planet. All politics everywhere is about this now.'

'Or about avoiding this,' I suggest. 'The curious thing is people are not afraid of ecological catastrophe. Whole societies, because of their divorce from the elements, have lost the knack of feeling this fear. Fear is healthy. But in the West we have instead neurosis – which is the deracination of fear. Or anxiety – which is the fear of fear. Or terror – which is fear in a state of paralysed panic.'

'You see, you are too sophisticated in the West. But don't worry,' he laughs, 'the Western model is out of date too. The elements will be coming after you soon enough.'

'In Russian politics, I think the ordinary man and woman are asking one question: who will protect us from the criminals?'

'Ah! Who will protect them? Another criminal of course! The growth of the mafia may be the first step towards decentralisation and make impossible the return of the totalitarian state. And since business is about the exploitation of others, mafia is the only way to give birth to a business class where no business class has existed before. This is why ordinary Russians are already sick to death of business.'

The tracheotomy party leave and the man gives another death-defying nod.

'You know this man?' asks Osip gravely.

'No.'

'Good.'

'Will, say, California survive?'

'There is a lot of New Age development there of course but also a very great tension because of its geological circumstances – the same is true of Japan. I don't know if either can survive. About survival I have an idea for a film. Cockroaches are extra-terrestrials. They arrived from outer space. They are the only creatures which can live in a nuclear reactor. We know this. So! I want to make a film about the colonisation of the Earth by cockroaches. The Japanese build special robots for copulation. You know there are many women living in the Chernobyl Zone. These are, let us say, witches. They are learning how to resist – or to live with – radiation. With these robots the Japanese impregnate the Chernobyl women with genetic material from cockroaches and eventually create a new race resistant to radiation. Good film, eh?'

'I read that some babies have been born with the AIDS virus from their mothers and have recovered spontaneously – that is, HIV has disappeared from their system.'

He buzzes appreciatively and says '*Some say* that new human beings will emerge with triple helix DNA instead of double helix. Triple is much more stable. And externally we move from bi-polar to tri-polar world: Russia, USA, China. All these things will be more visible in a few years' time.'

'Triple is not more stable in human relationships. A pair, a dual alliance, is always struggling to assert itself and eliminate the third. Will there be more Chernobyls?'

'Yes,' he says emphatically. 'I think the Caucasus region will be the next to go – because the UFO people want this area. The Rosicrucians have announced that the very critical period for Russia begins on August 15th. I think you are leaving just in time. Here – don't forget these.'

He takes from his bag several books and cuttings for Layla and a glittering iconic collage which he has made especially for me. Postcard size, it portrays the solar system and distant stars in a condition of prismatic iridescence against a purple background. Zipping round the Earth and out into the cosmic realm is a winged creature with love at its heart and far-seeing diamond eyes. (It's one of the most touching presents I've ever received and my god-children, when they came to the London flat, homed in on it immediately.)

'Coming here,' I say, 'it's like I suddenly stepped into a force-field.'

'At present St Petersburg is probably the most intense place on the planet. Which means the most emotionally and mentally alive. The unconscious is in volcanic eruption here – and *that* means our personal lives are out of control.'

'The effect was instantaneous on arrival at the airport, like a gas hitting you, the whole mind and body wound up in a second, everything supercharged. It was a shock and shock has been a theme. I have been shocked. And I have shocked.'

'People need shocks otherwise they slide down the spiral. We are shock-absorbers. That's how we grow. This is a very strange coincidence,' he says, 'because I have here in my bag a photocopy of Hexagram 51 from the *I Ching*. Look.' He pulls it out of the bag and shows me. 'Shock and the value of shocking. The upward movement of electricity, thunder. What is taking place in Russia now is not chaos. It is the accumulation of potential energy. The supermind knows what is happening. There is a special zone in Siberia where UFOs come very frequently. It is near the No. 35 Concentration Camp.'

'You know, Osip, it is all so unfamiliar – but I feel very at home in St Petersburg. I did almost from the beginning – even though it has often upset me and I've hardly been able to keep up with it.'

'Have you experienced déjà vu?'

'No. Not at all. It's more the opposite.'

'What do you feel?'

'That I had to come here. That I was pulled here – by the future. That certain things which hadn't happened had to happen. I'm not explaining it very well.'

'Maybe you will be reincarnated here in the future,' he says. 'The past, the present, the future are all combined here now.'

'In an eternal present?'

'No, not in that dead thing! But in *abnormal time*. And in *timelessness*.'

Is it possible to know a Russian? I go alone to the Dostoievsky Street Baths. Walking, walking, walking, always walking in this town, in hot sunshine, in hot rain, cut by sudden winds . . . to the Lux section, which is quieter, often only 3 or 4 customers during the afternoon . . . want to lie down, sweat, loosen the mind which has become rather tightly packed . . . The attendant, the attendant's friend, and a client in a towel are watching the Olympic Games on a portable television set in the cubbyhole beside the entrance. The attendant mumbles, smiles, hands over a sheet, and relocks onto the screen. It is uplifting to be here during the Olympic Games because Russians win almost everything and it puts the city into an affable mood of spacious self-esteem.

The sauna cabin is empty, and stretching on one of the lower benches, the body eases out of tension, taking the mind with it, and as the steaming cyclotron of the mind slows its revolutions a number of thoughts drop to the bottom and are expelled in a seemingly random sequence, but every idea connects with every other idea, as a swarm of bees compose a hive.

1. Russians are repressed but they are not puritan. And they are not philistine.
2. Russia is liberating. The West is free outside but rigid within. In Russia it is the reverse. Russians can be very free inside.
3. Russia teaches you not to believe in the world of appearances. America teaches the opposite.
4. Russia makes you feel young because here impulsive acts reap rewards.
5. So if you want something, don't stand there – try for it. It probably won't come round again.
6. Reason is indirect experience.
7. Closed minds create characters. All characters are fragments.
8. How ridiculous people appear when they behave true to type.
9. Mm, nice one. Here's another.
10. I want to be sentimental about the Russians – but they won't let me!
11. There are certain words in English – 'indigent', 'exigent' for example – which carry no savour. And others – 'labile' for example – whose savour is slight and quite other than their meaning. To use the word 'labile' is to mislead.
12. Feminist Film Party. She said 'You know the world is too small now for all this male testosterone, don't you?'
13. In order to grow we must be out of our minds.
14. The core of Romanticism: to succeed is to have aspired too low.
15. There is a chic centred on St Petersburg, not an aesthetic chic but an emotional chic.
16. Russian silence is often shyness – but it is often that they are stuck in ambivalence.
17. Balance is not possible in St Petersburg, but reciprocity is.

18. To live mythologically is to live *without recourse to myths*.
19. Russians are detached and passionate by turns – detachment permits the passions because one is unafraid of loss. People's sense of identity is liquid. Russia itself is a liquid.
20. Affluence reduces intimacy.
21. There is not one plastic person in Russia. Russia is Europe before clingfilm, and maybe Europe after clingfilm.
22. A Russian comes in and asks if it's OK to throw water on the coals and I say certainly and he does but it's still not hot enough for him so he tries the other room. Russians know about heat . . .
23. And they know about cold – Shalamov tells us that after 60 degrees below zero, spit freezes in mid-air.
24. Silence.
25. The process of growing intimacy between individuals has an added beauty here. With every meeting you must start afresh – and then you discover that it is not so, they do remember you.
26. Openness is overrated. The completely open person is the same for all, has no hierarchy of affections, is equally close to all, is impartially indiscreet, no respecter of confidences, and is without drama in his private life because all is public life.
27. Life is very big – and very short.
28. One should stop thinking of the present as temporary.
29. Don't be afraid of broken things. Broken things often work very well – with a little input from *us*. Therefore the broken is more *conscious* than the unbroken.
30. God has made us imperfectly. Why do the churches blame us and not God? We must try to improve God.
31. Russia makes one blasé about damage.
32. These notions continue to drop out. Sorry.
33. Perhaps one day I shall have sufficient money to buy a flat on the English Embankment. Does it get the sun? I must check. The position of the sun is another confusion. It seems to be all over the place in this city.
34. Oh, safe sex – what a bore! Where and when may the voluptuaries of mandragora slobber and hiss upon the thoughtless divan, indulging an injudicious concupiscence?
35. Where and when indeed.
36. Purity of race and culture is always provincial. Great nations and great cultures are always the result of chemistry, are syntheses.

37. One day Dima was fantasising about opening a little business in St Petersburg. I said 'The mafia will want 20, 30%' and he said 'Oh good. Before, the Government took 100%!'
38. All language is transitional, ie. it can be exact only in use, only when *moving*.
39. Happiness . . happiness . . . say the word a couple of times . . .
40. A man with no doubts is reduced to insect function.
41. There is so much a man doesn't understand. I must try to *live* that fact. The alternative is ignorance.
42. There are more minds in Russia than there are human beings. Serge the Estonian said 'The Russians – such genius people and so bloody bastards!'
43. Power moves like weather systems over the maps of world history.
44. Hot. I am burning here. All light comes from burning.
45. A society of total insecurity . . .
46. . . . will drive people apart . . .
47. . . . . . and together . . . in new forms of association.
48. Fitted carpets were not possible before the invention of the vacuum cleaner.
49. Is it possible to know a Russian? The deeper you go into people the more they have in common, until you reach the realm of lovers – and mobs. Too dry. Water on the coals.
50. Telepathy begins in intuition, an overlapping of dreams and expectations and understanding. 93% of communication is telepathic – which is roughly the percentage of dark matter in the universe. Sssss . . . Quieten down . . . . .
51. One glimpses this with horror sometimes in life, and in all cultures: the completely conscienceless person whose only morality is 'Can I get away with it?'
52. From 1850 onwards the Tsar's minister of education banned the teaching of philosophy in Russian universities.
53. What was that about a vacuum cleaner? No. Enough. Shut up.
54. What St Augustine, St Paul and the rest of them wrote on the subject of love are nothing more than treatises on cattle-breeding.
55. Sweat pours out like love . . . my body runs with tears . . . ha!
56. As Russia is high-octane for me, so the West is high-octane for Russians – but for different reasons.
57. The appeal of miscegenation: the charm of inappropriate couplings: the triumph of feeling over circumstance.

58. Without daring, without extreme daring even, there is no beauty. Who said that? Stop, enough, no more. Be quiet . . . . .

59. Cold water . . . More. Russia – first dog, first man, first woman, first crew into space! From backwardness and devastation to this in 40 years – it's Herculean. Oh yes, the Cold War had its primitive grandeur. How long ago seems the Space Age, the last age of Newtonian Man. We have since learnt that it is possible to travel further by standing on the Earth.

60. Or by lying in steam. Sssss . . . yes, quiet . . .

61. Boris: 'There are women who queue as a job. They sell their place in the queue and go to the back and start again. They queue all day. Sometimes people die in the queue.' Sss . . .

62. As a magnet requires positive and negative poles for its drawing power, so a magnetic or charismatic person, situation, must have pronounced positive and negative aspects. To be creative, the positive need exceed the negative by only a hair's breadth – but it must exceed it. To be destructive, the negative need exceed the positive by only a hair's breadth. Sssss . . . . sss . . . . .

63. I feel faint.

Up a metal ladder, over the lip, down a metal ladder, hit the cold plunge – its darkness is deep enough to reach the armpits and wide enough to permit a swim of 4 breast-strokes. When I return to the cabin, it is not empty. On the upper bench sits a small impish dark-haired boy with a pale muscular body. His knees are drawn up and he rests his arms on his knees and his head on his arms. 2 inquisitive eyes stare at me for quite a while but calmly. Then the whole face comes alive, and he says something in Russian. I reply in the few words I know. Does he speak English? There is an extended silence as he gathers his resources, staring fixedly at the pine panels of an opposite wall, until he draws his breath and exhales a reply: 'No.'

Communication.

He turns a deep red, but emboldened, adds 'Some. School. English 3 year.'

By pooling our skills we manage to have a fairly detailed conversation, aerated by long unpressured silences. His name is Ilya. He is 16 and a St Petersburg school running champion. We move to the plunge and the showers. The cold tap is painted blue, the hot tap red. A large metal rose gushes a great volume of water at high pressure – the Russians know how to organise these things properly. While we are soaping ourselves, he asks 'Will you come to Astrakhan with me?'

'When?'

'Now.'

'Immediately?'

'In 1 hour. We drive in big lorry with my friends. It take 2 weeks.'

See what I mean about this wonderful country? A stranger under a shower says 'Come to Astrakhan! Right now!', setting off in one's head a phantasmagoria of the Silk Road, the Amber Road, Marco Polo, the lost worlds of Gurdjieff and Paradjanov, of Cossacks and Tartars, and abandoned Ottoman forts and Byzantine monasteries where Europe melts into Asia, and had I not been returning to London so soon I should've gone with them juslikethat and it would have been another risible nightmare to talk of round the fire in old age about how we ran out of petrol 20 miles past Borisoglebsk whereat the Cossacks came down upon us from the hills, shooting rifles into the air, demanding plunder but Ilya pacified them by juggling 5 melons in the air and at night we gnawed roast fowl round bonfires while the Cossacks struck at us with inflated pigs' bladders, a local form of welcome.

Especially the young people of St Petersburg – they are so alive to change now. Always one is hearing of someone taking off in *an entirely new direction*. Internally too the shifts between tenderness – brutality – indifference can seem inexplicable. But elasticity, versatility, creativity, these are the qualities in demand. One's opinion of almost everyone and everything alters from week to week, from day to day, sometimes from moment to moment. To live always in this flux of unresolved situations is to live facing towards infinity.

A sequence is created by force of emotion and if this force be sufficiently strong a sequence may become a development. The distinction between pleasurable and painful emotion is sado-masochistically blurred in the leap towards life.

Russia remains very much a superpower – literally – but it is malleable now, its life wholly improvised and immeasurably quickened. Everyone is an entrepreneur. No, no – everyone is an impresario. Everyone can be Diaghilev! Every day is an experiment in possibility. Precedence is invalid. One feels very *futuristic* here in the city of kindred misfits. Like the artist, the Russian is every day reinventing reality in order to abolish his misfitness and find a place in life. Not absurd. Meaning splashes everywhere, causal meaning, but much more powerfully acausal meaning. The brain (being not a static computer sorting information but a dynamic organ bent on meaning) is more excited by the latter. The sense of significance is very great and it is this, more than frustration or self-pity or pity, which provokes tears.

How much more fascinating now is the world than it has ever been before. All is uncertainty! When I was a boy, I could not have, well – life is so much stranger than one imagined it would be. And in this pullulation of uncertainty, in this fizzing of ambivalences and possibilities, there seems only one recourse: abandon the struggle for meaning in the form of definition – meaning can be actual, not theoretical – take to the air and live! The universe is alive. Therefore the universe is dramatic. Therefore life is an adventure. Man is designed for the unknown.

Walking back along Nevsky Prospekt I pass the swing band opposite the statue of Catherine the Great, hot lemonade and warm champagne squirting from their horns. At the flower-seller near Gostiny Dvor I buy a dozen red, white and pink carnations (discovering only later that even numbers are bad, odd numbers good in the superstitions of this culture), take the underpass where a ringleted man sells puppies from a box and another man offers to change 180 roubles to the dollar, and rising up the other side, I stop on the street and turn round to face in the direction of Asia. I sense it tilting vastly beyond the curve of the Earth, far-flung, elusive and tantalising like a faint perfume, a word on the tip of the tongue. Then it is gone. I turn again, continuing westwards along the Prospekt, take a right under Rastrelli's great double arch, across the slanting sunlight of Palace Square, and so home.

The Mormon Boys sit on the sofa eating strawberry cake. I give Zoia the flowers and she says 'Very beautiful, thank-you', hurrying into the kitchen to hide her emotion. With a loud noise she smashes the base of the stems, puts vinegar and sugar into their water, and glows for the rest of the evening, bathed in their colours and scent.

To the Mormon Boys she says 'I shall not become a Mormon because you will not let me drink tea, coffee and vodka.'

I put on music – Nancy Nova: *The Force* – Stevie Wonder: *Do I Do* –

the Slow Twitch Fibres: *Let's Face The Music and Dance* – and ask her to dance but she pooh-poohs the idea.

'I declare you are afraid.'

'Russian women are not afraid of anything!' she informs us and launches herself across the carpet.

She's a great mover! catching the rhythm at once, and we want more of *this* song so run the tape back over and over again repeating the Slow Twitch Fibres' mad beaty rendition of the Irving Berlin classic. Moving chaotically and at the same time circling each other like planets, we dance and laugh at all the stupidity of the recent months, at all the stupidity there ever was in the world –

> There may be trouble ahead
> But while there's music
> And laughter and love and romance
> Let's face the music and dance . . . . .

– while the Mormon Boys grin at each other and outside the gaudy, glossy onions of the Church of Blood wink through the leafy arms of the tree. Oh yes, man is designed for the unknown and all that, but he needs the intimate pleaures of home, family, friends to make the unknown not only bearable but indeed possible. And love and romance? Perhaps that is what transforms the unknown into home . . . .

'Our country is very interesting, no?' she says, flopping red-faced into a chair.

'Oh, it's the best, Zoia, the best!' I say, giving her a hug. 'If you've got the stamina.'

Her face shines with a rejoicing delight.

When Boris returns we drink ice-cold vodka and eat gherkins. In bed I play the 3rd movement of Rachmaninov's First Piano Concerto. It glitters in gold flashes through the hot, dark blue night above the rooftops of St Petersburg. Mm, one day I'd like to do that drive to Astrakhan – *and beyond* . . .

At 3 am my eyes open and I catch remote sounds hanging in idle air, slip out of bed and pad down the corridor for a pee. The light is on in the kitchen. Boris is sitting at the table with his back to the door, staring silently at the opposite wall. While peeing I wonder 'Should I greet him? Should I say something?' but decide against it – he is so awfully still and silent. Padding back to the bedroom, I see he has his head in his hands. I pause, again wonder if I should, but continue down the corridor to bed. I fail. I should have touched him. This is my last memory of Boris. What disturbs his peace at this hour? That's a whole other story.

Dima telephones: 'You leave to-morrow. I want to say good-bye you.'

'Dima!' The line is very crackly and faint. Is he in Siberia?

'I found a telephone that is good,' he says.

'Where are you? Shall I ring you back?'

He says something. I cannot make it out.

'Where are you, Dima?'

He repeats it but I cannot make out the name.

'Dooncan, I want also to say that – '

There's a horrible noise.

'Dima, are you there?'

'Yes! I –'

More horrible noise.

'Are you there? . . .'

Crackles.

'Dima? . . . .'

The line goes dead.

POSTSCRIPT

The story was to have ended at that point. And looking back over it, I notice that even when I thought I wrote calmly and straightforwardly, I did not – there's a tremor running through the whole thing. Subsequent events make it necessary to add this postscript.

I returned to St Petersburg in the winter, renting my own flat which wasn't far from where I'd lived before (in my absence Khalturina Street had been returned to its old name, Millionaya). The bedroom had a view of the Moika and the Imperial Stables, with the Church of Blood behind. The walls were thick, the double-glazing very effective, and the heating high, constant and fixed – you reduced it by opening windows.

The city was no less wondrous than in the summer. The temperature outside moved between minus 25 centigrade and plus 5. With cracking and hissing noises the Neva and canals froze, thawed, refroze, their surfaces jagged with natural ice sculptures. The nights were long, from 4 pm to 10 am, and the snow fell like white fur. But there were many sunny days when the sky was blue and the snow city dazzled. 700, 800, 900 roubles to the dollar, the exchange rate continued to soar (and soon after continued way beyond 1,000 . . . 1,500 . . .).

Dima was at military college but we could meet and I came to know him much better. There were problems of course – all Russia was bewildered and on edge – but the atmosphere in our little corner was nervously optimistic. However one of the last things he said that winter, just quietly one day, was 'It's been so hard, Dooncan.'

I socialised much less than in the summer, spending many hours in the cosy flat writing a libretto for the opera *Gormenghast* while it snowed silently in the darkness outside. Dima and sometimes Valentina were my main visitors.

On returning to England I kept contact via letters and telephone. But Dima's life came under new pressures of some sort and altered rapidly. He left the Navy – I don't know how exactly. He left Valentina – I don't know why exactly. He planned to stay with me in London and study English and was very excited by that, as was I of course. But when we spoke next on the phone his voice was strange, his manner tight. Something odd was happening. Then – stop. Just like that. A complete break. He disappeared.

I never saw Dima again. I tried to trace him but my helplessness in the language made it a torture of frustration. Eventually, worried out of my mind, I co-opted a Russian-speaking friend to help. We sat on the phone in London for weeks calling St Petersburg, leap-frogging from number to number, from person to person. Some people were suspicious and put the phone down on us. Others said they knew nothing – perhaps it was true that they didn't. Some were out, away, living elsewhere, or we had incorrect numbers. You never really knew.

Then one afternoon there was a breakthrough. An acquaintance of Dima's, whom we'd tried before but he'd not been there, told us very matter-of-factly that Dima had gone to Novosibirsk for 10 days or so – no, he didn't know why – but that when he returned to St Petersburg there had been a fight. Dima was stabbed. He died in hospital a few days later.

No more can be written now – and anyway I feel I've put it all across so inadequately – except to say that on very bad days, or on very good days, I sometimes hold the piece of blue crystal in my hand and gaze at it and my mind plays a cruel but encouraging trick. I think – he was too bright to end that way – maybe it was another crazy stratagem – maybe he managed to jump clear of whatever sinking ship was dragging him down. And maybe one day, when I least expect it, out of the blue, the phone will ring. And I shall pick it up. And a slightly husky but light-hearted voice will say 'Hullo, Dooncan, how are you? . . . We can meet . . . At last I am free.'